T0090506

OPEN BOOK

THE RECOVERY *of* MY BROKENNESS

Carmen S Seguinot Matos

WESTBOW
PRESS®
A DIVISION OF THOMAS NELSON
& ZONDERVAN

Copyright © 2023 Carmen S Seguinot Matos.

All rights reserved. No part of this book may be used or reproduced by any means, graphic, electronic, or mechanical, including photocopying, recording, taping or by any information storage retrieval system without the written permission of the author except in the case of brief quotations embodied in critical articles and reviews.

This book is a work of non-fiction. Unless otherwise noted, the author and the publisher make no explicit guarantees as to the accuracy of the information contained in this book and in some cases, names of people and places have been altered to protect their privacy.

WestBow Press books may be ordered through booksellers or by contacting:

WestBow Press
A Division of Thomas Nelson & Zondervan
1663 Liberty Drive
Bloomington, IN 47403
www.westbowpress.com
844-714-3454

Because of the dynamic nature of the Internet, any web addresses or links contained in this book may have changed since publication and may no longer be valid. The views expressed in this work are solely those of the author and do not necessarily reflect the views of the publisher, and the publisher hereby disclaims any responsibility for them.

Any people depicted in stock imagery provided by Getty Images are models, and such images are being used for illustrative purposes only. Certain stock imagery © Getty Images.

Unless marked otherwise, all scripture quotations are taken from The Holy Bible, New International Version®, NIV® Copyright © 1973, 1978, 1984, 2011 by Biblica, Inc.® Used by permission. All rights reserved worldwide.

Scripture quotations marked NLT are taken from the Holy Bible, New Living Translation, Copyright © 1996, 2004, 2015 by Tyndale House Foundation. Used by permission of Tyndale House Publishers, Inc., Carol Stream, Illinois 60188. All rights reserved.

ISBN: 979-8-3850-1099-8 (sc)
ISBN: 979-8-3850-1101-8 (hc)
ISBN: 979-8-3850-1100-1 (e)

Library of Congress Control Number: 2023920578

Print information available on the last page.

WestBow Press rev. date: 01/02/2024

To all those who read *Open Book*.

May Jehovah-M'Kaddesh reveal to you what you need to hear, see, and understand in your life. May the Holy Spirit convict your heart of what you did not know, confirm what you do know, and prepare you for what He has in store for your life. If you are not a believer or if you have never accepted Jesus Christ as your Lord and Savior, may you be convicted to do so. And He will come and take up residence in your life as Jehovah-M'Kaddesh, Who will sanctify you.

ACKNOWLEDGMENTS

The author and perfecter of my life is Abba God Almighty; Elohim mighty and powerful; the Father, Son, and Holy Spirit; Yahweh, I Am, Jehovah. He is the Alpha and Omega, the Beginning and the End. He has carried me and sustained me through life. And He has assigned me many assignments, this open book being one of them. He truly is my Father, husband, and friend. To Him be all praise and glory, forever and ever. Amen.

I'm forever grateful to all the men and women who have played a part in rearing me spiritually—Dr. Charles Stanley, RIP; Joyce Meyers; Mike and Lori Kwasniewski; Lisette Vega,; Karen Wheaton; Collins Smith; Alistair Begg; Jimmy Evans; Tony Evans; Wilfredo de Jesus; Efrain Muñoz, David Marrero; and Jarixon Medina. You all played such an important role in my life. It was through your teaching that the Holy Spirit worked in my sanctification process that birthed the fruit of the Spirit in my life.

I thank each one of you for your obedience to Abba God and for submitting to His work of the building of His kingdom. You have been a blessing in my journey. May our Heavenly Father Elohim bless you sevenfold what you have blessed me. And may He continues to use you for the advancement of His Kingdom. In Jesus's name, amen!

Last but not least, I am grateful to Pelegrino, my dear husband; our daughters, Annette, Karen, Arisely, and Natalie; and our incredible grandchildren, Josiah, Niamiah, Jalin, Jared, Nadia, Micah, Jayla, Brence, Kyle, Akira, and Reign Shiloh, who are all the apple of my eye. They are my blessing from God and have been a constant reminder to check myself before my Heavenly Father Jehovah.

May our Heavenly Father Elohim bless and enlightened the eyes of their hearts to know Him and be able to walk in His righteousness. In Jesus's name, amen.

And I can't leave out my dear, dear Rafy, who blessed not only me but also our whole family in such a beautiful and powerful way and who continues to do so with his charm, intellect, and love.

TRIGGER WARNINGS

The point of warnings is not to prevent readers from engaging with disturbing content but, rather, to prepare them for it so they can engage with it productively.

Though I am epistemically (the philosophical study of the nature, origin, and limits of human knowledge) limited and, thus, cannot know exactly *all* of the content that might provoke reactions in readers—interfering with their learning and growing spiritually—I can provide warnings for *some* things. Child Abuse—mental, physical, emotional, and sexual—are topics in this book.

MY EARLIEST MEMORY

The earliest I can recall looking back at my life was about age four. It was late on a summer evening, and I was waiting for my bottle of Bosco chocolate milk, which was a routine for Lourdes, my younger sister, and me, before bedtime. I remember asking my mom for it, and she called out to my older brother, "Jose! No te dije que le diera la leche a Yaya y a Lourdes?" (Jose, didn't I ask you to give Yaya and Lourdes their milk?)

"Si, ya voy!" (Yes, I'm coming), he answered.

I recall him not being too happy about having to prepare our chocolate milk and mumbling under his breath, "You are too big to be drinking out of a bottle." Well, big brother was going to put an end to that foolishness. Jose was obedient and got our chocolate milk ready for us and brought it to us. That was when he decided to throw in his offer. "Hey guys, would you like to have a swimming pool you can play in?" he asked.

"Sure," we said.

"All you have to do is stop drinking your chocolate milk in a bottle. I will buy you a swimming pool, and you can play in it in the summer. Wouldn't that be great?" he asked. "Just tell Mami you do not want to drink your milk in a bottle anymore, OK?"

My sister and I agreed to his plan. We really believed he was going to buy us a swimming pool. That night, we stopped drinking our Bosco in a bottle and eagerly waited for our pool to arrive. Time went by, and I kept asking about the pool, but my brother always had a good reason why it was not given to us yet. I believe the last excuse he gave us was that he would buy it as soon as our parents moved to a big house because the pool was too big for an apartment, and we didn't have a yard to put it in.

This was such a big disappointment. It really hurt, as I had given up something I truly enjoyed and found comfort in for something that was not given—a broken promise. I had really believed Jose would get us a pool.

The disappointment was not over as time went by. Somehow, I seemed to remember it often. I was an adult when I asked him about it for the last time. "What about our pool? When are you going to get it?"

My brother laughed and said, "Hey, at least I got you to stop drinking from a bottle before you started school."

I knew he wasn't going to buy us that pool. Even though I was about thirty-six years old, I just had to hear it from him. I believe this broken promise was just the beginning of the accumulated events that built my untrusting heart with the lingering pain of a broken promise.

Toward the end of my kindergarten year, Mom came to school to enroll my younger sister. I was excited because we were really close—but it did not last too long. When my mom left, I found out that my little sister would be in the same class as I was the following year. I was being left behind for my inability to keep up. I did not understand it much. But for some reason, it did not sound like it was a good thing. I remember the nun telling my mom it may be good because I could make the transition for my sister easier. My mom explained to me that I would be helping my little sister in case she got scared.

Over the summer, my second oldest brother would tease me, chanting, "You flunky. You are in a baby class. You're going to be in Lou's class, kindergarten again. Ha ha ha!"

I felt deeply ashamed, and I didn't even know why I was being left behind. I just didn't understand what I had done wrong—what I was being punished for. I blocked the shame by thinking about how cool it would be having Lou in the same class and I had been tasked to take care of her. This had to be a good thing.

School started that September, and so did increased teasing at home. I blocked it out but still felt less than good enough. This played hand in hand with what I was already feeling at home. There was a sense that I didn't belong, something was out of place. But what was it? Why? From an early age, I recalled a lot of arguing between my parents. It always had to do with their children, especially the older ones.

We were a big family, seven children in all—three boys and four girls—plus Mom and Dad. I will explain it like this because this is what I saw and understood. It was how I processed our family setting. Whenever anyone referred to us, they would say, "Pablo's kids" or "Fela's kids." We were never mentioned as a whole family. There was a division and clarification of who was whose. This went on for a very long time, until I was about twelve or so. I thought I was adopted. Whenever my mom would talk about Eliberto, who was two years older than me, or Lou, who was one year younger than me, she would refer to us as "Pablo's kids." Then when she was talking about Elsa, the oldest, ten years my senior, Jose, eight years my senior, Pablito, six years my senior, or Martita, four years my senior, she would say "my kids." This cast some doubt about whether or not she was my mother. I would wonder, Did she adopt me? Or did both adopt me? I later learned that Eliberto and Lourdes both felt the same way.

The arguments were often because the older children seemed to get into a lot of trouble. I wished they would just stop and love one another. My mother would say, "If they were your children, you would not be so mean to them. Why can't you love my kids the same way you love yours?" (This was among other things I will share later.) We (the three younger children) were also included in a lot of the arguments. There was always a comparison between the two sets of children. I remember wanting so desperately for us to be happy, with no division and no difference between us kids.

A big issue was the difference in discipline by both parents. It was made clear that Papi was not to discipline my older siblings, which caused a lot of friction because they seemed to get in a lot of trouble. Oh yeah, and they did not call him "Papi." They called him, "El Gordito," the little fat one. There was all this conflict because we were a blended family. Dad had a previous relationship and a son, Edwin Seguinot, who did not live with us and just kept in contact by mail. And my mom had been married before and had four children by that marriage to Jose Marcano, who was known by the nickname Pepe. Mami did keep up with Edwin. She had a natural caring and affectionate heart.

The flip side to all of that was the great family times. We did things together, like going to the movies at the San Juan Theater on Division Street. Every so often on a Saturday afternoon, the theater also held live performances. I was fascinated by performers like the Lloroncita (Alma Quezi), Joselito (Jose Jimenez Fernandez), Jose Miguel Class (el Gagito de Manati), and Jose Luis Rodriguez (El Puma), among others. Or during the evening, Mom would have us sit around her in the living room and tell us spooky stories or play Que Veo? (What Do I See?)—a guessing game. That was so much fun. She would make a big batch of homemade hot chocolate (from a bar, not the powder in a can) with *queso de bola* (Holland cheese), *salchichon* (Puerto Rican pepperoni), *guayava* (guava), and *galletas de lata* (Keebler's cracker in a can).

One of my favorite things to do, which I can't leave out, was the family fishing trips to Fox River or the countless days out to Humboldt Park. Another favorite was when my older siblings played superstars and sang and danced for us. Jose was always Elvis, Sandro de America, Rodolfo, Raphael, or Fabian. He could even imitate Sammy Davis Jr. pretty well. Pablito would play the guitar. He was good at it! Mami loved to sing and had a tremendous voice. I was always front and center, attentive and admiring them with all my heart. Martita was a great dancer, and she would imitate the Supremes and the Temptations with rhythm and style.

And one of my top favorite things to do was to help my dad count the bolita (lottery) money when there was a payoff!

Our home was also known as the favorite spot for hospitality and family gatherings. But unfortunately, it wasn't always just family. There wasn't much difference between friends and family. Everyone was treated as family. Mami always made room for others, and they often stayed over. One in particular was an older man called Johnny, who claimed to have no family. He was a military veteran and worked for Cinderella's Fashion, a very popular women's clothing store at the time. He befriended the family and would spend the weekends at our apartment all the time, and he babysat if my parents went out on a date night. He showered everyone with treats and gifts. He was about fifty-five years old.

One day while Mami was helping me out of the bath, she noticed a lump on my right side, just above my private area. She took me in to get it examined, and it was diagnosed as a hernia. It was so big the doctor said it had to be removed immediately. When I came home after the operation, our so-called family friend, Johnny, asked me to show him where my "ouchy" was at, and I did. This was the first time I was sexually molested. I remember feeling scared—terribly, terribly scared. But I was even more scared to say what had happened. I'm not sure why, but I was.

The apartment seemed to be busy all the time and when my parents were not at home we were watched by our older siblings, and they usually had friends over. They would normally go into one of the bedrooms and shut the door. I was curious and wanted to go in, so I knocked on the door, and they let me in. Little did I know the reason they closed the door was because they would play inappropriate games, where the boys would take turns on the girls. One of them pushed me on the bed and proceeded to molest me. I was about six or seven years old.

One day, when I was passing by one of the rooms, Johnny called me into the bedroom. He said it would only be a minute. But as soon as I stepped in, he grabbed me and put his hand over my mouth and proceeded to molest me. It was a long time. But there was no other adult in the house, so I guess he knew it was safe. Then, when he was done, he hugged me and said that I had been a very good girl. He

5

reminded me I could not tell, or I would be a tattletale and handed me a dollar. He was always giving out money and treats to all of us.

I can't explain what I felt—if it was anger, fear, or what. I ran to the window, staring out in search of my parents. I didn't move until they got home, which, thank God, was shortly after.

When I was about nine, my parents were gone again. This time, my second oldest brother snatched me, put me in the closet, and covered my mouth, saying, "If you make any noise, I am going to really hurt you. So, just be a good girl and be quiet." When he was done, he said "Whenever I ask you to do this for me, you have to do as I say." He was pretty strong. Once before when I'd tried to get away, he had twisted my arm, which was very painful. He said this time I had been good. He said, "See. I didn't have to hurt you this time."

Such a situation is addressed in scripture:

> "No, my brother!" she said to him. "Don't force me! Such a thing should not be done in Israel! Don't do this wicked thing.
>
> What about me? Where could I get rid of my disgrace? And what about you? You would be like one of the wicked fools in Israel. Please speak to the king; he will not keep me from being married to you."
>
> But he refused to listen to her, and since he was stronger than she, he raped her.
>
> Then Amnon hated her with intense hatred. In fact, he hated her more than he had loved her. Amnon said to her, "Get up and get out!"
>
> "No!" she said to him. "Sending me away would be a greater wrong than what you have already done to me." (2 Samuel 13:12–16)

When I first read this passage in the Bible, I cried profusely. I could not believe what I was reading. But it gave me revelation as to how and why this same thing had happened to me in my life. It was called sin, committed by one who cast off the fear of God and the restraints of decency. My brother was in complete darkness and had no idea what he was doing, other than to feed his fleshly desires. By the time I was ten, this brother left home. (He wouldn't be able to touch me again.) He became involved with a female friend; I believe he started staying with her. He was into so much trouble and even physically lashed out at Mami once. I was very happy he was gone.

Then I come across a good memory—a time when my oldest brother came to my defense. I had an innate love for people and to serve others that was seen at a very early age. There was a neighbor next door to the apartment we lived in at the time who had a handicapped son. I noticed she had brought him in from the hospital or a doctor visit one day, and I wanted to go next door to visit and ask her if she needed help. We were not allowed to do that without permission, but I did it anyway (I was disobedient). My dad was calling me. "Yaya! Yaya! ¿Dónde estás?" My older brother let me know, and I ran back home. When I got there, Papi started to take off his belt to spank me. My older brother got in the way and said, "Don't hit her. It's not her fault. I gave her permission to go. So, if you're going to hit someone, hit me."

My dad scolded me and put his belt back on. Wow, that was close. I was so grateful to my brother. The best part of the memory was that I was able to help the lady feed her son before Papi started calling me.

Then there is the memory of my dear brother El. He had been attentive to me since birth. Mami would tell the story of him standing in front of my crib, chanting, "Yaya, Yaya, Yaya," calling out to me. So, they started calling me Yaya. And later in life, some family members would say Yayie instead. Family and close friends still call me Yaya or Yayie.

When I was about seven or eight years old, our parents took us to the beach on a hot summer day. Lourdes and I loved the water. We were told to stay near the shore. We ran in and started playing. We held each other's arms and started jumping up and down, laughing and enjoying the water. We did not notice that we had drifted to the deep, and we started drowning. We tried yelling for help, but we were not able to. It was the scariest moment ever. My brother Eliberto notice and ran in and was able to save both of us.

Another rescue was in the school yard. An older boy pushed me. My brother Eliberto came to my rescue, and that big bully never bothered me again for sure.

Eliberto has rescued me throughout my life. God gas always sent him at the right time on so many occasions.

My baby sister Lourdes and I still laugh when we recall her wanting everything I picked at the clothing store for myself. She would not come along when Mami and I went shopping. I would pick out my clothes, and Mami would pick Lourdes's. When we got home, Lourdes always wanted whatever I had picked for myself, and I would end up giving it to her.

The third time around, Mami told me, "Don't tell Lou what you picked is yours. Make believe her items are yours. When she says she wants yours, you will still have what you originally picked for yourself. I did just as Mami told me. And sure enough, it worked out just as Mami had said it would.

Into adulthood, Lourdes has always been big on her wardrobe collection. My baby sister always made sure I was styling as well. I would get lots of compliments on my clothing. Whenever someone asked where I got them, I would answer, "Lou's Boutique."

My second oldest sister's best friend, Mimi, had a big family too—three boys and four girls just like us. Both her parents worked as hard laborers in a factory and held the second shift, 3:00 p.m. to midnight. Mimi and her siblings took advantage of the fact that their parents were at work and were not expected back until midnight. She lived nearby. One day, my sister went to her house (without permission) to hang out; it was a house party. We typically were not allowed outside the house on a school night. I don't recall how exactly Martita got out of the house, but she did. And of course, my mom went looking for her when she noticed she wasn't home. She headed to Mimi's house and found her in one of the bedrooms with one of Mimi's brothers, the one they called him Smiley. She got the beating of her life. This incident also caused secrets to come out. Martita told Mami this was not the person who had taken her virginity and that she had been molested by one of our uncles, sadly my godfather.

That started a family feud for sure. Of course, my uncle denied it. My dad blamed my mom for allowing us to spend the night over at his house on two occasions, him being a bachelor and all. My dad said that, once you dishonored the family, you were not allowed to live in the home, at least that's what I understood. But I didn't understand the why. It just got really, really, bad. My mom was torn, completely devastated.

Before we kids realized it, we were on a plane to Puerto Rico. My mom had decided to leave my dad and start on her own with us kids, the four who were left at home—Martita, Eliberto, Lourdes, and myself. We were staying at my Uncle Regino's house with his wife and six children, two boys and four girls. This was also the first time Martita met her biological father (Pepe). She was fifteen at the time.

I think that was one of the happiest times of my life—if I can say happy time. Even though I missed my dad greatly, I loved living in Puerto Rico. My siblings hated it. They all wanted to go back to Chicago. I was the only one who wanted to stay. Things didn't go well financially, and housing was very difficult. My dad kept asking my mom to come back. He was reluctant to move to Puerto Rico. I'd heard him say throughout my life that he would never set foot in Puerto Rico again. I never found out why. Whatever the reason, he was not going there, and my mom ended up going back home to Chicago. But she did not return to Chicago with her four children. She left Martita behind.

Before I turned eleven, all my older siblings from my mother's side had left home. Home without them was very different; it felt peaceful and more like a real family. I didn't have to be scared any more.

Mami took care of toddlers for her friends. One of my enjoyments was playing with the babies she took care of and, later, caring for my nieces and nephews and other family members' children. That's how

I got the hernia in my groin area—by lifting them up and carrying them around.

Because I was fond of kids and responsible, Mami would allow me to babysit my four nieces and two nephews for my older sister when she had to step out. On one occasion, when my sister came back from her outing, she told me her friend was willing to pay me thirty-five dollars if I let him be with me. I immediately said, "*No! No way!*" From that point on, I refused to stay with her kids in her apartment any more.

Years later, around 2005, she had accompanied me on a visit to a friend of mine. While I was driving, she said, "Yaya, I have been wanting to tell you for a long time why I agreed to try and get you to let my friend be with you."

"Huh?" I said. "What?"

She went on to explain, "Remember Ernesto's friend Zurriyo?"

"'I think so," I responded.

"Well, he had told me that, if I got you to be with him, he would give you thirty-five dollars. And if I didn't, he was going to hurt Mami or one of the kids. That's the only reason I accepted. I wanted to say that I am sorry for doing that. I was afraid."

"Oh, that's all right. I understand and forgive you," I answered her.

It wasn't that I had forgotten. Rather, I had rejected the thought whenever it came up in my mind. I just wanted our family to be equal and loving to one another. To the day of this writing, this has been my life's emotional battle, and it remains my sentiment. I claim it in Jesus's name.

When I was about eleven, one of my adult cousins asked Mami if I could babysit for his kids over at his house. My mom said yes. He picked me up and, on the ride there, talked about one of my older sisters and how truly special she was. He explained how important it was for family to be close and love one another. He added that there was no stronger love than the one of family willing to do anything for one another. While he was talking, I could not help but think about how much I yearned to be loved by my mother's family. My second oldest sister was very popular and was highly esteemed by the family. I guess, since I had the notion that I may be adopted, it was important to me to be loved by them and accepted.

Before I knew it, he had stopped in a parking lot and said he would be right back. Then he returned and said, "Come on out. I just want to rest for a short moment. He took me into a room that he opened with a key. I asked him, "Is this place yours?"

He laughed and said, "Just for a little while. I want to teach you how to be better than Martita—because you could be."

I said, "No. I want to go to your house and take care of the kids. That's what you said I was going to be doing."

Well, he went on about the secret of a great family and the power of love that is given to one another. Then when I saw what he was doing, I figured it would be faster if I just did what he said. It felt like forever, and it did not seem like he was in a hurry to leave, so I started to complain again. I did not feel anything that he explained earlier. I felt sick, just sick.

This happened a few times before I had to leave home.

His brother did the same thing when I was eleven years old. His wife, who I love dearly and to whom I became attached to (she was my childhood mentor so to speak) wanted me to spend the night. He came to pick me up. On the drive to their home, he pulled over and had his way with me and then continued to his home as if nothing had happened. I believe he knew I was already convinced to look the other way. He did say, "Even if you tell, I would deny, deny, deny. And no one would believe you."

So, I learned to look the other way and keep quiet. I believe he regretted it or was fearful that his wife would find out (she was very fond of me), because he never touched me again. Thank God Almighty!

Again, scripture speaks clearly against the behavior of these men:

- No one is to approach any close relative to have sexual relations. I am the Lord. (Leviticus 18:6)
- Do not have sexual relations with both a woman and her daughter. Do not have sexual relations with either her son's

daughter or her daughter's daughter; they are her close relatives. That is wickedness. (Leviticus 18:17)

By the time I turned thirteen, I had no concept of right or wrong in my mind. I just went day by day with thoughts that turned on and off flying around in my mind about everything that surrounded me. I wondered about the why of many things that didn't seem right. Mostly, I yearned for love and acceptance and unity in our family. The fact that my older siblings didn't live at home didn't remove what had already happened. Neither did my desire for us to be a normal family, like the family on the TV show *Father Knows Best*, disappear.

In early April 1974, Mami received the worst news a parent can receive. A call came from my Uncle Regino from Puerto Rico. He said, "En el radio, salio noticia de una muchacha que encontraron muerta en la carretera en frente del Hotel Flamingo. Dicen que se conose ser La India. Fela creo que es Martita. Nesesitan que venga a reconocer el cuerpo" (On the radio, there was news about a girl found dead in the middle of the road in front of the Flamingo Hotel. They said she goes by the name La India. I believe it is Martita. They want you to come and identify the body).

Mami flipped out, clenching her fist tightly and raising it in the air and yelling out "*Nooooooooo!*" She argued with God out loud, asking how He could allow this to happen.

Shortly after the call, she readied herself to fly out to Puerto Rico to identify the body. She told me to get ready. She wanted me to go with her to make the arrangements. As I was getting ready, I heard a big bang on the floor. I ran to the kitchen, and there was Mami, lying on the floor and not responding. I called 9-1-1, and she was taken to the hospital. She had tried to kill herself by taking an overdose of Valium prescription pills. Thank God she got to the ER on time. Her stomach was pumped, and she was kept for observation and then discharged the next day. She flew to Puerto Rico on the next flight out.

Mami's greatest fear was confirmed. Her daughter was dead. She was identified via pictures, which the authorities there gave to

Mami. Martita had been beaten badly. It was said that her assailants had used a wooden object like a bat or a two-by-four and had run a car over her body, breaking her hip and other parts of her body. She was killed fifteen days before her eighteenth birthday. Mami would look at the pictures all the time and cry.

After a while, my younger cousin's wife took the pictures from Mami and said she needed to stop looking at them because it was hurting her, and it would not bring Martita back. Mami wanted to believe that it was not true, and every day she waited for the mail, in hope there would be a letter from Martita saying she was alive and well. She waited ten years, if not more, hoping for good news.

Martita had sent Mami a letter two weeks before Tio Regino's phone call. It told Mami how well she was doing and how she was seeking God. In the letter, she had asked for Mami's forgiveness. She'd added a drawing of Jesus Christ with a symbol of a heart and torch on fire on the center of His chest and His left hand touching the heart. So, Mami waited for another letter from Martita saying she was alive. How could she not wait for another beautiful letter like that? After all, she believed in God and His miracles.

Years later as I listened to His whispers, Abba God revealed to me truths about our passing from one life to the next:

- The righteous perish, and no one takes it to heart; the devout are taken away, and no one understands that the righteous are taken away to be spared from evil. / Those who walk uprightly enter into peace; they find rest as they lie in death. (Isaiah 57:1–2)
- Now there is in store for me the crown of righteousness, which the Lord, the righteous Judge, will award to me on that day—and not only to me, but also to all who have longed for his appearing. (2 Timothy 4:8)

We also must accept death, as it is allowed by God when a person's time here on earth has expired. Only He knows the why and when of each person's expiration date on earth. For this is what scriptures tell us. There is "a time to be born and a time to die, a time to plant and a time to uproot" (Ecclesiastes 3:2).

Around this time, my older cousin (of the two who lived in Chicago while I was growing up) had a party celebrating his thirtieth birthday, which happened to be in April. There was a live salsa band playing. Back then, it was custom to have a live band play at a house party. The band was actually really good. I don't recall personally meeting any of the musicians, but I believe it was a group of four or five men. I do recall seeing the leader of the band interact with other people, including my mom. He was very friendly and definitely a great musician. When the party was over, everyone went home and resumed his or her routine life. I was thirteen at the time.

Monday morning at lunchtime, I went out to visit with Vicky (my older cousin's wife). I would normally walk to her house during lunchtime and watch soap operas with her. They lived about half a block from the school I attended at the time. I was walking toward the building when I heard my name being called out. "Yaya!"

I looked immediately because only my family knew me by my nickname. Turning, I saw a man in a sky-blue and white Cadillac.

"Yaya! Come here for a minute," he said.

I walked over to his car, and he said, "Hi. My name is Joey. Do you remember me? I was the leader of the band at your cousin's party."

I realized who he was and said, "Yes, I do remember you."

He went on to ask, "Where are you going? Can I give you a ride?"

I responded, "No. I'm just going down the block to my cousin's house."

He insisted, and I agreed. As he drove, he continued to state how he'd had his eyes on me that whole night at the party. And then when he stopped, he expressed how much he really liked me and would love to take me to lunch.

"No. But thank you for the ride," I said and left.

The next day when I got out of school for lunch and started walking toward Vicky's apartment, there was Joey sitting in his car.

This time, he stopped me before I crossed the street. I don't recall why, but I accepted the invitation to go to lunch with him. I must have felt flattered that he would want to befriend me.

Well, there it was—the beginning of a relationship with an older man. I was thirteen, and he was twenty-seven. At this time in my life, I really didn't know what OK was and what was prohibited. I don't recall having any type of boundaries in the area of relationships explained to me. There was so much incest that, even now, I still wonder how it wasn't noticed and dealt with. Maybe it was that no one dared to speak up out of fear. I did not know what it felt like to be an innocent child—or that that state even existed. But I definitely knew I wasn't an adult.

Joey and I went to lunch a couple of times. He seemed to enjoy spending time with me, and he never tried getting physical with me. Our time together just involved good conversation about things like music and art, all the things I enjoyed. I was starting to feel special.

On one occasion when I was babysitting for my older cousin and his wife, Vicky asked if I would mind having an extra baby that night. Their friends didn't have a babysitter, and they would really appreciate it if I watched him too. I agreed. He was the cutest little boy with big blue eyes. I did not meet his parents because he was already there when I arrived. I don't recall who told me—it may have been my other cousin's wife (my childhood mentor) or it may have been Vicky herself—but I ended up finding out after that night that the baby was Joey's son Little Joey. Wow! What a mindblower. I decided I would never see him again.

A couple of months down the line, my sister threw a big party for her stepdaughter Barbie. It was at a banquet hall, and there was live music. To my older sister's surprise, guess who was there? Yes, Joey. He seemed to know my family well. I recall him trying to talk to me, and I really wasn't paying too much attention to him because I had told myself I would not see him again. None of my siblings who still lived at home were there. Only I attended the party.

When it was time to go home, Mami came to pick me up. I recall her coming in; saying her hellos and; yes, speaking to Joey

15

briefly. When she finished socializing, she headed out the door, went downstairs, and got in the car to drive home. My Aunt Benita was in the front seat. I got in the back seat, and Mami drove off.

I looked back through the back windshield and saw Joey trailing Mami's car. Before long, Joey was beeping the horn, trying to get our attention. Mami ended up pulling over. He ran to the car, spoke to her briefly, and then got in the back seat of the car. We headed to downtown for a cruise, with Joey in the car. This was so awkward. I never understood why my mom had allowed him to join us or why we ended up at Buckingham Fountain.

It was at this time that he apologized for not telling me about his girlfriend and his son before. He added that he was no longer seeing her and that he wanted to continue to see me. I accepted his apology, and he continued to stop by the school to see me. One day, he insisted on stopping by my parents' house to ask for their permission to date me. I recall my dad's immediate response. He did not want to speak to him. But somehow, he ended up coming in. My mom met with him, and she agreed that he could date me. I don't recall having a say in the matter. It was official. I was dating an older man.

I remember Joey coming by on the weekends. Sometimes, he took me out to the theater, and my youngest brother and younger sister tagged along. Joey was very attentive and called me all the time. One day, he stopped by and said he wanted to go cruising, just us two. We drove around Humboldt Part for a little bit, and then he said he needed to pick up something. We drove to his apartment. Well, the bit about him needing to get something was a complete lie. He turned on the music, and before I knew it, we were in bed. This became our regular outing.

Once during a visit, I found out that my oldest cousin (his best friend) was staying with him because he had left his wife and needed a temporary place to stay. My cousin went to take a shower while Joey and I were listening to music. Joey got a phone call, and about the same time, my cousin called out for a bath towel. Without delay or thought I got a towel and took it to him. Oh, my goodness, that was like the worst thing ever! When my cousin left, Joey started yelling at me, asking me why I would do such a thing and saying how I'd disrespected him and myself. I had no clue why this was so bad. He would not let up yelling, and I started to cry. He took me home and would not talk to me for a couple of days.

When he got over his anger, he picked me up. Right away, he jumped into asking me a lot of questions about me and my family. Then he went on to explain that what I had been doing was wrong and why. I was deeply ashamed. I thought to myself, *How could this be so wrong when so many adult people in my surroundings were doing it?* He told me he did not want my cousins, brothers, or uncles kissing or hugging me anymore. Suddenly, I didn't feel safe without Joey, but I felt badly about telling him about what went on in my family because now I felt dirty. Joey didn't understand that I just wanted to be part of my mother's family and be like my older sister because they loved her so much. It never entered my mind that him pursuing me and getting involved with a thirteen-year-old was not right either. But of course, he was not the one on trial.

What I did feel was that I was damaged and should feel grateful that he even wanted me. I wished I could change what had happened. When I took a bath, I remember crying and scrubbing hard, wishing I could remove all that I had already allowed to happen to my body. But I did not see my involvement with him to be wrong.

On the contrary, I was a big hit at school. My neighbor had spread the rumor that I had a twenty-seven-year-old boyfriend, and that must have been a big deal for my peers. Joey showered my mom with gifts and would get me whatever I asked for. I noticed, when he paid for things, he would pull out a thick stack of large bills like the stack Papi had when there was a payoff for the *bolita* (lottery).

I was going to school (sixth grade) and volunteered at St. Mary's of Nazareth Hospital as a candy striper. My life was starting to look and feel good. Then I started getting sick a lot, particularly in the mornings at school. I was nauseous and tired, had headaches, and often vomited. The school called and had me picked up a couple of times. In my classroom, there was a teacher's aide, and we often had deep conversations about life. Once, she asked me if I was pregnant. I responded to her I had no idea. Actually, I didn't even know I should keep a record of my monthly cycle. The teacher's aide said, "I believe you're pregnant."

I was terrified.

She said, "You can have an abortion nowadays. What you need to do is go to the abortion clinic, register, and have an abortion. And no one will know."

I informed Joey that I was pregnant. He was thrilled! But I was too scared and didn't want to go through the pregnancy. I suggested the abortion to him, but he was completely against it. He told me that, if I wanted it, I would have to do it on my own. So, that's exactly what I did. I started the process of the abortion on my own. The teacher's aide gave me all the information I needed, and I started taking the steps toward aborting the pregnancy. I was thirteen, but I looked a lot older than I really was physically, so that wouldn't be a problem—or so I thought. I knew my mom had medical assistance for my older sister Martita, who was now eighteen years old and was still active on Mami's medical card. I took the medical card from my mom's purse and scheduled myself an appointment to have an abortion. Wow! I can't imagine how I came up with that idea, but I did.

On the day of my appointment, I was terrified. I went in, registered, and filled in the questionnaire using a dictionary because I could barely read. I had difficulties spelling even the word "that"— this was how poor my spelling was. They gave me a gown and asked me to take off my clothes and enter the waiting room, saying someone would call me when they were ready for me.

When they called me in, the nurses walked me toward the exam table and helped me up to it. It was cold. There were all kinds of poles with big lights facing different directions, a big machine near the bed (the exam table), and a little table with wheels that you could roll around with wrapped-up items on it. I was here at an abortion center, getting ready to get rid of my big mistake. (I didn't know it to be sin as I understand sex out of wedlock to be today). Mami and Papi would never know. That was the important part. Once it was over, I could continue school, continue volunteering at St. Mary's of Nazareth Hospital, and stop seeing Joey. And everything would be back to normal.

I didn't think of praying or repenting because I didn't even realize or understand that I was committing a sin by being sexually active. Little did I know that what I was about to do was a sin and considered committing murder. I did not understand, but I knew I was in big trouble. Ironically, I believed that God was helping me get through this, to cover up my mistake. Or was he?

I found answers from the Bible on Got Questions:

> Before I formed you in the womb I knew you, before you were born I set you apart; I appointed you as a prophet to the nations" (Jeremiah 1:5)
>
> (This tells us that God knew us before He formed us in the womb.)

- For you created my inmost being; you knit me together in my mother's womb. / I praise you because I am fearfully and wonderfully made; your works are wonderful, I know that full well. / My frame was not hidden from you when I was made in the secret place, when I was woven together in the depths of the earth. / Your eyes saw my unformed body; all the days ordained for me were written in your book before one of them came to be. (Psalm 139:13–16)

  (This passage speaks of God's active role in our creation and formation in the womb.)

- If people are fighting and hit a pregnant woman and she gives birth prematurely but there is no serious injury, the offender must be fined whatever the woman's husband demands and the court allows. / But if there is serious injury, you are to take life for life, / eye for eye, tooth for tooth, hand for hand, foot for foot, / burn for burn, wound for wound, bruise for bruise. (Exodus 21:22–25)

  (The passage prescribes the same penalty—death—for someone who causes the death of a baby in the womb as for

19

someone who commits murder. This law and its punishment clearly indicate that God considers a baby in the womb to be just as much a human being as a full-grown baby. For the Christian, abortion is not a matter of a woman's right to choose to have a baby. The baby is already present and living. Abortion is a matter of the life or death of a human being made in God's image.)

- Then God said, "Let us make mankind in our image, in our likeness, so that they may rule over the fish in the sea and the birds in the sky, over the livestock and all the wild animals, and over all the creatures that move along the ground." / So God created mankind in his own image, in the image of God he created them; male and female he created them. (Genesis 1:26–27)

- Whoever sheds human blood, by humans shall their blood be shed; for in the image of God has God made mankind. (Genesis 9:6).

After a few minutes, a doctor came in, introduced himself, and explained to me what he was about to do. He sat in front of me and asked me to pull myself closer to him. He started to draw the light near the area, and then he stopped. He explained I should have a physical exam done before the actual abortion.

I said, "OK." Then took a deep breath and exhaled.

After the doctor examined me, he asked the nurse, "When was her last menstrual cycle?"

The nurse proceeded to read the information on the chart to him, and he interrupted her, saying, "No this can't be. She is too far gone for this procedure."

Apparently, instead of being twelve weeks pregnant, I was fourteen weeks pregnant per his examination. He continued by apologizing and letting me know I was not able to get the abortion I had been scheduled for. He added that there were other measures I could take, and the nurse would explain those to me. The doctor left the room, and the nurse instructed me to follow her back into the dressing room. She asked me to get dressed and said she would come back for me. I was devastated, filled with anxiety and fear.

I was called into the office to speak to someone regarding what other procedures could be done at this stage in the pregnancy. It was explained that there was a procedure that could be done in a hospital setting. It would be a little bit more complicated, and I would have to be put to sleep completely and spend the night in the hospital. Of course, I absolutely agreed and started the arrangements to have that type of procedure done. Right away, I called the teacher's assistant and explained the situation to her. I asked her if she would help me, and she agreed. She was going to ask my parents if I could spend the night over at her house, and then she would drop me off at the clinic, where I could be admitted and stay overnight to have the procedure done. She promised to pick me up the next day and take me home. Wow, this was great! I would be able to have this done and over with after all.

Everything went as planned. The aide asked Mami for permission, it was granted, and everything seemed to be working as scheduled. That same week, a day or two later, Joey wanted to see me. I said yes, and we went to his apartment. Shortly after I arrived, there was a knock on the door. Joey tried to ignore it. But then we heard a loud call. "Joey my son, abre la puerta. Soy yo, Fela" (Joey my son, open the door. It's me, Fela.) It was my mom in her Spanglish calling out for Joey to open the door.

Oh no. I was in big trouble now.

Joey got up and opened the door. She came in and greeted him and went straight to the point. "Yo vine para haserte una pregunta. Yo tengo sospecha que Yaya esta enbarasada y quiero que tu me lo confiese para poder tomar los pasos necesarios, como llevar la a un médico" (I have a question I need you to answer. I have reason to suspect that Yaya is pregnant. I need to know in order to take the necessary steps, like taking her to see a doctor).

Oh my goodness! I couldn't believe this was happening. It was almost like I wasn't even part of this whole situation. Yet I was. No questions were directed at me at all. Joey answered her quickly,

21

saying, Si, es verdad. Yaya esta enbarasada" (Yes, it's true. Yaya is pregnant).

My mom asked him the big question, "Y tu, que piensas haser?" (What do you plan to do about it)?

Joey responded to her, "Yo me quiero casar con ella pero su esposo se opone" (I want to marry her, but your husband is against it).

"No te preocupe de el. Yo le hablo esta noche cuando llegue del trabajo" ("Don't worry about him. I will talk to him tonight when he gets home from work), Mami responded. She added she would take me to the doctor the next day to get the pregnancy confirmed and that he could pick me up on Friday. "She'll be ready to go with you," she concluded. "You will be married shortly after that."

Wow, that was it. I was speechless and didn't know what to think. I just felt this enormous emotion deep down in my heart and soul, telling me my life was over.

The next day was Tuesday. Everybody was getting ready for school. El was always the first one ready. Lou and I were getting ready. Mami walked in our room as Lou was walking out. "Yaya, you are not going to school," she said. "I'm going to take you to the doctor." As she was walking out, she turned and added, "Oh yeah. Your father doesn't want to see or talk to you ever again."

We read about this situation in scripture. "If, however, the charge is true and no proof of the young woman's virginity can be found / she shall be brought to the door of her father's house and there the men of her town shall stone her to death. She has done an outrageous thing in Israel by being promiscuous while still in her father's house. You must purge the evil from among you" (Deuteronomy 22:20–21).

Thinking about it now, I realize I was truly blessed. Had I been born earlier (between 1200 BC and 1500 BC), I would have been stoned to death.

Without my realization, the curse that had been said earlier when I was a little girl (around eight) was coming to pass. My father would pay, through me, for his unloving heart toward my older siblings whenever they were disobedient. My mom had stated this during a couple of their disputes regarding his disposition toward my older siblings' behavior.

Another phrase that had been spoken out loud, this one by my older brother, was that I would be the worst prostitute in the city of Chicago. Oh, my goodness, what had I done? Was this what was next in my life? Would my brother's statement also one day be true of me? I didn't understand much of it. But what I did know was that I must be this awful person and that my dad had to pay, through me, for the pain he had caused my siblings.

I had no clue what I had done that would cause them to wish such awful things. Today, I understand why I was put out of my home. It may not have been the right thing to do, but it was what my parents understood to be correct. In their rearing, losing your virginity and becoming pregnant was dishonoring your family name, and you were not allowed back in the house. That was my dad's understanding and belief, and it was probably why my parents argued so much about the older children's behavior. This was why the curse had been made— why it was said that Papi would pay for his intolerance of my siblings' behavior through me. Again, without understanding or even having a clue about it all, I allowed it to come true by the choices I made. Even just being quiet about what had happened to me earlier on in my childhood was a wrong choice.

My mom telling me my father never wanted to talk to me or even see me after all of this truly destroyed me inside.

Lou and El went to school, and Mami took me to the doctor. I was the main topic in the doctor's office. The staff kept talking about a baby having a baby, and my mom added, "She even beat me; I was seventeen when I got pregnant."

I was somewhat confused. Was this a good thing or bad thing? The nurses had me do a urine pregnancy test. And yes, I definitely was pregnant. I recall Dr. Hernandez saying, "*Wow*, a baby is having a baby." I would hear that phrase often for the next few months. While they talked about me, in my mind, all I kept hearing was, *Your father does not want to talk to you ever again.*

We headed back home, and I went straight to my room. I was

too embarrassed to face anyone. And I definitely knew I wasn't to address my dad at all.

My dad went to work. My mom continued with her regular routine. I thought, *If Papi doesn't want to talk to me ever again, then I don't want to live any more.* I recalled that, earlier that year—when Martita died and Mami got the news—Mami had taken some of the little blue pills. When the firemen came, they'd said she almost died. I decided that would work for me. If I stayed in my room, no one would notice, and the pills would work. They hadn't worked for Mami because I was always behind her, and when she had fallen to the floor, 9-1-1 had been called immediately. I would stay in my room, and no one would notice. I would not be Papi's shame anymore. He would not have to suffer the shame I had caused him.

I waited for the opportunity when no one was looking, and I took my mother's prescription Valium. I drank the whole bottle. Whatever was in there went into my stomach. When I became drowsy, I went into my room and lay down. To my surprise, Joey dropped by. He wanted to know the result of the pregnancy test. Mami called for me to come out of the room, and I didn't respond. They came in and found me passed out on my bed. They rushed me to the ER.

In the hospital, my stomach was pumped. I kept vomiting, which was what the pumping was supposed to do—in order to clean my stomach. Mami and Joey yelled at me. I remember thinking, *I can't even get this right.* I didn't want to be here. I didn't want to live anymore. I was crushed. I could feel my dad's pain and, for the first time, the shame I'd caused him. When I got home, I went straight to sleep.

The week went by faster than I would have wanted it to. Before I knew it, Friday was here. My siblings went to school, and Mami woke me up and said they were taking me to the store to buy me some items before Joey picked me up. Not even that cheered me up. (I couldn't understand why. Really, what was the point?) I was still distraught that my dad was not speaking to me. I dreaded the car ride. Papi would be right there. I wondered how I would get through this. But I knew I had to face him sooner or later.

I was the first one in the car, as usual, and he was the last one in the car, as usual. When he got in, I felt my heart racing, as if it was pumping a hundred miles an hour. As Mami started driving off, Papi looked back toward me and said, "Yaya, tu tienes chavo que me preste? Estoy pelao" (Yaya, do you have money you can lend me? I'm broke).

I kept quiet. I didn't know what to say.

So he repeated the request. "Yaya, que no me vas a prestar dinero? ¿Que me vas a comprar de comer?" (Yaya, what? Aren't you going to lend me some money? What are you going to buy me to eat?) He looked back and smiled at me.

Oh my goodness! I couldn't believe he'd spoken to me; he'd even had a smile when he was speaking. That was the greatest "I love you" I had ever heard. He may have said a group of words asking me a question. But I heard, *I love you.*

In Psalm 103:13, we read, "As a father has compassion on his children, so the Lord has compassion on those who fear Him."

I wanted to say I was sorry and would never do this again. But I didn't have the courage or the words. I didn't pick out anything at the store like I normally would. I let Mami pick whatever she wanted.

That afternoon, my mother took me to city hall to give her permission for Joey and me to get married. But she was rejected. It was illegal for me to get married before the age of sixteen, even with a parent's signature. We left, and Joey went back to his place to take care of some things.

When evening came, Joey arrived to pick me up. I had a small suitcase and my organ. I knew my life had ended. I did not know what to expect. But I knew one thing for sure. I could never come back. Everything had gone as planned by Mami and Joey. It was the saddest day of my life. It was the beginning of my role as a wife and mother-to-be and *the end of me being a child.*

FACING LIFE / ADULTHOOD

As I see it today, my protection/blessing was that I didn't get pregnant by a family member. After all, they were the ones who'd had use of my body until Joey came into the picture. Part of me was content; I did believe I loved Joey and Joey loved me—at least in terms of what I understood love to be at the time. We did have good times together. I figured it probably wouldn't be that bad. I had made my bed; I had to lie on it, as the phrase goes. I don't know how I did it, but I had Joey drop me off by my parents' apartment and pick me up when he got out of work every day (for a couple of weeks at least until I got used to not seeing my parents daily). Then it was a daily call without fail.

I still have a hard time understanding how all that sexual abuse could take place without notice and without someone doing something about it. But I am reminded that I never voiced what had happened. Even at school, instead of getting good counsel, I was taught how to cover up my sin by having an abortion before my parents could find out. I was confused most, if not all, of the time. In a strange way, it was a blessing getting pregnant. It was the first time I started understanding what had been happening to me and how it was wrong and should not have happened. But I carried the shame, fear, and guilt forward into my adult life.

I have experienced a great deal of sexual abuse and harassment, even in my marriages and in the workplace. It's like a plague that won't go away. It made me go through several different insecurity issues. It created inner anger in me that I did not understand, a violent instinct whenever I felt threatened or anyone I knew was threatened in anyway. I don't remember what it feels like to be a child. In fact, I don't think I ever was a child. In addition to the sexual abuse, I was the peacemaker. I found it necessary to find ways for everyone to feel loved, accepted, and respected.

That fearless inner me caused me to get into situations I shouldn't have. Now I had added fear that turned into a hidden anger I did not understand until much later in life.

I ache for my four older siblings, as I know they, too, were abused in many ways. They were separated from Mami for about four years before she was able to send for them. Johnny had his way with them as well, among other things.

I ach for my parents. They did not know how to do things differently. They had no proper education, much less the psychological tools to successfully handle a blended family with chaos happening all the time. They were doing better than they'd experienced in their upbringing. Getting the wrong advice from people they trusted had not worked in their favor.

I recall Mami telling the story about being pulled out of school in the second grade in order to help out economically at home. She had to work in a different town as a nanny and maid for wealthy families at the tender age of seven. She would be given shelter and food plus twenty-five cents every two weeks. At the end of the work period, she was given the twenty-five cents. My grandfather would pick her up at the end of the road. When she was getting close to him, he would extend his hand out, and she would greet him by putting her quarter in the palm of his hand. She was allowed to stay home for a couple of days, and then she had to return to work again.

Mami had many gifts in the arts. She loved to sing and crochet and was an excellent seamstress. She made most of our clothing and loved doing it all. She was very affectionate with all people, regardless of their race or economic status.

My papi was an introvert and a man of few words. The little he shared of his past was about attending school. It was important for us to know that he did graduate. At his passing I found his diploma of the six grade. He had a vending cart he would sell goods from without much prosperity during his life in Puerto Rico. He loved to recite poetry, and I loved to hear him do so. Papi did not say much, but when people would talk about visiting Puerto Rico, he would say, "I didn't lose anything there to have to go back." He would tell us that we were of French descent, not Puerto Rican. We never really found out why he seemed so reluctant to return to Puerto Rico.

I hurt mostly for my children. They got a child for a mother, and my fears caused me to overly protect them. That may have hurt them more than helped them. I was quick to discipline and, at times, was too harsh. I cringed at the idea of them getting older. As I understand it today, I disciplined them with the inner anger and the fear that was knitted within me, trying for dear life to protect them from the experiences I'd had.

The hidden blessing, the one thing I am grateful for, is that all the abuse, betrayal, deceit, adversity, storms, valleys, turmoil, pain, and fear served to lead me to the foot of the cross. Even if it took over three decades, it came to be.

In the first couple of months, living with Joey was not too bad. I got to see Mami and Papi every day. Joey took me out to eat a lot, and I started meeting some of his friends. Of course, they were all fifteen or more years older than me. But they were very nice people, and they became fond of me.

The reality of life started to kick in. I had to learn how to cook, clean the house, and so on. Joey taught me what he knew, and I would call Mami or my cousin's wife to walk me through other recipes.

Joey was a perfectionist with OCD. Everything had to be sparkly clean. Clothes had to be completely wrinkle-free. I recall one occasion when I had cleaned the apartment and thought it to be well done. But when Joey got home, he made me do it over again. The center table or coffee table had a clear glass plate on top of a design carved into wood. He made me remove the glass and, with a toothbrush, clean the carvings on the table design and then polish the woodwork, clean the glass on both sides, and place it back on the table. Wow!

I learned that clean meant detail clean, or it was not clean at all. This reminded me of my siblings getting hit for not doing a good job at home. And Mami would say, "Cuando agan algo, agalo bien" (When you do something, do it right). I didn't mind being taught. In fact, I enjoyed it. I liked working. And learning how to do things right was a plus. I wanted to be the best wife ever. So, whatever he said, I did. This was no different from how I had been raised in a very clean home, with perfection being the model.

Everything in life has two sides to it, even human beings. Joey was romantic and thoughtful. He would bring me a rose almost every day. And whatever I wanted, he would buy for me. Money wasn't a problem in the beginning. Even though I didn't ask for anything, if I mentioned I liked something, I was sure to get it at some point.

I was happy with my Pepsi or Coca-Cola, sunflower seeds, candy, and cigarettes. Yes, I started smoking regularly. I had been taught how to smoke by Martita before she left home. I didn't smoke after she taught me until after I had left home myself. It was funny because Joey did not smoke or drink alcohol, other than a glass of wine socially. I think, in a sense, smoking was the only thing that made me feel grown up.

I was always told what to do and how to do it, just like being at home with my parents. Joey was a man who'd just walked into my life one day and somehow owned me. Whatever emotions I had for him were all mixed up. I liked him as a conversationalist and artist. I liked how sociable he was with people. I enjoyed that he cared to spend time with me. But I did not understand much about defining other emotions.

When I was about six months into my pregnancy, a knock sounded at the door in the middle of the night. It was loud and scared me awake. Joey jumped up and said, "Put on your coat. Run to the back porch. Under the steps, there is a hole. Put this bag in there and come back to the bedroom. I was scared and did not understand what was going on. But he was upset, and I just did what he told me to do.

Meanwhile, he was trying to calm the man at the door, yelling, "I'm coming," as the knocking grew louder and louder and the beams of flashlights shone through the window. "This is the police," they called. "Open the door."

There was snow on the ground. I slipped and fell, but I got up quickly and hid the brown bag as Joey had instructed me to do. I ran into the bedroom and climbed back in bed under the covers.

Joey opened the door and let the policemen in. They searched the apartment and did not find a thing. Surprisingly, they did not go out to the back. They only searched inside of the apartment.

When the policemen left, I tried to ask Joey what it had all been about, but he refused to give me any information. He said that he was holding something for a friend, and he did not know what the police had wanted or why they had come to the apartment.

The event was terribly frightening. The four officers weren't wearing police uniforms. If nothing was wrong, why would they come at that time of night? And why had there been four officers, not just two of them? So many questions arose from that scary event. I wanted to know what was in the bag I'd hid under the stairs and wondered why Joey kept a gun in the apartment.

Questions started to race through my mind, and I didn't feel safe anymore. I didn't have any place to go. Who could I ask about these things? Oh yeah, I had made my bed, and I had to lie in it. I didn't feel like a wife but, rather, the student of a man who wanted to create the perfect obedient wife for himself in the way he wanted her to be.

He would tell me how I was supposed to be as a woman and wife. Rule number one, I was not supposed to ask too many questions. Rule number two, if he stepped out, I was to accept it and never question it, no matter what time he came in. Rule number three, if he was at a nightclub, and a woman offered herself to him, I needed to know he had to accept the offer because he was a man and not a homosexual. And of course, the list grew as time passed and our lives unfolded.

On one of his manly nights out, he told me he would be going out with one of my cousins. That night, he came home at 4:00 a.m. I did just as I was taught. I asked no questions, just happy he was home.

A couple of days later, I was at my younger cousin's home hanging out with his wife and the older cousin's wife. One of them asked me, "What time did Joey get home last night? Where was he at?"

In my naiveness, I answered her without any hesitation, "He was at a club and got home at 4:00 a.m."

A few days later, Joey and I went to visit my younger cousin, who lived upstairs from my older cousin (Joey's best friend). After twenty minutes, Joey went downstairs to the older cousin's apartment, and minutes later, he called me down. He asked me in front of my cousin and his wife what I had told the women a couple days earlier.

"I answered their question. You went to the club and came home at 4:00 a.m. Why?"

He slapped me with the back of his hand and told me I was not supposed to gossip. If I ever did it again, I would really get it. I tried to clear myself, but he told me to be quiet, and we left.

I had never spoken about what my cousin was doing. All I had done was answer a question about where my husband was and what time he got home. I didn't know what gossip was, and I didn't think I had said anything wrong. My cousin's wife never apologized for getting me in trouble. Nor did she explain what I had done wrong. I never told her anything again. Joey started going out and spending less and less time at home.

I lived with Joey out of wedlock for two years until I turned sixteen. In December 1976, my mother kept her word to Joey. They took me to city hall, and we were married. My sister Elsa (the oldest of the seven of us) served as a witness, along with my mother. Wow! Sadly, I still did not know I had rights. (I'll say more about that later.)

As time progressed, I noticed that Joey would spend long periods of time in the bathroom or in the guest room. I would often find the cap of a soda bottle, matches, and a glass of water left behind after he would leave the room. It was strange, but I was not to ask questions.

One day, he was watching TV in our bedroom. Our bed frame was handmade by him and had an extended headboard. On one end, he'd built a shelf for the phone, and he'd installed mirrors as the wall between that and the other end, with a built-in space for the alarm clock. The mattress was round, extra thick, and huge. The bed was beautiful and special because it was made by his own hands, and he took a lot of pride in that.

Joey was sitting up, leaning back with his arms extended out and resting on the headboard. I noticed some red marks on his forearm. Out of concern, I got close to look and see what was wrong with his arms and asked him, "Are you OK?"

Immediately, I was pushed away and told nothing was wrong. After that, he would try not to make his arms visible to me, wearing shirts that covered half his arms. That was not a problem, because he would make his own clothes. Yes, he would make his own clothes. Imagine that. He also made drapes that matched the bedspread and pillowcases. Joey had gifted hands. God had truly blessed this man with multiple gifts. Unfortunately, he let the power of drug addiction rob him from the blessing to use his gifts to benefit God and for God's glory.

I had few people who I could confide in. I had become close to my younger cousin's wife, and she became my "go-to" person. My younger cousin was strict with his wife and home. He did not allow any visitors in the apartment unless he was at home and had approved the visit. I would sneak into their place when he was off to work and sneak back out before he got home. Actually, I'd learned how to do that when I was still at home with my parents. I'd ditched school a couple of time to spend the day with his wife and kids.

Those were fun times I spent with her. One of the first things I noticed was a Bible on top of her end table. I was drawn to the big book and asked about it. I didn't ask to read it because I could hardly read at the time and had a fear of doing so. She said it was the Bible, and she would normally read it after my cousin would leave for work and before the kids got up. She was always alone with her kids, and we became very close.

One day, I asked her if she knew what the marks on Joey's arms could be. She asked me if I had ever read his track about his life. I said no, and she went on to explain what it was. She said, "It is a little folded piece of paper that talks about his life." (I have added a picture of that track in the end of my story. Joey shared it with me later on and told me the whole story and how he served for ten years in the Teen Challenge movement.)

A couple of days after, I was watching *The Phil Donohue Show*. Drug addiction was the topic that day. In fact, Donahue became my resource center for all topics. Most of what I learned in the first couple of years was from that show. I watched it daily and gained some knowledge about the world around me.

Every time we went out, Joey would spend those long periods of time in the restroom. One day, he was in there for a very long time, longer than usual. When I heard a large *bang*, I pried the door open. He was lying in the bathtub with one leg hanging out and some blood present. Foam was coming out of his mouth, and his skin was purple. I tried moving him, but I couldn't. I ran upstairs for help. The upstairs neighbor came down. But when he saw Joey, he said he couldn't do anything. He was clearly scared and ran back upstairs.

I started pumping his stomach and praying, *God, help me*. Out of nowhere, a punch flew across the air. He gasped for air and started trying to get out of the tub. "Get out of here," he yelled. "I told you never to bother me when I'm in the bathroom."

I had mixed emotions. On one hand, I was glad he was OK. But I didn't understand why he didn't acknowledge that he had just been lying there dead. And had I not come in the bathroom, he would have died—period. I was terrified. He acted like he had just walked in the bathroom, and I was disturbing him. How absurd was that?

This was the first overdose Abba God Almighty saved Joey from, using me, in our time together.

The second time was in 1977 before I got pregnant with our second daughter, Karen. It was not an overdose; it was more like a suicide due to hallucination from barbiturates. He was, once again, trying to kick the heroin addiction and was taking some methadone and street-bought barbiturates. I brought up his plate of food—pork chops, mashed potatoes, and green beans. He threw the plate and said there were insects crawling over it. I ran down to put the plate away and get something to clean up the mess. When I got upstairs, he was trying to throw himself out the second-floor window. I caught him by his feet and pulled him in. Again, thank You, Jesus. This was only You, my Lord. Thank you, Jesus. Amen!

The third time was in 1978. This was after Karen was born, and Annette was three years old. Again, he was locked in the bathroom for a long time. This time, I heard water running, but it sounded like overflowing water. Abba God, thank you for my excellent hearing, as it has been very handy in many situations! My daughter jokes about it all the time. I knocked on the door. When no response came, I busted the door open. Joey was lying naked in a tub full of water. I proceeded to do the same thing as I had the last time. And yes, God was merciful, and Joey responded.

Whenever we would go out, he would doze off constantly, no matter where we were. Everyone was talking about him, saying he was an addict. One time, he was shooting up in my mom's restroom and left blood on the ceiling and floor. Elsa told my mom, and they told me to tell him not to do that in their home.

I was deeply embarrassed. Oh my, what had I gotten myself into? But I would remember. I made my bed. Now I must lie in it. That was a saying I heard a lot, and I picked up the phrase. The truth of the matter was I had sinned against God and was paying the consequences for my sin. This is how I understand it today.

I remember exactly what moved Joey to seek help. It was a pamphlet I found at the local public aid office when I accompanied my cousin's wife, who was there to take the free GED test being offered. Reading through the brochures, I found one that offered help for drug addiction. I asked a lady who worked there about it, and she added some information that sounded great. I took the brochure home, and Joey followed up and went for treatment at a local outpatient clinic called Rincon.

My cousin's wife was deeply upset that I'd asked questions about the subject. She asked me, "Aren't you embarrassed? You shouldn't be sharing that with people in public."

I didn't understand what was wrong with what I had done. If you needed help to get out of a bad situation, you could only get help if you shared what the problem was that you needed help with. Right?

This happened when Annette was about eighteen months old. I was very happy that Joey agreed to go to the outpatient clinic. I also had him explain about his past a little more. I was shocked that he supplied the information without getting upset. That was a plus—a move in the right direction.

Sometimes, I would accompany him to the clinic and would stay in the car with Annette. It was during the summer months, so I would keep the door of the car open to avoid the enclosed heat. A couple of the ladies tried to befriend me. They made some conversation, and one of them asked me, "Where are your tracks? What area do you shoot up at?"

I said, "I don't shoot up. What are you talking about?"

She responded, "Sure. You know, where you hit yourself at. I don't see any marks."

I told her, "You see no marks because I don't have any. I don't use any drugs. All I do is smoke cigarettes." I thought it was ignorant that these women would think that, just because I was married to Joey, I must be using too.

She said, "Well, I didn't do drugs either when I met my husband. But then he turned me on to pot and then a hit of cocaine. And before I knew it, I was shooting up."

"That was you, not me. I didn't, and I haven't, and I won't do any of that," I responded.

To the glory of Almighty God, I can say that I did not and have not. Thank you, Jesus! But like it is said, tell me who you walk with, and I will tell you who you are. I would hear this often when growing up and even later in life. Then God revealed it to me this way:

1. The righteous choose their friends carefully, but the way of the wicked leads them astray. (Proverbs 12:26)
2. One who has unreliable friends soon comes to ruin, but there is a friend who sticks closer than a brother. (Proverbs 18:24)

3. As iron sharpens iron, so a friend sharpens a friend. (Proverbs 27:17)
4. Walk with the wise and become wise; associate with fools and get in trouble. (Proverbs 13:20)
5. You can trust what your friend says, even when it hurts. But your enemies want to hurt you, even when they act nice. (Proverbs 27:6)

When I was ready to deliver our first daughter, Annette, Joey had to inform my mom, not so much because of the good news that I was going to deliver but because, legally, he could not take me in himself. I didn't realize this fact at the time. It wasn't until later in life that I came to understand the true reality of my situation. Mami met us at the hospital, completed the admission documents, and then came to the exam room I was in. She told me she had to go home now. "When you get any pain, don't scream or yell. Just pray. Ask God to give you strength." Joey had left the hospital too. It was just me, the baby to be, and God.

It felt like forever. At first, they tried to induce labor because my contractions had ceased. But everything they tried was failing to work. She just did not want to come out. Labor took seventy-two hours, but it felt like a lifetime. Dr. Rodriguez was very gentle with me. Everyone in the hospital was talking about the baby having a baby. She was born at 4:00 a.m. The doctor came up to me and said, "I am so proud of you. You did great. You have a beautiful baby girl. Who should we call?"

I said proudly, "My mother and let her know I didn't scream." I thought to myself, *Wow I'm a mom. I have a baby.* "I will never let anything happen to you," I whispered to her.

After the delivery, I was moved to a regular room. Everyone came to see me. Doctors, nurses, everyone wanted to see the baby who had a baby. I did just as Mami told me to. I did not cry, scream, or complain, not once. I prayed and prayed until Annette was out, and she was placed into my arms.

How I thanked God for my little one and regretted ever wanting to abort her. Sadly, I could not breastfeed her because I was a smoker, and no one ever suggested I should stop smoking. I was clueless about what to and not to do. Shortly after I was settled in my room, the nurses brought me some formula, a set of bottles, and an extra bottle with water. Before I knew it, there my little one was, snuggled in my arms. What joy! And she was all mine. I fed her and burped her so naturally it looked like I had previous experience. But no, I did not. None of the other children I had taken care of had been newborns. She was the first.

The woman next to me was having problems feeding her baby. She called for help, and the nurse said, "Look. She is only fourteen. She is a baby, and she is not having any problems feeding her baby." It was not nice of the nurse to say such a thing. Everyone is different. But I was surprised to hear the compliment. I just smiled and continued enjoying what came so naturally to me—feeding and loving my baby.

Mami came later that morning. She had a beautiful outfit and a crocheted coat she had made while waiting for Annette to arrive. Funny, it was yellow, as we hadn't known the gender of the baby. But I'd always felt I was carrying a girl. I didn't want a boy anyway. Everyone else did.

My beautiful baby girl had blue eyes and blond hair. Her skin was pink as a flower in spring. She had perfect little hands and tiny, tiny little toes. She had the chunkiest little cheeks, despite her thin, tiny body. I recall that was the first thing my brother Eliberto noticed when we brought her home.

Oh yeah, I was not allowed to go to Joey's apartment for the first couple of days. I had to stay at Mami and Papi's. And when we were leaving, they wanted me to leave the baby because *el sereno de la Noche* (the night air) would harm her. I had a tantrum, crying until they had to let her go. There was no way I was going to leave my baby behind. I didn't recall anyone at the hospital with me when she was born, just God the doctor and me. I understood instantly that Annette was my responsibility—not Mami's, not Papi's, not even Joey's. She was mine to take care of.

Joey loved his baby girl. Yes, he did. She was his queen, pride, and joy. He protected her like a hawk, and she could do no wrong. She was perfect, a real queen. The nursery was decorated with hand-painted cartoons done by him. The door had a sign that read "Queen Annette," in a half-moon arch and drawn in a combination of French script MS and Monotype Corsiva writing, white bold letters and black outline with baby blue backings.

Right away, he gave me the first thing instructions related to her: She is to be held by no male. Absolutely no one is allowed to kiss her on her lips, only on her forehead. And she is not allowed to be dirty at any time. Those were nonnegotiable rules. I felt the same way, so it was not a struggle for me to obey the commanding chief.

As time passed, many things happened, both good and bad. One that Joey was thrilled about was September 15, 1976, when I turned 16. He was quick to remind Mami that she had promised to sign to give us permission to get married. Papi was still against it, but nevertheless, Mami, my sister Elsa, and Joey took me to city hall, and we were married. Wow, just like that. Again, I had no say so in the matter. I was dealing with things as they came along. I was starting to understand a few things but not much. So, I went along with what I believed was my responsibility after making the choices I had made. There was no joy, one way or the other. I just did what I had to do.

Back to Joey being an overprotective dad. On the one hand, he could be too protective of Annette. We lived in an apartment that Joey had agreed to rehabilitate for my older cousin in exchange for free rent. It had two floors. The bedrooms, one bath, an art room, and the laundry were on the second floor. The living room, dining room, guest room, bath, and kitchen were on the first floor. There was a long staircase up to the second floor. Joey was an artist and had beautiful pieces of artwork framed and showcased on the wall of the stairs that led to the second floor. They were hung in a staircase style.

One day, Annette was coming down the stairs and placed her hand on the wall, sliding it along as she walked down, which of course caused one of the paintings to fall down. He was furious but not at her. He grabbed her, kissed her, and made sure she was OK, saying, "It's OK, Mamita, it's OK." Then he yelled at me and said it was my fault for not watching her.

That temper of his fired up more often. During this period, he was clean of all drugs, and he never really was an alcohol user. So, it was all of him, and that temper was triggered off by any small thing. I knew it was impossible to keep the children by me constantly. But he may have been right. It must have been my fault. I should be more attentive. I was reminded again this little one was my responsibility, all mine.

By this time, we had two precious little ones. Yes, I had a second child while taking birth control. I could not believe it. Again? Life was hard enough with just the one, especially with neither of us holding jobs for long periods of time. I was discussing it with my cousin's wife and expressing the fear of not being able to support them. She said, "Don't worry, Yayie. Where there is for one, there is for two, or ten." And she laughed, adding, "You have a long way before the baby is due. Things might get better. Don't forget. Joey is very talented."

I knew I didn't want an abortion. And it was true Mami would always say, "Donde come uno, comen dies. Dios probera" (Where one eats, ten eat. God will provide).

One week after getting the news I was pregnant, I received a letter from the Stevensen Building Swimwear Co. It read:

> Dear Ms. Seguinot,
>
> You have been recommended by Fashionette Swimsuit World (Mr. Morris Greenblatt, Proprietor) in the Stevenson Building of downtown Chicago and Chosen by Innovations Finishing School and Model Agency for an opportunity to represent us as a contestant in a swimming pageant scheduled in August.

That was on May 14, 1977, and the deadline was May 28, 1977. I was devastated. I had been recognized by one of the finest stores in swimwear in downtown Chicago, and I had to turn them down. In August, I would be in my sixth month and definitely not in bikini shape or any state to be in a swimwear pageant. I felt the opportunity of a lifetime slip me by—all because I had not been careful enough. Again, I had failed. First, I'd ruined the years of my youthful education and tarnished Papi's family name. Now, I was having to pass an opportunity that any young girl would dream of. How had I managed that on the pill? I could not understand.

But yes, a second child was on the way, and I was only sixteen, with very little education. One thing made it a joy for sure; Mami loved babies, and she started planning the next crochet sweater suit, this time yellow and green in case it was a boy. She never showed anything but joy at the announcement of a child being born, and that somehow gave me peace of mind.

This time, the delivery was early, after one false alarm. The scenario was the same. Mami took me to the hospital, and she picked me up when the baby was born. The labor and delivery was not as bad this time, only forty-eight hours! Joey did not wait because he had planned to go out (clubbing) that night, and Mami of course had my siblings and dad to go home to. But I knew what to do—don't scream and pray.

Dr. Rodriguez was sweet and gentle and very attentive. Again, he asked, "Who do we call?"

And yes, I said, "Mami."

When he announced, "It's a girl," I was very happy, even though I knew Joey wanted a boy. I was happy that this new little one was a girl. When I saw her, I felt a strong sense of commitment. The responsibility became much greater. It was now a commitment to two precious little lives that depended on me to protect and care for them.

Oh my goodness, she was so beautiful. And she had a head full of hair! Oh, and it was black, just like mine. Her skin was light, but the cuticles on her fingers were tan. They had to believe she was mine for sure. She had a cute dimple on her chin, just like Joey. I felt so blessed and thrilled that she looked somewhat like me.

When we left the hospital, of course, we had to stop by my parents' apartment first. Papi was absolutely tickled over Karen. He loved both granddaughters. I caught him, for the first time, baby talking to Annette when I brought her home from the hospital, something he had done with no child, not even his own and now did the same with Karen. With this second grandbaby, there was something about her (Karen) that drew him. He even changed her name from Karen to Karina. As the girls grew, he always remembered to bring Karina a snickers bar whenever he went to the grocery store. I believe it had to do with the fact that she looked more like me and that she also had cataplexy, which I'd inherited from him. Funny, years later, after his passing, I found out she felt the special bond between them.

After having Karen, I knew I needed to get another job. I had been blessed in getting jobs whenever I applied. Over time, I worked at Jupiter's department store, McDonald's, and a clothing store. What I remember about the time I worked at the store was being harassed by an older man who owned the jewelry store right next door. His daughter worked in the same store I did and had been there for several years. He would come in the store and say stuff to me all the time—asking me out to lunch or dinner and so on. I would ignore him and always kept myself busy to avoid talking to him. He kept inviting me to dinner and would not take no for an answer. He said he would make it worth my while and that he just wanted to get to know me better. One day, when I walked to my car, which was parked around the corner, this man was standing next to my car. He again extended the invitation, and I declined.

I was so upset at his persistence that I told Joey about the incident. Joey gave me a very different response than the one I was expecting. I was expecting him to have a word with this person, asking him to leave me alone. To my surprise, Joey said, "That is a good thing. Don't look at it as negative. If he owns a jewelry store, he may, in addition to taking you to dinner, give you a gift. I'm sure it will be a piece of jewelry. Don't be ignorant. Accept the date. We can sell whatever piece of jewelry he may give you."

I was deeply upset. I shared the incident with Mario, my

sister-in-law's brother. He normally helped me get methadone for Joey when he sent me out for it during episodes of detox withdrawal. He said, "Don't worry. I will take care of it."

Sure, enough, the next day when I was going home, I walked to my car, which was always on the same street around the corner from the store. And yes, the man was by my car. Before I realized it, there was Mario on his ten-speed bike, pulling up right next to my car. Wow! Thank you, Jesus! I wouldn't have thought of saying that at that time, but I say it today. I was very happy. I was not a newborn Christian at the time. Had I been, there would have been a whole lot of hallelujahs being shouted. Mario asked the jewelry store owner what he wanted and made it very clear that he was to stay away from me in the store and on the street, or he would be answering to him. It was God who sent my dear friend Mario. He also explained to me that, normally, when a person is doing heroin, he will often get his wife or girlfriend hooked on it too or will prostitute her for his fix. Joey was not even using heroin at the time. I cannot imagine what might have happened if he was shooting up. He wouldn't have forgotten the offer as quickly as he had. He would have pushed the issue.

Jesus protected me without me even knowing it. There are many stories like this in my life. I am so blessed to have lived to be able to talk about it. Let me move on to where I was going.

It was great having the two girls, and Joey was doing well at staying off heroin and off the streets. Now, I had peace of mind, instead of the constant worry of him overdosing, getting hurt on the streets, or getting arrested for any reason. That peace of mind was short-lived.

Joey had a younger brother named Ando, who, for whatever reason, wanted to come to Chicago. And yes, he ended up staying with us for a while.

One day while Joey was not home, Ando started acting strange. I was in our bedroom, previously the dining room before Joey converted it into a bedroom by making curtains to divide it. Ando started crawling under the curtains into our bedroom and started trying to grab my legs. I kept saying, "What are you doing? What is wrong with you?"

Since he was not answering me and kept acting weird, I jumped off the bed, grabbed the two girls, and ran out the door. His behavior was incredibly frightening. I started calling my neighbors, Professor and Pamela, who lived across from us. Their building had a tall fence surrounding it that was kept locked. So, when they came out, they grabbed the girls and pulled them over the fence, and then I jumped over. Professor wanted to go after him, but I did not want to get Joey upset in any way. So, I asked him to just let us stay until Joey came home. I waited a couple hours and had Professor check to see if Ando was still in our apartment. But thankfully, he had left. I chose not to tell Joey what had happened to avoid him from getting upset and turning back to heroin. God was so good that it ended up being that one time, and Ando never again tried to disrespect me during his stay in Chicago.

A few months passed, and my older cousin made Joey a proposition. He had bought a two-flat building, but it needed a lot of repairs. He asked Joey if he would be willing to live in the building rent free in return for Joey fixing it. He would buy the material and put in the labor in exchange for rent. Joey thought it would be a good deal. He estimated the repairs needed and knew he could do it and keep his day job, working on the apartment in his spare time. It seemed like a wise deal.

One day, I needed something from the store, so I asked Ando to keep an eye on the girls for a few minutes. When I came back, Karen's diaper was loose on one side. I picked her up to fix it, and I saw blood on her diaper. I panicked and started checking her all over. There were no cuts that I could see. I immediately called Joey and he ran home from work. His brother could not tell us what had happened. He said he did not know. We took her into the ER, and she was examined. They said she was OK and had a little split on her feminine area, but they said there was no signs of sexual activity. But due to the nature of the injury, they had to notify DCFS. An investigation was started, which lasted for a few months. Joey's first reaction was violent. He wanted to kill his brother. My older cousin allowed him to stay at his place until he was able to return to Puerto Rico.

Well, that surely triggered Joey's addiction to start up again. He lost his ability to deal with the whole issue and started using heroin again. My younger cousin's wife suggested that the girls be baptized immediately. She and my younger cousin could be their godparents. That way, if the state felt the need to take the girls, at least we could request they be placed with their godparents, and we would have access to them regularly. This was devastating. I couldn't understand why he ended up using again. I felt he should have gotten other help, instead of turning back to the demon of heroin.

After all was cleared with the DCFS and the case was closed, he started doing better again. Now my older cousin requested that we pay rent. Joey had transformed the apartment from a big mess and had rehabilitated it to a beautiful state. He'd spent more money and hours of labor than it would have cost to rent the place. We had no savings and could not pay the rent my older cousin was asking for.

About a week after he requested the rent, a sheriff knocked at our door and served us with an immediate eviction notice. We did not even get a chance to do anything. They started taking our furniture out of the apartment and placing it on the street. Oh, my goodness! There I stood, with my one-year-old in my arms and the three-year-old holding the other hand. Joey tried pleading with them, but it was to no avail. All our things were being placed on the street. This took him back to using it again. We were on the street without notice, and all our earnings were invested in my cousin's apartment.

Thank God I was a stay-at-home mom at the time. I was able to be with the girls when this happened and handle it accordingly.

This reminds me of time going back to when Annette was about nine months old. Joey had decided it was time I helped with the finances. So, he gave me an address that had been given to him by one of his friend's wives. She worked at the Hyatt. I went and applied and was blessed. They hired me. I lied on the application and said I was nineteen, when I was only fourteen.

This was great! I loved what I was doing, and I was earning what I needed to help raise my baby. Funny, I shared about my job with my younger cousin's wife, and she said she hated the idea of me cleaning beds and toilets for other people. I, on the other hand, enjoyed it. I was really good and put a lot of pride in my job. About three months into the job, I was offered a supervisor position, but that was short-lived.

One weekend we were invited to my uncle's home for a get-together he was hosting. It was nice. Everyone was there—Mami, my siblings, my two cousins, and their families. We had a great time. When we were going home, I was looking for my wallet to stop at the store. It was nowhere to be found. Joey started accusing my family, saying that my uncle's place was the last place we had been. I knew that was impossible. I called my uncle, and he reassured me that I had not left my wallet there. I just chucked it up to it being gone, and I couldn't do anything about it.

The next day as I was getting ready to do laundry, I was moving things around in the trunk of the car. And guess what I found? Yes, it was my wallet. It empty of cash, but at least my IDs were there.

I stopped by my younger cousin's house to talk to his wife, and she said, "I told you not to be working there. You are cleaning toilets so that he can shoot up. You should quit. He cannot take what you do not have."

I did not delay. I quit my job the next workday. Joey was not thrilled, but I told him I had been laid off. He really could do nothing about it.

Today, I know that was the wrong approach to the situation. We should never resort to any kind of deceit in order to handle a wrongdoing. Nor should we pay evil with evil:

- No one who practices deceit will dwell in my house; no one who speaks falsely will stand in my presence. (Psalm 101:7)
- Do not repay evil with evil or insult with insult. On the contrary, repay evil with blessing, because to this you were called so that you may inherit a blessing. (1 Peter 3:9)

I got a job quickly after that whole ordeal of getting evicted from my older cousin's building. I started working for Medical Arts Pharmacy. I did very well there. I was the cashier at the front of the store. I learned quickly and did my job well. The owner of the store was very fond of me.

Joey was still using. It wasn't as much. But still, he was back on heroin. I was just living day by day, trying to do all I understood to do to raise my two little ones and help Joey financially. But of course, his addiction was difficult to deal with because I did not understand a whole lot of things. I knew of God and understood I was a Christian. But I did not know much else regarding spirituality and how to have a true relationship with God. I did not understand that prayer is the key to our relationship with God, and it plays a significant part of your daily life. Instead, I would go to my younger cousin's wife for just about everything.

A couple of months into my employment, a customer walked in the store and left a roll of film to be developed. He befriended me by asking my name. I had always had a joyful spirit and love for people. I smiled and said, "My name is Carmen."

He in turn said, "My name is Julio Arzuaga." He then invited me out for lunch.

I declined his offer. He took out a small piece of paper and wrote his phone number on it and handed it to me. I did not take it right then. But when he left, I picked it up and put it in my pocket.

Back in those days, photos did not come in right away. It took a few days for them to be developed and returned to the store. In a few days, Mr. Arzuaga stopped by to pick up his pictures. I handed him the photos and charged him. As he opened the envelope, he began a conversation with me about the pictures. He shared that they were of his mother's birthday celebration and started looking at them while standing in front of me. The store was not busy. Actually, he was the only customer in the store at the time, so I allowed him to engaged with me in conversation.

He asked me why I didn't call him, and I answered, "I am married."

He said it didn't matter. He just wanted to take me out to lunch or have a cup of coffee at Woolworths (which was next door.) He then asked, "Do you know who I am? I am Julio Arzuaga."

I answered, "I'm sorry. I don't know who you are."

A customer came in the store, and I ended the conversation by excusing myself to take care of the other customer.

He walked away saying, "Call me."

He stopped by the store a few times that week. He walked around looking at items and ended up approaching the counter to purchase a pack of Juicy Fruit or Double Mint gum before walking out. During my next visit to my younger cousin's house, I shared the incident with his wife.

She shouted in reply, "What!? Julio Arzuaga?" She continued, "Do you realize how many women would love to get that invitation?" She called me *sangana* (foolish).

Wow! Apparently, Julio Arzuaga had a television program on Channel 26, and he had recorded a few records (they were vinyl records at the time). I was like, "Really? Well, how was I supposed to know that? And so what? I am married, remember?"

A couple of days later, it was payday. Joey stopped by to pick me up from work. Joey was not working at the time and would help Mami with Annette and Karen. Normally, he would take the girls to the park and then pick me up. On this occasion he asked me for my paycheck—not some of it but all of it. I was very upset. But I knew I had better give it to him and not have him blow his temper or steal it from me later on.

I went to my younger cousin's wife to vent about what had happened. She became so upset over his behavior. She said, "El compai Joey merese que se la pegue" (Joey deserves to have you cheat on him.) "Why don't you call Julio and let him take you out to lunch? Ha ha ha." She laughed.

Guess what? Yes. The next day I called Julio, and he was thrilled, to say the least. We scheduled a date. I called off work and spent the day with Julio. Oh my, was my soul captivated by his charm and attention and all the beautiful things he had to say about me! He saw a great deal of potential in me that no one had ever noticed before. He continued to demonstrate his interest by stopping by the store frequently for no real reason. I knew nobody needed to buy that much gum!

This started a whole new chapter in my life that I truly knew nothing about. The emotions were intense. Worst off all, I committed adultery, spoken against in Leviticus 20:10, which says, "If a man commits adultery with another man's wife—with the wife of his neighbor—the adulterer and the adulteress are to be put to death.).

According to my understanding today and what the Bible says, a person would have been stoned to death for what I did. The penalty was death. Even in the secular world, you can be killed, and Joey would have been that type of man who was capable of retaliating in that way. Wow! Even then, Abba God was protecting me when I did not even deserve it.

It is so easy to fall into sin when you are clueless about what you're doing or by listening to someone else's opinion about anything. Even if you have great respect for a person—someone who seems wise in your eyes—he or she may not be giving you the right advice. Just because people you know have an opinion, it does not make that opinion right, no matter how highly you think of them. If someone is not giving you godly advice (providing they have a true relationship with Abba God) confirmed by the word of God, then you should let it go with the wind and not give it a second thought. (Protect your heart from all unrighteous influence.) Here again, the last piece of advice I had been given applied. "He cannot take what you don't have." I foolishly quit my job at the pharmacy.

Julio left Chicago to go to New York or Puerto Rico on a business trip. I was devastated. How could the greatest thing that had happened in my life, besides my daughters, come in like a whirlwind and disappear just as quickly? I would drive around at night in his neighborhood in hopes of seeing that man wearing his black three-piece suit. But he was nowhere to be found. It seemed like a fairy tale out of a book or a dream that did not last very long. I had to move on.

Joey found a job in a mattress company doing what he did best, sewing, one of his many art trades. I, in turn, found a job in a bank downtown. I had a sixth-grade education and a third-grade level in spelling, comprehension, and reading and walked around with a mini pocket dictionary in my purse to get by. But God was right there getting me through life, putting me in great places, and opening doors I wouldn't have imagined.

We started saving money. Joey was back on methadone to help wean him off the heroin. My younger cousin and his wife had just purchased their first private home about six months earlier. She knew of a few properties in the area that were up for sale. She also knew of a program for first-time homeowners that would really benefit us. She gave me the information, so Joey and I started the process of getting our first home. God was faithful in blessing us. We got approved for everything we needed, and we bought our first home right across the street from the school I'd attended when I was eleven.

Our new home was perfect! It had a huge front and back yard that were fenced in by a black steel fence, tall enough to protect the girls yet not so tall as to hide the beauty of the property. The girls could play in the front or back without the worry of them getting out into the street. It had two full baths, three bedrooms, a living room, a kitchen with a dining area, and a two-car garage. I felt safe within its stone frame, which meant less chance of losing it to a fire.

I was starting to be a real adult, productive and wise (so I thought). Everything was going well for us as a couple and as individuals. The girls were healthy and well cared for. And Jose, my older brother, moved in with his wife, Mimi, who I absolutely loved.

Martita, who was four years older than me, had passed away in April 1974, a few days before she would have turned seventeen. Mimi kind of took her place. Jose and Mimi had come across some hardship and were going to stay with us for a while. She would help watch the girls, which took away the stress of taking them out daily.

Joey had his glass of wine and smoked marijuana socially. But so far, he was staying away from the heroin. He was at home more now that he had a regular job, and he was also doing some work to upgrade the house. I enjoyed the girls, our home, and learning new things while working at the bank. It was truly a blessing. Yet things had never really been confronted and had no closure as far as our relationship in the marriage. I did not have a true sense of feeling complete or whole as a couple. He was still master Joey and could do whatever he wanted, and I was Yayie, submissive wife to the king.

One morning, we got up late. I rushed up, got out of bed, ran downstairs, and made him his coffee and lunch taking care of him before he drove off to work. Then I ran back up the stairs, got ready, and ran out to catch the bus, trying not to be late for work. When I got home that evening, Joey was already home because he got off work earlier than I did, and he drove, which cut the traveling time to get home. I was saying hello to Mimi and the girls when I heard Joey call me.

I ran upstairs. He was in the middle of the little family room in the center of the upstairs between our room and the girls' room. He called me into the bedroom and asked me, "What is this?"

I responded, "What?"

He looked over to the bed and repeated, "*What* is this?"

"What?" I responded again. "I was running late, and I forgot to make the bed."

He started walking back to the other room, saying, "We need to talk."

I sat down on a bedroom bench we had sitting against the wall facing away from our bedroom. He sat across from me and said, "This is not acceptable. What do you think, that just because you started working in a bank you are a big shot now, real important, huh? Well, guess what? You are not. And you don't neglect your responsibilities just because you work at a bank. If that's the case, you will have to quit that job." He got up and walked toward me. And just that fast, he slapped me so hard with the back of his hand the glass from my glasses dug into my cheek. "Let that be the last time you ever leave the bed unmade. Now fix it!" he said.

I took my glasses off; held my cheek; and, as the tears ran down my face, went into the bedroom to fix the bed. Mind you, it was almost time to go to bed anyway, and only he and I were going to see the bed. But I did as I was told.

I went to my younger cousin's house and told his wife what had happened. She was so upset and said, "You shouldn't stay there."

I agreed. I called Mami and did what I had always dreaded ever having to do. I asked for shelter. The answer was yes. I could stay for two weeks until I got my own place.

And that's what I did. Taking only a few items for the girls and myself, I headed to Mami's.

Well, staying with my parents was not the same as when I was at home before getting pregnant. Karen was almost two, and instead of walking, she would run. Oh boy, was that not a good thing. The landlords lived downstairs, and Mami and Papi were very strict about any noise.

My first weekend there, I found out that Julio had come into town and was going to be live at the San Juan Theater Friday Saturday and Sunday. Wow! This must be fate. It was going to happen some kind of way that I could see him again. To think, I hadn't known who he was, hadn't known a thing about him before he introduced himself at the pharmacy. I asked Mami if I could go to the live show, and she surprisingly said yes. This had to be fate, I told myself again.

This was the first time I had gone out by myself to an event since I'd left my parents' home in November 1974 with Joey, the father of my unborn child. I must admit I was a bit nervous. I didn't know if my nerves were due to the opportunity to see Julio again or if it was just the fact that I was alone and ready to face who knew what.

I wore shiny, skin-tight black pants; a black, short-sleeve body shirt; a brass-covered one and a half-inch belt with a big oval buckle in the center; and pointy, closed-toed black patent leather shoes with one and a half-inch heels and a strap around the ankle. My hair was loose, full, and curly with a red flower on the left side. I wore black eyeliner, light blush, and black coffee bean lipstick. I have to say, I was feeling pretty good about myself.

I got to the theater and paid my way in. It was packed, to say the least. I wanted to know if Julio had already arrived. I asked the young man at the ticket booth. He said, "I'm not sure, but I can find out for you." He came back and said, "Yes, he is here. If you go through this first entrance, down the aisle toward the stage, and ask someone there, they should be able to get him for you."

To my surprise, he came out to find me. Normally, performers don't come out until the end of the show. He saw me talking to the young man. I don't know how he found out I was there looking for him. It must have been the way the young man had described me or something. Whatever the case, he approached me and said, "Hi!" He looked me up and down and said, "Who is doing the show, you or me?" and laughed. He added, "I will see you after the show is over. Just stay put until I come out for you."

And that he did. As soon as the show had ended, he came out walking extremely fast, grabbed me by the hand, and rushed me out the door into a cab.

I did not get to my parents' apartment until 4:00 a.m. I walked in and started tiptoeing into the room. When I looked over, Mami was sitting on the sofa crocheting. She asked in a harsh tone, "Esta son horas de llegar?" (Is this the right time to arrive?)

I was terrified, I would never have imagined her waiting up for me. I stayed quiet. She continued, "Que sea la primera y la última vez que te atrevas a llegar a esta hora. Ningunos de tus hermanos ni tu padre se han atrevido a llegar a esta hora" (Let it be the first and the last time that you ever arrive at this time. None of your brothers, not even your father has ever dared to come in at this time).

Lesson learned. I never again did such a thing. That would be easy—no struggle at all—because Julio was gone. He went out of town again.

Into week two of staying with my parents, Karen's inability to walk instead of run was constantly complained about. I was reminded that I was in week two and needed to find an apartment. On Wednesday or Friday of that week when I came from work, I was told that Joey had called and that he would call again.

Joey called, and we talked for a while. He was apologetic and asked for the girls and me to return home. I thought about it and decided it would be best for us to go home. I had to make sure I did everything right. There was no room for error, and I hoped he would not lose his temper again. With no delay, we went back home. I did miss Mimi and my little home.

One night we went out as a group—Joey, Jose, Mimi, Evelyn, and me. I don't recall the occasion, but I do know it was in the fall. We didn't go out together much in the evenings since the girls were born. Normally, it was just Joey going clubbing or whatever he did to kick it, while I stayed home with the girls. Remember, I was not to question or complain because he was a man. But I also don't recall anyone saying happy birthday, so it could not have been that. I guess it was a night out just because. Evelyn was having problems with her boyfriend, so she was spending the night. I considered her my best friend. She was Mimi's younger sister, and I was Martita's (RIP) younger sister. We had that kind of relationship, like family.

We all had a great time. We got home really late, and everyone went straight to bed. I woke up not sure if it was morning yet because it was still dark and went straight toward the bathroom. I had to pass the girls' room to get to the bathroom. As a habit of mine, I looked into the girls' room as I walked up to it.

Oh my goodness! I could not believe what I was seeing. Evelyn was lying face down, and Joey was with her. Frantic at what I was seeing, all I could say was, "Joey, what are you doing?"

Joey yelled, "Get *downstairs!*"

I ran to our room, got dressed, and went downstairs, sobbing uncontrollably. It was strange how, despite all the times I had known he was with other women, especially when he came home infested with lice, I had not ever actually thought of it as him having sex. Even stranger was the fact I'd had an adulteress affair. Yet I never saw it as being unfaithful or unloving toward him, because I made sure I did everything I was told. Maybe it was because there was so much of that stuff going on in the circle of people I had grown up around. Or maybe I was just completely blind to what it really was—sin.

Maybe the big hurt came from the fact that it was someone I truly trusted and believed was a true friend, more like family. This should not have bothered me, since that was what I saw all around me. This is how completely blind we can be in life when we don't know Jesus:

- Satan, who is the god of this world, has blinded the minds of those who don't believe. They are unable to see the glorious light of the Good News. They don't understand this message about the glory of Christ, who is the exact likeness of God. (2 Corinthians 4:4, NLT)
- But their minds were made dull, for to this day the same veil remains when the old covenant is read. It has not been removed, because only in Christ is it taken away. (2 Corinthians 3:14)

Jose had a blank look on his face and avoided looking at me. Mimi kept busy. When Evelyn left, Joey and I did not really talk about it, other than him saying, "Nothing happened. Let it go."

But on Monday when I got home, everyone was there—Joey, Jose, Mimi, Evelyn, and their brother Smiley. "Why is she here?" I asked.

Joey answered, "We are just hanging out."

I said, "She needs to leave."

To this, he replied, "This is my house, and I say who can and cannot be here."

I started crying and walked to my younger cousin's house. I explained to them what had happened. They told me, "That's your house, too, and your daughters' house. You should state that. If he refuses, tell him he is going to have to talk to your lawyer."

I learned the hard way, that *most people who give advice mean well. But not many will stand with you, ready to take the blows for you.*

I followed their advice, and when Joey heard me, he said, "Oh, so you have rights, and I am to talk to your lawyer?" He got up off the sofa where he was sitting, entertaining Evelyn. And as he got closer, he swung a right punch, and I fell back. The wall behind me broke my fall. Mimi ran toward the living room, where we were.

She reached out her hand and grabbed Joey's next punch while it was still in the air.

Jose grabbed her by the waist and dragged her out, saying, "We need to get out of here."

Smiley and Evelyn followed them out.

Well, it was time for business. Joey punched me again. This time, I landed on the floor, but I got up again. I kept protecting myself the best I could.

He said, "Oh yeah, I almost forgot that I taught you how to fight. I am going to need a two-by-four for you." He looked in the special corner where he kept his two-by-four, and by the grace of God, it was not there. He came back and continued to beat me. I curled into a fetal position, trying to cover my face. He continued punching and kicking me. He used to wear platform shoes, which were very hard. I guess he got tired because he stopped and went upstairs.

Jose and Mimi returned, finding me on the floor hardly able to move. I could hear Mimi saying, "Oh no, see Joe—"

Jose said, "Come on. Stay out of it." He took her to their bedroom.

Suddenly, Joey yelled out for me to come upstairs. I got myself up the best I could and went upstairs, where he proceeded to have his way with me.

God is amazing. Only He could have gotten me up the next day and ready for work. And that I did. I arrived at work that morning. As soon as I got to my station, my supervisor pulled me to the side and asked, "What happened to you? You cannot stay here like that."

I explained that I was all right and that I needed to stay. I was told that, either a family member could come pick me up and take me to the hospital, or they would have to call the police and have them take me to the hospital. But I couldn't stay there working in the condition I was in."

I don't recall if someone from work called and asked a family member to pick me up or if I did. I was taken to the ER and treated. X-rays showed I had a dislocated jaw, a broken nose, and three broken ribs. And I was covered in bruises all over my body. Papi and

Mami came to see me. That was the most painful part for me. Papi had tears and definitely said unloving things about Joey.

I was in the hospital for about ten days. The hospital wanted me to press charges, but I couldn't get myself to do it. I heard that Papi wanted to hire a couple of gang members to have Joey taken care of. But he did not know any gang members, not even someone who knew one. So, his desire to avenge me never came to fruition.

Around this same period, my Aunt Ana was packing and getting ready to move into the new Palmer Square Apartments. Mami, Aunt Ana, and my younger cousin's wife came up with the idea for me to sublease her apartment. I agreed. As soon as I got out of the hospital, I met with Titi Ana's landlord and subleased her apartment. Titi Ana gave me a kitchen table. Mami was also in the middle of moving into the Palmer Square Apartments. So, about a month later, she gave me her sofa. Someone else gave me a folding cot that was a little bigger than a twin-size bed for the girls, and my sister was getting a new bedroom set, so my parents gave me her old one.

I went to the house to pick up the girls' things and mine. I was using someone's car. I went in to gather our items. I would take one bag out to the car. And while I was getting another bag, Joey would have someone take the bag out of the car. I went back and forth a few times. And then I just gave up; it was not worth it. I started moving quickly because I had to work, and I did not have transportation. It was all done by footwork.

Catholic Charities had a great program for needy families. I gathered my information and started my task of building a new home for my little ones. I got winter clothing for the girls—coats, shoes, boots, and so on. I was able to get them even better things than the ones that Joey would not allow me to take out of the house. I got dishes, pots, and other needed home items. Mami and Titi gave me bedsheets and a thick blanket for the girls. I inherited my brother and sister's portable record player and a small portable TV. My younger cousin's wife gave me bus fare. I went to public aid, and they gave me emergency food stamps. Catholic Charities also gave me vouchers for the light and gas. What a blessing, *yes*! God was taking care of me every step of the way. I still had my job, which I definitely needed. Mami agreed to keep the girls Sunday night through Friday. That way I could go to work without worrying about the transportation to and from her apartment during the work week. God is *good, so good*.

FACING LIFE ALONE

This was a whole new chapter in my life. Not only was I a parent. Now, I was a single parent. And I had to keep my eyes open to any trick Joey may have up his sleeves. He most definitely did not help with the girls' financial needs, and I did not want his assistance if it was going to put me in debt to him. The tables were a bit different now. In fact, he asked me for money the one time I allowed him to spend the day with the girls. When he brought them back, he asked me for ten dollars. It was late November. What a time for this to happen. It's not that there is a good time for it to ever happen to anyone. But it was the month man has chosen to give thanks to God. And I was very grateful to God, for all the protection and the blessings He bestowed on me.

This was also the month Julio would come into town for the "Show Jibaro" at the San Juan Theater. He was one of the performers who played in the show, El Show Jibaro Navideño (The Jibaro Christmas show). I stopped by to see him; it was the first time I was doing so as a single woman (or I thought I was). I admit I felt free and liberated from the bondage I had been living. I told Julio what had happened, and he did not believe me at first. He thought I was joking. So, I lifted my skirt and showed him the remaining bruises on my legs and around my rib cage. He was taken aback at it all. Of course, we hadn't behaved in holiness and obedience. We, too, were in need of a savior. I didn't understand that myself then. This is called living blind to your sin.

I invited him over, and he agreed to come. Julio came over a few times, and we definitely were bonding. He would tell me many stories and often quoted the Bible, which was very impressive. I was drawn to him even more. Julio would encourage me all the time. He even convinced me to enroll in a GED course at Well's High School. I enrolled in the classes and was truly enjoying it. I would get home late, a little after 9:00, maybe 9:30, 9:40 at the latest. But, to me, it was absolutely worth it. I was able to get back what I had thrown away by getting pregnant.

My abuelo and my Titi Benita lived in the same building on the first floor. My Titi Ana would still come to the building to visit Abuelo and Titi Benita, along with her next-door neighbor, also named Yaya. They would play dominos. The game was our family's favorite pastime, and they were all very good at it—and very competitive.

Guess what? My ins and outs were being watched. I would go to work, get out, go straight to Wells High School for the GED class, and go straight home after that. There was no time for anything else. I would pick up the girls from Mami's on Friday night and take them back to her on Sunday. I attended school on Monday, Wednesdays, and Thursdays. And what little time I had left, I spent studying. This arrangement was short-lived.

One day, Mami called me and asked me to come pick up the girls. She said she would no longer be able to keep them. Besides they needed *calor de madre* (a mother's warmth)—they needed me to be rearing them.

Wow! What a blow to the abdomen. I'd thought I would be able to finally get my education. It wasn't only a desire but, rather, a need. I could barely read, and even what I did read, I did not understand much. My spelling was very poor. And math? I don't even want to think about it. I was blessed to always have a calculator and really caring people in the workplace willing to help and never criticize me. But I wanted to be able to read and spell and do math without needing a calculator and a dictionary. I wanted to be able to feel complete, which I did not. I felt broken and incomplete deep in the core of my soul. And even though I responded in love to the rejection I'd received as a little girl, it left a hole in my heart—along with Joey's constant adultery and absence from the home. Mami told me to come pick them up now—not at the end of the week but now. And when Mami said something, I was obedient. There was no talking or reasoning.

I went to my younger cousin's wife, and I explained to her what had happened. She shared that Titi Ana had been stating how I would come in late—past 9:00 p.m. at night. She made it sound like it was all the time, not just a couple nights a week. She added that she may have told my mother something to that effect.

Oh no! But it did not matter if it was many nights or just one night a week. If Mami thought I was out goofing off, she was not going to have any part of it. So, yes, I had no choice but to quit my job at the bank, which I loved. It was a shame, as management was considering giving me a supervisory position soon, providing I kept up the good work and kept being punctual. Wow! I still feel the pain of having to let that job go.

Julio was in disbelief, but it was what it was. He was leaving town, trying to promote his next record album (LP). He had asked a few days earlier if I wanted to go with him, but I would not be able to bring the girls. So, now that the time was here, I knew I could not leave them even if I wanted to because of the whole calor de madre bit. I understood that, even if I wanted to, I could not go.

The next day, he said, "I want you to meet someone." He took me to his sister house. Her husband was a pastor and knew about getting help for families in need. They were very nice, and the pastor gave me some phone numbers and addresses that would help me.

The next day, Julio was off to Puerto Rico in hopes of landing a recording deal for his new album. As he walked down the long staircase, he turned, looked up at me, and showed me his key. "I will see you as soon as I get this deal done," he said.

I was heartbroken but had no reason to doubt that he would be back. I had some things I needed to work on. I was out of a job and back on the footwork road of survival for my little ones and me. I was able to use the information I was given, which I believe I knew of already, from the beginning of my role as a single mom. I did get some emergency food stamps and some financial help, along with a medical card from public aid and some extra help from Catholic Charities.

I have much reason to be grateful for the Catholic Church and their programs for families in need, in fact for all individuals in need. They did not discriminate. It didn't matter, if you were single, married, black, white, Asian, Polish, Jewish, Mexican, or whatever. They just considered the need. You didn't have to be a member or even believe in God. They just considered the need of the individual, just like Jesus did. I have seen them do great things for the common families in the neighborhood (any neighborhood), and I am one of them.

I was getting things done and really receiving blessings—not that I was practicing my faith. I was a Christian and had completed all the sacraments I was required to do through the Catholic faith. But I was not practicing my faith. I would pray in my own way. I did not know how to do it like my Uncle Regino and my mom, and I did not have a rosary anyway. I knew I was blessed by God because Mami had taught us that everything we have comes from God. I started looking for a job. And in a short time, I had one.

My sister Lou told me about the owner of the store where she normally shopped. It was called Armitage Boutique. I went by the store, introduced myself, and was hired immediately. It was great. The owner had two other men working for him, Lionel and Danny. I was the only female. The owner grew fond of me in more ways than I would have liked him to. He knew some of my story and was always offering to help me. He even wanted to pay for my divorce. Invitations to dinner, the movies, and any outing I wanted came daily, and he did include the girls. I was just not interested. I was doing fine with just the girls and me. I still hoped that, one day, Julio would pop back into my life, and we could start our lives together.

I talked about the shop owner's advances with my younger cousin's wife whenever we talked. One day, she said, "You are foolish not to go out with him. You are just selfish and daydreaming of un *pajarito en el aire que no va a llegar nunca*" (a flying dove that is never going to come back). "Don't be foolish and pass up a future for someone who will never come. You need a man in your life, and the girls need a father figure to have a complete family. You are being selfish and foolish not to go out with him and get to know him better. You may be surprised at what you could be throwing away."

I continued working, but the money I made was not enough to pay for rent, food, utilities, transportation, and our other basic needs. So, I started looking for another job. The store was not for me, and I didn't want to feel the pressure of the owner's desire for me to go out with him. We did become close, and I did not want to see our relationship get ruined over what could be avoided.

I started working for another bank. I just needed a sitter, as Mami was not going to do it anymore. I shared my latest good news with my younger cousin's wife, adding that I needed a sitter. She told me to ask my Titi Ana. I did. And guess what? She agreed. Why then had she made up stuff about me before to Mami? Well, the important thing was that I had a babysitter. And she would come by my place. I did not have to take the girls out.

As for the job, it was a great place to work, and I fit in immediately. I was off public aid and was doing well for the girls and me. I had no need to ask their father for any financial help. In fact, I got a call from Mr. Vargas, the insurance agent who we had gotten our home policy from. He wanted to meet with me to discuss the policy. I didn't understand why he was contacting me, as I no longer lived with Joey or in the house. Nevertheless, I was being held responsible. He came over and explained to me that Joey had stopped paying the policy on his life insurance and that it was going to lapse. He was not going to be able to hang onto it. He wanted to give me the chance to save it from lapsing. It was twenty dollars a month. I took over paying the monthly premium for the life insurance.

I continued to go to the Armitage Boutique to shop for mine and the girls' clothing. Yes, the owner still insisted on asking me out. During one of my visits with my younger cousin's wife, the subject came up again. Again, she said, "I told you, you are being selfish.

Think about it. Julio may never come back to Chicago. The owner of the store even wants to meet the girls and take them out with you to the movies. What's the harm in that?"

I said, "I don't want the girls to meet anyone. I didn't want to confuse them."

I just continued working and missing Julio all the more. If he would only call.

Time went by, and Julio had neither called nor written. There was no sign from him at all. I was too busy to go around trying to find out what was going on. It seemed this was something he did— he'd leave town and then pop in when I least expected him to. But now it was different. I was single. I had my own place. Why didn't he call or write? I had so many questions going through my mind. Now, I was starting to doubt that he would ever come back.

Spring was around the corner. The freshness in the air was encouraging and motivating. Beautiful things started happening in March. The weather started to warm up, and new possibilities started to flow in the air. My spirits were hopeful. I refused to believe that all those beautiful things he told me were not true. He said I was his first love and then explained why. He said I could satisfy any man. I was a 100 percent plus woman, and I would make any man happy. This could not be a lie; he had no reason to lie.

He would list attributes that explained what he was saying about me. He quoted scriptures from the Bible; I couldn't believe he would lie. I knew, if I concentrated on work and the girls, before I realized it, he would be back. This was my frame of mind and my way of staying encouraged.

This would be the first time I was filing taxes on my own. When I went to the tax preparer, the representative ran my social security number. I was told I could not file because I had already filed jointly with my husband. What?! I did what? With my husband?! The tax preparer said I had a return of $1,275, and it had already been paid out. I knew there was foul play going on. The week before, Joey had visited the girls and had bought them each a pair of gym shoes, for a total of $10. But he could not pay the premium of the insurance on the house? This led me to believe he was struggling financially.

I contacted Joey and confronted him. I told him the copy of the tax return had been shown to me, and it had my signature on it. But I knew it was not my signature. Then he confessed that Evelyn had signed for me. "Oh yeah," he added. "I forgot to mention that Evelyn kind of moved in."

I was furious. But what could I do about it now? I could not believe it. He'd bought the girls a pair of gym shoes each, for a total of $10 with the income tax return he'd received only by forging my name. How could anyone do that? *These are your kids*, I thought. He could have kept even $1,000 and given us at least $275. I let it go and continued moving forward. Now, I needed to find out how I could prevent this from happening again. A new task lay before me. Joey kept away from me and didn't ask to spend time with the girls after that.

I continued waiting for Julio. It seemed like his return was my one hope of anything good in my life besides my girls. As time went on, waiting on him was no longer a concern because I was so busy with work and the girls.

Before I knew it, it happened. He was back in town. I was so happy words could not explain it. He came over, spent the night, and explained how great everything was going. In the morning, he added to his story, letting me know he was going to perform that night at a nearby club.

He said he would not be coming over that night because he had to stay at his brother's apartment. He went on to explain that his ex-wife was a music promoter, and she was going to be in town that night. He would have to stay at his brother's apartment with her. She would also be at the night club that night. I did not understand, but he promised that it was all business related, and it had to be done that way. He would be back when the deal was closed after the tour.

I asked if I could attend the show, and he said, "I will not be able to pay any attention to you. I am going to be busy performing, and Mercedes will be there. I will have to attend to her. If you want to attend the show for the performance, sure, you can. I don't want you to expect any attention from me because I will be busy working."

I knew where the club was, and I made sure I attended. I got a babysitter, slipped on a black dress and my heels, and I was off. I arrived and saw it was not that big of a place. I got myself a soda and kept it low-key. I did not see Julio anywhere; he must have been backstage. That's what artists do, right?

There was a photographer walking around with a big camera. I stopped him and introduced myself as a big fan of Julio Arzuaga and asked, "Would I be able to take a photo with him when he gets done with his performance?"

He said, "Sure. It will be $10. Leave me your number, and I'll call you when it's ready. You would need to pick it up at my studio."

"Sure," I agreed.

As soon as Julio's name was announced, I made my way to the front of the stage. I had made sure to have a handkerchief on hand. And when he ended the first song, I stretched out my hand and gave it to him. This was a routine I'd started when I'd first started seeing him perform. I handed him a handkerchief to dry the sweat from his forehead. When he was done and came out, I made sure to stay by the photographer to get my picture taken. That was the last I saw of Julio. The show was over. I had nothing else to do there but go home.

I hoped that all he'd told me was true and that I would soon hear from him. Some time passed. I had become close to his brother and his girlfriend, with whom he normally stayed when he was in town. I'd also met Julio's daughter Maria Nelly, who had just come in from Puerto Rico a few weeks earlier. It was amazing how much she looked like her dad. We got along great. She had two little girls just like me. She was about two years older than I was.

Shortly after I'd met her, Julio's daughter called me with a personal problem. She was having problems with her husband. It had gotten bad, and he was going back to Puerto Rico, leaving her with a dilemma. She didn't want to go back with him. She asked me if she could stay with me until she got on her feet.

I said, "Yes, absolutely."

Her aunt's husband was against the idea. He said there were *diavlijos* (devils, wicked spirits) in my apartment. Why would he say such a thing? I don't know. But I knew what it was like to be down on your luck with no place to stay. So, I opened the door of my humble little apartment.

A couple of weeks passed, and Maria Nelly was notified that her dad had come into town. He was not staying at her uncle's apartment like he used to. He was staying at her tia's and pastor's house. They had extended an invitation to come by if she wanted to see her dad. She invited me to come along with her, and I did. It was strange that he would not stay at his brother's, but nevertheless, I was going to see him.

It definitely wasn't the reunion I was expecting. But here I was, waiting for him to come down the stairs. Her aunt and her husband had asked us to sit down, before going to the kitchen to prepare some *café y aperitivos* (coffee and snacks). Maria Nelly went upstairs to get her dad. He came down, and his wife was right behind him. Wow! I was shocked.

I felt like running out the door, but I wanted some answers. They walked straight into the small kitchen. As they sat down, her aunt called me into the kitchen to join them. I got up and joined them, and her aunt served the café. I was sitting across from him, and his so-called ex-wife was sitting between the two of us. Maria Nelly stayed in the living room. I guess she wanted me to have the opportunity to get some closure.

He was avoiding my eyes. I was sitting straight up, looking straight at him. His sister placed the cup of café in front of him. He looked down, stirring the sugar into the café still avoiding my eyes, while I looked dead straight at him. The pastor tried making small talk, but it was obvious this conversation was going to happen. Maria Nelly called the pastor into the living room. At the same time, his kids were needing his help upstairs, and he went up to assist them. Julio's sister kept busy in the kitchen and then joined her niece in the living room.

Julio finished his café and finally looked up at me and said, "Hi."

I stared at him and said, "Hi."

He went on to ask, "How are you?"

I replied, "Fine."

He said, "I know you are wanting to know what happened with my return. It is a lot more difficult to explain than I'd like it to be. The reason I left was to record the record, remember? But it got a little complicated, and now I am back with my wife. We will be leaving in a couple of days, as we are on tour. So, I need you to understand that I will not be coming back because I can't. Things have changed."

I let him finish, and then I said, "Do you think this is a story you are writing on a piece of paper that you can simply erase to change the scene of a play?" As I was talking, I was writing on the table and erasing just as I was stating it. He said, "Mi amor, tu no entiende" (My love, you don't understand).

His wife said, "You do not owe her any explanation. I'm your wife, not her."

He yelled at her, pounding his fists on the table and saying, "Stay out of this!" Then, in his frustration at not being able to explain why he was not coming back as he had promised, he got up and rushed upstairs.

I ran out of the house crying, completely broken. I ran and ran, and finally I dropped to the ground. As I raised my head and looked up, I saw I was in front of St. Aloysius Church. I was crying uncontrollably, and as I saw the church, I felt even worse, because I was asking for a person God Himself had appointed to His service. I said, "God, I am so sorry I am asking for someone You have appointed to serve You." I felt I had no choice but to let him go and wish him the best in life. It was easier said than done. It was not that simple.

Thoughts of us raced through my mind all the time. I thought I finally had someone in my life who was concerned about my moving ahead in life. He believed in me. He said I could make any man happy. So, what had gone wrong? His daughter could not understand it either.

The word was that he was on tour and was going to be giving his testimony at a local church. His daughter was planning on attending the event. Guess what? I was too. I wanted to hear that testimony myself. On the night of his testimony, I not only attended, I wore a white A-line, clingy, spaghetti strap dress he had bought me that Christmas. I was in pain, and I wanted him to see and recall what he was saying goodbye to. The service was actually really good, but I had my mind set on stirring up his emotions.

Julio gave his testimony, and I wanted to die. It was not true. I was there that night, and nothing that he said happened, at least not while I was there. I had the eight-by-ten photo of us to prove it. The night before, he had spent the night with me and not with his so-called wife. This was a hoax. I was crushed, but I could do nothing. I responded to their testimony in my flesh. I started throwing him kisses from my seat as he spoke and sat at the altar. He kept wiping his forehead and neck. He was sweating heavily. That was not nice of me. But then again, neither was the lie they were displaying. Today, I understand that you do not pay evil with evil and that you reap what you sow. Scripture makes this clear:

- Do not repay anyone evil for evil. Be careful to do what is right in the eyes of everyone. (Romans 12:17)
- Do not repay evil with evil or insult with insult. On the contrary, repay evil with blessing, because to this you were called so that you may inherit a blessing. (1 Peter 3:9)
- Do not be deceived: God cannot be mocked. A man reaps what he sows. (Galatians 6:7)

Keep in mind, this was before I came to Christ, and I was a complete mess.

The cards were dealt out on top of the table. Guess who left and did not come back? I was crushed. Yet in a hidden place in my heart, I still had the hope that he would one day come back—especially since I could not believe it was all true about the restoration of his marriage and all. I did pray to God that, if it was true, He would forgive me and bless Julio. I always prayed for good things for him, and I could not even hold a grudge against him. I continued believing all he had said and knew there was a reason for his deceit. I never stopped loving him. I would try to figure it out and could never come up with a justifiable answer. Today, I understand that love never fails (1 Corinthians 13:8).

Time moved on a lot more quickly than I wanted it to. I was still in touch with the boutique owner. He would tease me about my Prince Charming and his delay in coming after me. He was still willing to pay for my divorce whenever I decided to get it. I normally shopped at his boutique for myself and the girls. But I was not interested in anything else, just the friendship that had developed.

I had a lot to do, since Annette was turning five that year in a couple of months, and I had to get her ready for school. I went to my favorite place for additional school clothing. Yes! Catholic Charities. I kid you not when I say they were a great resource—a refuge and a complete blessing for me during those days.

Well, that moment came. My baby turned five and was ready for school. Of course, we had a little birthday party for her at Madrina and Padrino's house, her favorite place in the world to be during those tender years of her life. I couldn't believe it was already time to enroll Annette in school. This was a tough one for me, but I had to face it. My heart was breaking at the thought of leaving her in class. This was horrible.

Talk about a task rearing your child. She had just started, and shortly after, I received a call from the office, a complaint about Annette's behavior. She had bit the principal. It was not even a teacher; it was the principal! Oh my, this was not starting out right. I knew I would have my hands full if this kept on. My aunt was not going to be able to handle stuff like this.

A few months had passed, and I was having a hard time emotionally. I was not lonely; it was more of a feeling that I wasn't accepted. The sense of rejection that stung my heart was polluting my thoughts with unworthiness. I was feeling less than. All those thoughts that said there must be something wrong with me had tormented me since I was a little girl. If I only hadn't done this or that. I comforted myself with his words—how he'd said I was more than 100 percent woman, and I could satisfy any man. What did that mean anyway? What about when he'd told me I was his first *love*?

I was not having a smooth time; I was more nostalgic than I wanted to be. I went shopping at my friend's store. He was still inviting me to dinner, despite my constant no. I shared the conversation with my younger cousin's wife, and she said, "That dove is not coming back. Let it go and let someone else give you what you deserve."

I went home and thought about it a lot. And before I knew it, I was on the phone calling the store owner, retracting my no and saying yes. We agreed to meet at the store that Saturday at 7:00 p.m. I was really nervous. I asked my sister Lou to stay with the girls at my place that night. My plans were set.

Saturday came. I picked up Lou and my cousin Carmensita; they were going to babysit for me. On the ride to my apartment, my sister asked if we could drive by the neighborhood to see if she saw her boyfriend, Angel. I agreed. I took a detour and drove through their neighborhood. As I drove, Lou and Carmensita kept an eye out to see if they saw Angel. Lou yelled out, "There he is. Stop the car."

I looked over and saw two guys walking. One was carrying some dry cleaning over his shoulder. I pulled over, and Lou and Carmensita got out of the car. They talked for a few minutes. Then I said, "OK. We have to go."

They said their goodbyes, and we were off to my apartment.

During the drive, Lourdes was saying to Carmensita, "Did you see his brother? He has the biggest upper arms and a big wide chest. Did you not notice that?" Carmensita agreed with Lourdes about how handsome Angel's brother was. But she did not seem interested. I was thinking, *They are so silly. Kids will be kids.*

Can you hear that, how I thought of them as kids? Lourdes was only one year younger than me, and Carmensita was a year or two older than me. Is that what happens when you have children? You think of yourself as an adult and mature when you truly are not? It takes a whole lot more to be mature than a couple of children and a few responsibilities.

When we arrived at my apartment, I got ready. I was wearing a ivory skirt that fell just below the knees, with a split in the middle of the front that came up about three inches above my knees and a black, skintight, spaghetti-strap body shirt. My hair was pulled up in a French roll with a red and white flower on the left side. I had made up my face (which I rarely did)—blue eye shadow, blush, and coffee bean lipstick. I was ready for my first night out since that dreadful night when I went to see Julio sing, only to know he would be leaving with someone else that night and not coming by the apartment.

To my surprise, when I got to the store, the owner was not there. His friend Lionel was alone. I engaged in small talk with Lionel, but the owner did not seem to be arriving, and it was already past seven.

Lionel said, "Carmen, I will be honest with you. He is not going to show up."

I asked him "Why not? We did have a date."

He responded, "Maybe because you said no to him so many times before. This is his way of saying no to you, by not showing up."

I said, "That is so silly. Why would anyone do that? But that's OK. I will just go home."

Lionel said, "Well, you are already dressed. Why don't you accompany me to the Concha Night Club? I have a girl meeting me there, and I would prefer not to walk in stag. I will pay your way in and buy you a drink. When my date arrives, you can leave."

I agreed, and that was just the way it played out.

After Lionel's girl arrived, I was finishing my soda and getting ready to leave when this guy came up to the bar to get a drink. He asked me, "Do I know you?"

"I don't think so," I replied.

He said, "Yes. You are Lou's sister, right?"

I said, "Yes."

He said, "Earlier today, you drove her by my neighborhood. My brother and I were walking home from the cleaners."

I said, "Oh yeah, that's right."

He invited me to join him and his brother at their table, and I accepted. He introduced me to his brother, Pelegrino, and we started talking. Angel stepped away and continued to mingle with their friends.

Pelegrino asked me if I wanted a drink.

"I don't normally drink, but sure," I responded.

He flagged a waiter and asked for a mixed drink—rum and Coke. Little did I know it was a drink we would share, not a drink just for me. I didn't mind. I was not accustomed to drinking alcoholic beverages.

Pelegrino asked me to dance. We spent most of the time on the dance floor. When it was getting close to closing time, Pelegrino asked me if I wanted to step outside for some fresh air. I agreed. We were both smokers, and so we enjoyed the night breeze; conversation; and, of course, our Kool cigarettes. We were in what is called a "cubbyhole," a doorway to a storefront upper apartment. It was not a big space, kind of narrow, but we did not mind.

At one point, Pelegrino was facing the street, smoking, and blowing his smoke out the opposite direction from where we stood. I was right behind him, looking over his shoulder. Suddenly, Pelegrino turned around quickly, grabbed me by my waist, and kissed me. I was not pulling away; it was a magical moment. Maybe the whole atmosphere, the time of day, and being in a very vulnerable place emotionally made it feel that way. Or was there some real chemistry between us? I didn't know, but it was a magical moment.

We made our way back upstairs. I saw the photographer walking around with his big camera, and I asked him to take a picture of us. Looking back, I see that we really looked good together. But that was not even close to crossing my mind. You see, I had never been attracted to members of the opposite sex by their physical appearance. We danced some more, and then it was time to go. The performance was over. The lights were starting to come on. Here were all the clues that it was time to go.

We made our way downstairs, and there was the question. "Can I take you home?"

Before I could answer, Angel added, "That would be great. I could see Lou. So, can we come over?"

"I guess," I replied, "but just briefly."

We started walking. I asked, "Where is your car?"

He said, "I don't have a car."

"But you asked if you could take me home," I said, surprised.

"Yes," he answered. "I meant walk with you."

"Oh, OK," I consented.

It started to rain. Pelegrino had a long black umbrella that looked just like a cane Papito (my grandfather) had. He opened the umbrella right away.

You would never guess what happened next. The umbrella had a hole, and some of the water was coming in. Angel said, "Hey, bro. There's a hole in the center of your umbrella."

He replied, "That's OK."

He did make sure I was not getting wet. We walked from California and North Avenue to North Avenue and Western, where my apartment was located (close to eight blocks).

When we arrived, Lourdes was happy to see Angel, even though she was surprised because that was not the plan. During this whole ordeal, I kept thinking about what my younger cousin's wife had been telling me for some time—about letting go and giving other men a chance. Not that I should be hunting for anyone, but maybe she was right.

I could not picture me and anyone else other than Julio. I wondered if I could even function that way. Not recalling the kiss earlier, it just seemed wrong. There I went again, trying to make sense of what I had been told. I put myself to the test. I told myself, *Let me see how I feel with someone else.* I went in my room and got comfortable, and after a few minutes, I invited Pelegrino into my bedroom for some privacy. We listened to some oldies and talked about what a good time we'd had and how great the band was.

Then it happened. Before long, we were intimate, and there was no turning back. I had allowed it. Afterward, I could not believe what I had done. I had allowed this to happen, and I could not take it back. We did not sleep; we spent the night talking and listening to music. A little before sunrise, I showered and got dressed.

I came out and started getting breakfast ready. Lourdes and Angel were in the kitchen talking, and Carmen was also up talking to them. The girls were still sleeping. I went to my room to get a cigarette, and Lou followed me. She asked me, "Did you have sex with him?"

I was trying to avoid the question and mumbled, "No."

She said, "Look me in the eyes and tell me you didn't have sex with Angel's brother."

I could not look her in the eyes and say no. I said, "Yes, I did."

Lou said, "Oh no. Now his family is going to think I'm promiscuous."

I felt horrible. "I will make up for it," I said. "I will prove to him I am not promiscuous.

DETERMINED TO PROVE I
WAS NOT PROMISCUOUS

Well, I kept my promise to Lourdes. I made sure after that day I called Pelegrino often. I tried hard to prove I was a good person and that I was dedicated to my children and home. He thought I was running after him because I was attracted to him when, all along, I was trying to prove myself to be a decent mom and home girl, in hopes of preventing their family from thinking wrong of Lourdes because I was her sister.

As we read in 1 Corinthians 15:33, "Do not be misled: "Bad company corrupts good character." This is how a person can really mess up his or her life without even imagining that's what is happening—trying to fix a situation one shouldn't tamper with.

I should have just let it go and never seen this person again. Lou was off to college. And who was there to really judge her because of my poor choice? How would my actions affect Lou when we were two completely different individuals. We were not tied to each other so that my actions could compromise her character. We did not even live near each other or under the same roof. We didn't even live in the same city.

But again, just like the patient at the Rincon Clinic said that idea that we would be judged according to who we are acquainted with made me feel guilty. So, I had a sense that it was my responsibility to clear up her name by my actions—to show through my actions that I was not promiscuous. I tend to want to fix things that are broken or wrong, especially if I was the cause.

Today I know it's not because of the world that we should be wise about who we hang around with but because of what God tells us to do in His word. "Walk with the wise and become wise, for a companion of fools suffers harm," we are told in Proverbs 13:20. That means we should be a righteous a reflection of who God calls us to be in how we live our lives.

I would invite Pelegrino to dinner, and I took him to meet my family, my younger cousin, his wife, and even my parents. I did this just so he could get a true picture of who and how I was, in hopes his family would not judge Lou according to my bad behavior. I did not feel anything for Pelegrino during this period other than a good friendship. He was easy to talk to and the first person I dated who was my age. We would go cruising down Humboldt Park, listening to oldies and the current hits as well.

While at home, I was always around my older brothers and sisters. They were ten, eight, six, four, and two years older than I was. My two cousins were fourteen and fifteen years older than me, Joey was thirteen years older than me, and Julio was twenty years older than me. So, I was always around people who were way above my age. Spending time with Pelegrino was different. He was a good listener, he was funny, and we both enjoyed dancing. We did become close.

One day, just after I'd first left Joey and started living by myself with the girls, I was visiting my younger cousin's wife. "Yayie, you know this is a good thing in a way because Joey was so abusive," she said. "But now you have become a threat to women and an invitation to men."

I said, "What? I don't understand."

She went on to explain that, now that I was single, I was going to be a temptation to men and a threat to women because men are so sinful that they will try to get with other women, even if they are married.

"What? That is not right" I said. I did not understand why she was saying this to me. These words were impressed in my heart forever.

My younger cousin's wife and I were very close. For the first couple of years, I was the only one who could sneak in and out of her apartment without my cousin catching on (I followed her rules on how to be discreet). We spent a lot of time together. She had been unable to be close to her family since leaving her home at age eighteen. My cousin, being as strict as he was, made it hard for her to do much socializing, unless he was around. He did not welcome people into his home very easily.

We would clean the house together, listen to music, and even dance. She was a joker, always had something to say, and had a smart crack for just about everything. She had a soft heart for people who were hurting and no tolerance for those who did not measure up to her standards. She made it very clear when I first started hanging out with her that she would not forgive anyone who would cross her in any way. She claimed she was just like her father. This, too, was impressed in my heart.

Back to Pelegrino and me. Pelegrino had just been released from the penitentiary. He had served two years of a two and a half-year sentence for breaking and entering in a private home. He mentioned that he was staying with his sister, her live-in boyfriend, their two daughters, and Angel. Pelegrino would sleep on the floor. He hadn't completed high school; he had dropped out in his second year. He had taken a bricklaying course in the penitentiary and had graduated. He'd had a lot of afflictions in his young life. He had two siblings, an older sister and a younger brother. He came from a broken family. His dad had left them when he was about twelve. He lost his mom when he was about thirteen or fourteen years old, and there was abuse in his young life as well. We did have a lot in common.

I told him about my marriage to Joey, our breakup, and my relationship with Julio. I told him how he was the love of my life. It would have been obvious because I had pictures of Julio displayed in my living room. That special one with him and me. One was taken on the dreadful night of his testimony that tied up with the LP recording and changed the course of our lives.

Pelegrino shared that he did not want to have any serious relationships. He was simply out having fun. I was fine with that because I was waiting for the love of my life, and I could not afford to have anything get in the way. This turned out better than I thought. I had a friend.

Well, now Lou's dignity was not the reason for our relationship. Pelegrino and I actually had things in common. And what about that little chocolate chip, my Karen, grandpa's Karina? The second time Pelegrino came over, he knocked. When I answered the door, he walked in, and Karen/Karina came running, saying, "Papi, Papi!" (Daddy, Daddy). Where did that come from?

Pelegrino was surprised at her welcoming him by calling him Daddy. But he picked her up, hugged and kissed her. I think they had love at first sight.

He started staying over more and more. Whenever he did leave, I would feel bad because I was sleeping in a nice, warm comfortable bed, and I knew he was on a cold, hard floor. So, one day I asked him if he would consider staying with us until he got himself together. But I made it very clear that he had to leave as soon as Julio came back into town. It was an agreement.

He took me to his sister's apartment to meet her and her boyfriend. I even met his brother Angel again. His sister's name was the same as mine, Carmen. She had two little girls from a previous marriage, just like I did. She was a smoker like I was. And she loved café just like me. I met some of his cousins (male and female), his grandmother, his aunt, and his friend Bitin, who was very nice and respectful. I loved his family. I thought they were very nice and loved their closeness. That was something that meant a lot to me. As far back as I could remember, I was always wanting a close family. For them to get along as well as I believed they did was a plus in my book.

I was doing well at work. No matter how late we stayed up, I was out the door on time every day. My aunt was still watching the girls and, yes, keeping watch over my day-to-day activities. She told me one day, "The person you trust the most and tell all your affairs to is the one dragging your name through the mud." Wow, what a blow to hear those words.

There was only one person I shared my life with. That was my younger cousin's wife, with whom I had shared everything in my life since I was eleven years old. She seemed to be very concerned for me and for the girls' well-being. I couldn't believe what my aunt was saying; no, I didn't want to believe it. Or was there some truth in what she'd told me? But her younger son's wife didn't even go out of her house without him. Could I be the topic of conversation at the table gathering at her home? Why?

One morning shortly after I arrived at work, I was notified that I had a call from my mom. She was on my emergency list of personal contacts with access to me at work. She said, "Que lindo, mientras tu estas en el trabajo hay un hombre grande y fuerte durmiendo en tu cama" (How cute. While you are at work working, there is a big strong man sleeping in your bed). That did not sit well with Mami. She said, if I could get up and go out to work, then every adult who slept in my apartment needed to get up and go to work. Oh boy, I had to talk to Pelegrino about this. Funny, she did not pay my rent or any of my bills. She did not even take care of the girls for me anymore. But she was mom. Out of respect and after thinking about what she'd said, it did make sense. I definitely followed her correction.

I had a talk with Pelegrino about it when I got home that day. He explained that he had little education and did not even know how to look for a job or how to move around in the city. He had never traveled out of his neighborhood. I understood. But I made it very clear that, if he wanted to keep staying with me and the girls, he had to get a job or something. Pelegrino agreed to look for a job.

A day or two later, I guess during the time he was putting his clothes away, he noticed some male clothing that still had tags on them. He asked about the items, and I explained it was a gift I had for Julio, and I hadn't had the opportunity to give it to him.

He said, "Well, since I have to start looking for a job, and I don't have dress clothes, can I have them? He is not coming back anyway."

"Yes," I said, "he is. But since you need clothes, you can have them. When he comes back, I will buy him some more."

Now, this was a whole new challenge. I had someone who lived with me and needed to get a job, had very little education, no motivation, and limited traveling experience in this big windy city. But in order for him to stay, the right thing for him to do was to get a job. If he wanted to live in the apartment, he had to contribute (according to Mami). I bought the *Chicago Tribune* and the *Chicago Times* and started showing Pelegrino how to look for employment. I gave him some money, and off he went in search of a job. (Or so I thought).

Fall was here, and the weather had changed. It was flu season. My little chocolate chip, Abuelo's Karina, the one had first called Pelegrino Papi got sick. I took her in to see Dr. Chajub. and he had her admitted to the hospital. She was diagnosed with bronchitis. I called Joey right away to let him know that Karen was really sick and had been admitted to the hospital. I explained that she had been diagnosed with bronchitis.

Pelegrino went with me to see her the next day. We walked into the hospital lobby and up to the front desk and asked for passes to see Karen. As we started walking toward the elevator, I looked up to see Joey walking toward the front exit door. He paused, first looked Pelegrino up and down, and then looked at me before he continued on to the exit. I sensed trouble. Sure enough, as we walked out of the hospital, I noticed Joey's car right in front of the hospital, north bound. When Joey noticed that we had spotted him, he pulled out his hand and pointed his .38 Magnum at us. I told Pelegrino to walk on the inside of the street so I would block his body from Joey's aim. It worked. He followed us for a short distance and must have noticed that, if he shot at Pelegrino, he was going to get me in the process. I'm sure he did not want to be seen by other people either. He was forced to put the gun away and drove off.

God was definitely with us. Just as Joey was capable of beating me almost to death in a moment of rage, he could have been blinded by rage once more and simply pulled the trigger and killed both of us. But at that moment, my life was protected. Praise God Almighty and our Lord Jesus Christ!

Pelegrino and I walked to my younger cousin's—about a mile and a half from the hospital. It happened to be my younger cousin's birthday (October 31). His birthday was a big deal every year because it landed on Halloween, and his wife liked to make a big deal of it. I recall what Pelegrino and I were wearing. He had on a black knitted sweater and gray dress pants. I wore a black body blouse and gray dress pants. I guess that night has stayed imprinted in my mind, and every detail just comes back to me. We left the party late that night, leaving Annette to stay at my younger cousin's house overnight for safety, given our encounter with Joey and the fact that we did not have a car and were using public transportation.

When we got to the apartment, we felt safe. We went to sleep. But shortly afterward, we heard banging on the door. It was Yaya and her husband, yelling, "Fire! Fire! Open the door!"

We woke up frantic and each grabbed a pair of pants. We tried to put them on and then noticed that he had mine, and I had his. Quickly, we switched pants and opened the door. We all ran through our apartment out the back door and downstairs to safety.

Well, that put a halt to a lot of things, and we ended up with no apartment because we had to vacate immediately. Pelegrino went to stay with his sister, Carmen, and I stayed with my younger cousin and his family until we found an apartment. That put an end to my aunt watching the girls, which led to me losing my job at the bank.

Pelegrino and I went apartment hunting every day until we found one. Pelegrino did not find a job, but he did get information about a program that paid you for taking your GED, the completion of the high school equivalence test. They gave you $76 and tokens for transportation. Every little bit was needed because my rent was going to be $200 more than it had been at the previous apartment.

Since I lost my job at the bank, I had to get busy looking for a new one. I was blessed to find one at another bank. It was quite a distance from where I lived, but it was an open door. My younger cousin's wife agreed to keep Annette during the week. Darlene agreed to keep "her baby Karen" (she would tell people she was really her baby) during the week. Darlene was pregnant and was staying home for the rest of her pregnancy, which worked out for me. This arrangement was only until I could figure out how to get the girls to and from school and day care and so on.

It was all this hardship that started building Pelegrino and I up as a couple. In the mornings, we would leave the apartment at the same time and walk to Western Avenue and Diversey to catch our bus to school and work. We would stand in the middle of the road and kiss goodbye. Then he would go to the bus stop on Western Avenue going southbound, and I would go to the bus stop on Western Avenue going northbound. While waiting for the buses to come, we would run, meet each other in the middle of the street for a last kiss, and run back to our bus post. We managed to get at least three kisses in before our buses arrived. It was fun.

We would pick up the girls on Friday and bring them back to my cousin's wife and Darlene on Sunday night. By December, Pelegrino started staying out, hanging around his old neighborhood. I knew something was wrong. He was acting very immature and not committed at all. Although we were not married, this was a red flag for sure that I should live alone with the girls. I talked to Pelegrino about the situation, and he responded in a controlling way. He said, "I am not leaving anywhere. I gangster you and everything you have. I am not going back to sleeping on a floor when there is a perfectly good bed right here."

Oh no. What had I gotten myself into? I thought about it all the time and knew I had to get rid of the relationship somehow. I thought and thought and regretted ever going out the night I met Pelegrino. I felt foolish. I remember praying and praying for God to make something happen that would set me free of our relationship and what felt like an invasion in my life at this point. I knew of God, but I didn't know God the way I know Him today. I did know how to pray in my own words. Papa Dios is Abba God yesterday, today, and always. Back to that later.

About two weeks before our argument, I had been hemorrhaging. Dr. Rojas admitted me to the hospital, where the doctors performed a D&C. He clearly explained that I needed to be careful because, after a D&C, a woman could become pregnant quickly. I promised myself that I would not have sex until I got the clearance from Dr. Rojas. A couple of days after our argument, Pelegrino did come home at the proper time. We went to bed at a good time, which was surprising because he normally liked to watch late TV. I fell asleep quickly. Sometime after, I was awakened by the pressure of his body on mine.

I pushed him off, saying, "What are you doing? You know I am not supposed to have sex for four weeks."

Pelegrino replied, "So, now you can have my baby. That's right, if you can have a baby by someone who beats on you, you can have my baby."

I jumped up and ran to the bathroom. I washed up and hoped I was OK.

I couldn't understand how a person could stay after being asked to leave. I recalled he had come from the streets and had the whole gangbanging mentality. But he was also sweet, gentle, and a good listener. He was playful with the girls and strong when I needed that extra physical strength. He did smoke marijuana from time to time, but that was it. Why did he have a need to stay out? Why was it so hard for him to understand that we were supposed to be responsible, committed people when we were adults? You couldn't just do whatever you wanted when you had kids and were trying to rear them correctly.

Oh yeah, he didn't have kids really. I could see why that was not a trigger for him to act responsibly as parents are supposed to.

I started questioning my whole separation from Joey. I started acknowledging that I wasn't perfect either. I didn't even think of the beating he had given me. Rather, I focused on the idea of a family unit—husband, wife, and children—and the roles we played in that unit. I knew he had a lot of things he needed to deal with and work on, like his addiction and temper to start with. But at least he was the girls' father, and he did act more responsible in that sense. Not to mention, he was my husband—even if I did not understand the meaning of commitment. Wow, I really messed up.

(Here is a typical example of my life with Pelegrino. It is

Valentine's Day on the day I am writing this chapter, and his priority is to spend time with his friends and addiction, rather than to come home. He got off work at 1:30 p.m., and it's 4:50 p.m., and he isn't home yet. God has helped me in this area. He's helped me carry my cross in humbleness and love.)

Back to the story.

Would you believe it? A couple of weeks later, I was visiting my younger cousin and his wife. And guess who dropped by? Yes, it was Joey. I was surprised to see him. He asked me to step outside for a few minutes because he had something to talk to me about.

"Sure," I said.

"I want to start by saying I am sorry for all that has happened," Joey said. "I know I need to get my life back together, especially in regards to kicking the heroin addiction. I miss you and the girls and would like to have you back home. I need help with kicking the habit. And my mom, being the Christian woman she is, would be a great help to me in accomplishing that goal. She has yet to meet you and the girls. I think that, if we move to Puerto Rico and get a fresh start, she can help me with my addiction and get the chance to meet you and her granddaughters. I believe it will be great. I know it will. Would you be willing to come back home, and we can start fresh away from Chicago?"

As Joey was talking, I was thinking about my cry for a way out of my relationship with Pelegrino and how I had started appreciating what I had left behind—him and our home. I said, "Yes, sure. We can try that."

Joey asked, "When can we go pick up the tickets?"

I replied, "My next day off is on Tuesday."

"OK then. We will purchase the plane tickets on Tuesday. I will pick you up at 1:00 p.m." Joey gave me a kiss. He put his hand on my stomach and added, "I will give the baby my name."

"What?" I said. "What baby?"

"This baby," he replied, rubbing my stomach. "I will give the baby my name."

"You are not right, Joey. I'm not pregnant," I said.

"OK. But I still will give the baby my name. You will see. I am right; you're pregnant."

January 6, 1981, Tuesday, was that magical day that would make everything right. Here was our second chance at being a family. I got the girls ready and took our regular two buses to my younger cousin's house. It was about 10:00 a.m. when we arrived. His wife and I did our normal routine. She did her domestic duties, I helped, and then we had café, talked for a bit. Then it was time for *General Hospital* at 1:00 p.m.

It was about fifteen to twenty minutes into the show when there was a knock at the back door. She got up, answered the door, and then walked back toward me, saying someone was looking for me. I went to the door. The man standing at the door asked, "Are you Joey's wife?"

I said, "Yes, I am."

He replied, "Joey is dead. He died this morning."

"What?!" I yelled. I could not believe what I had just heard. I can't even explain the emotions going through my mind, body, and soul. I can still feel the stabbing pain in my heart at the sound of those words. How could this be? I had just talked to him on Sunday. We were going to pick up the tickets to go to Puerto Rico and start over again. He was going to get help and be clean from his heroin addiction. I was going out of my mind, and racing questions kept circling. And how could I tell the girls? That was my greatest pain. And his mom. How could I call and tell her that, instead of us arriving as a family to start a new life, I would be bringing her son in a casket. The man at the door could not even tell me how it had happened or what had happened.

My younger cousin's wife, bless her soul, tried to calm me down. But she was as thrown as I was. I started calling places like the hospital, funeral homes, and so on. Still today I ask, how could this have happened? Why? Only God knows the answer to that question. And while I am still waiting to hear an answer of some kind, through much study of the Word of God, sermons, and other testimonies I have heard, I can get a pretty good idea of the why. One thing is for sure. This book is the product of that awful experiences, as well as many others in my life.

I was not able to see Joey, which broke me up inside. I would have to wait until the funeral home picked him up and laid him out. I wasn't there when it happened. I should have been. Or was this God protecting me from what I did not know was to come by reconciling our marriage?

There was a lot of work ahead of me. I started making calls to find out what to do. Finding a funeral home was one of those necessities that was on the immediate list. I chose Anderson Funeral Home, right next door to the practice of Dr. Rojas and Dr. Chajub. I made all the arrangements needed to get Joey's body to Puerto Rico, his home, mom, and family. I wanted to give him a beautiful burial.

Next, I had to build up the courage to tell the girls, really Annette. Karen was too little. She was only two years old. I didn't know to pray before addressing her, but I did say, "God help me." I don't recall the exact words I started the conversation with, but I do recall saying, "Papi Joey has been sick, and he died. God took him to heaven." (At least it was an illness. His lungs collapsed from walking pneumonia. It wasn't a drug overdose).

She responded, "It's your fault. You didn't take care of him!" And she cried her little eyes out.

That was worse than the news of his death. It broke me completely inside. Oh, how I carried that guilt for years. The tons of what–ifs, should haves, and could haves ran through my mind constantly. I had dreams and nightmares all the time. It was my fault; I was sure of that. I did not stay. I ran away and took the easy way out. I made my bed but didn't lie in it. All he needed was a strong person next to him. I had failed. Oh, how I failed. This was the thing with me. I had been given an assignment, and I'd failed to follow it through—first as a daughter when I hurt my dad and ruined his family honor. Now as a wife, I'd failed to stay by his side. And by failing him, I'd failed my daughter as a mom and caused her to lose her Papi Joey. Failure seemed to have followed me since kindergarten.

Through this ordeal, who was with me trying to console me?

Pelegrino. Yes, that, immature man who I was running away from was there to dry my tears. The punk, as my friend, the store owner called him. This gang member / street hoodlum—who was worse than the first one, as Papi said when he met him—was right there holding me and telling me that it was going to be all right. Pelegrino was a very good listener. That helped a whole lot. But he wasn't God. That's who I needed, and I did not realize it.

You see, I should have been going to God. But I didn't even know I was far from Him. He would have consoled me without any consequences to follow. I did not understand that He was the one I had to be concerned about when it came to my feelings and behavior, not people or anything in this world. But again, all things happen for a reason. Without question, hardship will take us closer to God. We just don't see it or understand it in our darkness. We are told in scripture:

> Consider it pure joy, my brothers and sisters, whenever you face trials of many kinds, / because you know that the testing of your faith produces perseverance.
>
> Let perseverance finish its work so that you may be mature and complete, not lacking anything.
>
> If any of you lacks wisdom, you should ask God, who gives generously to all without finding fault, and it will be given to you. (James 1:2–5)

Part of the funeral arrangement was my duty to take Joey's body to San Juan, Puerto Rico. I was to bury Joey in his hometown of Ponce, Puerto Rico. I had to leave the girls with my younger cousin's wife. I couldn't leave them with Mami because she was on her way to Puerto Rico. Just a couple days before I got the news of Joey's death, my Uncle Juan had died of cirrhosis of the liver. He would also be buried in Puerto Rico. I was twenty years old, traveling by myself, on the way to meet my husband's family for the first time, and the occasion was not a happy one but, rather, the worst kind, his death.

When I arrived, Joey's family received me with open arms and warmth. I was sick the whole time I was there. I even passed out at the burial site a couple inches away from the grave. Despite all this, meeting his family was a beautiful experience. I wished all the more that the occasion would have been different. I couldn't understand the why of anything.

We kept in touch and built a relationship via mail until the girls became adults, and then they continued communicating with Annette. Mami Santa died at age ninety-three. My desire was for her to meet the girls before leaving earth. Unfortunately, that did not happen. A couple years after Annette and Karen left home, I just lost track. My life became so busy, and I failed to keep in contact with Rosa (Joey's sister) and Mami Santa.

When I got back to Chicago, I was still sick all the time. My younger cousin's wife said it may be my nerves acting up due to Joey's death. I went to the doctor, and the diagnosis was, "Congratulation, you are pregnant!"

Oh, my goodness. No! I thought to myself. *This cannot be.* I hadn't been sexually active. Then Joey's words came back to me. "You are pregnant." And as I tried to figure it out, I recalled the incident when I'd woke up to Pelegrino's disobedience to doctor's order and him saying, "Now you will have my baby. If you can have children with someone who beats you, you can have a baby with me."

I went into panic mode. The only thing I could think of was getting an abortion to get rid of this big, big mistake. I never wanted to have children with different men. Abortions were popular in the '70s and '80s. It went hand in hand with women's lib. I called my sister and, without hesitation, the money was made available to me.

Once I got the money, my conscience started to disturb me. Suddenly, I felt it to be wrong. I did pray about it. I talked to Abba God, asking for his approval. Funny, I was so naive that I asked God if I should have an abortion or not. "Thou shall not kill" (Exodus 20:13). It could not be clearer than that. But that's what happens when you are a Christian, yet you do not have a relationship with God. You don't read His Word—the very place where he speaks to you. Nor do you have a full understanding of His commandments.

(What is a Christian? This may be a topic for another book.) In my conversation with God, I believed He was telling me that my pregnancy was a life for a life. He had taken Joey and was giving me a child. That's what I understood. The fact that Joey had known I was pregnant without me knowing it myself was really something to think about. I repented for the thought of having an abortion and received the pregnancy as a gift from God.

I discussed it with my younger cousin's wife. She said I should give Pelegrino a chance. She said, "Remember how much it hurt being rejected by Julio? Well, why would you reject someone the same way? Besides, you are waiting on a flying dove that may never come back again. A man is needed in the house when you are raising children, and it is his baby."

I am sure my cousin's wife meant well. But she was so very wrong on all counts. I thought about it. She was older and, a wise person in my eyes. I decided to tell Pelegrino about the pregnancy.

This was great news for Pelegrino. I had decided to give the relationship a try, even though I did not really want to because of his need to be gone so often from the home. This was his child I was carrying. So, I figured it would be best to try and make it work. I did not trust myself to stay single or to avoid getting involved in another relationship. I did not want to take the chance of yet another child with a different man. I did not know I could stay celibate, raise two little girls, and get ready for another one coming without getting involved with someone just by having a true relationship with God. Not that I was planning to, I just did not know all I needed was God in my life to be successful in rearing my daughters. I chose to believe my younger cousin's wife may be right. The answer was right there in Philippians 4:13, "I can do all this through Him who gives me strength."

MY RELUCTANT SUBMISSION

Once more, I was beginning a new chapter in my life.

Here we were, the perfect couple, both misfits in our society from dysfunctional families with the bare minimum of education and a whole lot of baggage, raising two little girls and one on the way.

Joey's death left me some work to do, in addition to getting him buried and to his family's home. The life insurance I had taken over the payments for paid off. I was able to arrange his funeral and burial. Funny how some of his family thought he had left some wealth behind. I found out that the house had several liens on it for lack of payment, one from People's Gas and one from Commonwealth Edison. He had gas and electricity racked up unlawfully; however, legally, the gas and electricity were both shut off for failure to pay the bills. This was my new adventure into adulthood.

I was not able to keep the house. It needed a lot of repairs, and it also had a bad memory I did not want to deal with. The light and gas company debt, all the funeral expenses, and the back-owed mortgage payments were all paid off at his death. I was able to sell the house and put the balance in a secure account for Annette and Karen. It was not much, but it was something.

My mom would have wanted me to keep it and give Elsa and Jose a place to live, but it was not possible. I was already dealing with too much to take them on my shoulders. Bless her heart, always finding a way out for them.

Pelegrino was a great support. He helped me clean out the house, getting it ready for the bank to take over. He was willing to go with me wherever I needed to go and was a great listener. My younger cousin's wife pointed out an empty apartment across the street from her. She said moving there would be a good idea. I would be close to her. And when Annette started school, she would be able to attend the same school as Gladys and Al. Pelegrino and I looked at the apartment. It was kind of small and sat at the back of the building with no front windows (which I don't deal well with). But it was affordable, and it had a big backyard, so we took it.

I was having a tough time with morning sickness. It was getting the best of me, but I dealt with it just like I had with the other two. Pelegrino was around more, and I started getting close to his family. My brother El and sister Lou were away pursuing their college education, and I had no one here other than my younger cousin's wife. Elsa and Jose were so much older than me and had their own set of friends, who they preferred to hang around with.

Funny, my younger cousin's wife was also way older than me, but it didn't matter. I enjoyed staying home and being close to Mami and Papi and my younger cousin's wife, who my mom loved dearly as well.

Everyone in my family liked Pelegrino and treated him like family. We did fun stuff together and always had something to do and somewhere to go. There was never a dull moment. We went to the park, visited each other's families, went to the movies and out to eat, and attended many holiday gatherings. We would always visit both our families without leaving anyone out. The girls were with us all the time. We mostly traveled on the CTA bus; it did not bother us at all. We were both very family and people-oriented and seemed to do extremely well in crowds.

Pelegrino's brother-in-law had an accident at work and lost most of his fingers on his left hand. He was awarded some money for his loss, and Pelegrino's sister and their little family moved to a house in the far north side of the city. They no longer lived in the neighborhood, and Angel went with them. That was a blessing for me. Pelegrino now had fewer excuses to visit the old neighborhood. It was Angel who he'd normally hung out with.

I was receiving financial support that allowed me to stay home for the pregnancy. This was another blessing because I was sick most of the time during the pregnancy. Pelegrino's sister and his brother-in-law were excited about the baby, as were most of his family members, especially his grandmother. This was a big difference from when I'd had Annette and Karen. Now, I had people in my life other than Mami, Papi, and my younger cousin's wife. They were cool, loving, and funny—great people to be around.

OK, the time came; I was having those so-called contractions. Pelegrino was not around. He had started hanging around the neighborhood again and was not home when the contractions started. I did not want to get alarmed; I'd had a few false alarms with Karen and did not want to go to the hospital prematurely. But the contractions kept coming. I called Pelegrino's sister, and she rushed to my apartment. She asked for her brother, and I told her he must be in the neighborhood. She put me and the girls in the car, dropped Annette and Karen off at my younger cousin's house, and drove straight to the neighborhood.

She stopped where she thought Pelegrino might be, but he wasn't there. She shouted to one of the guys, "Tell Pelegrino I'm taking his lady to the hospital. She is having the baby. He needs to get there now."

She flew to the hospital, left me there, and went back to find her brother. It was awesome. Pelegrino got to the hospital and was brought straight to the exam room I was in. He looked nervous and excited at the same time. He held my hand and kissed my forehead. Before we knew it, I had another contraction. The nurse came in the room, checked me, and said, "It's not time yet." She told Pelegrino, "If she has another contraction, it may be that she needs to use the bathroom. You should just put this bedpan"—she handed him a bedpan—"under her."

Pelegrino said, "OK."

A couple of minutes after the nurse left the room, another cramp, along with desires to push, came. He got the bedpan, and as I was lifting to position myself, a stronger one came. Out came the tip of the baby's head.

He said, "Oh no!" and started yelling for the nurse.

I had his arm and would not let him go. Sure enough, it was time. And this time I was not alone. The nurse came in and took over. He stepped out and joined his sister in the waiting area. It was so different from the last two deliveries, and with a couple more pushes, baby Arisely was born. The nurse went and got Pelegrino. He was a proud daddy, and he did not even mind that it was another girl, not a boy (as most men desire when becoming a dad for the first time).

She had the fullest head of thick black hair, and she also had it all over her little body. She looked so much like Pelegrino; there was no way of denying she was his. And he made sure that he stated it. "I told you she was mine!" Yes, she really was his baby.

I felt blessed. It was as if I had been given life—another life for the loss of Joey. But it was more than that. I had listened to God and not had the abortion I'd wanted when Dr. Rojas had first told me I was pregnant.

My grandfather was right. It was a girl. And I gave her the name he gave me the day he touched my stomach and said, "You are having a girl. Name her Arisely."

Pelegrino's sister was extremely excited about her first niece. In fact, the whole family was excited for us. My sister Lou was excited because she was going to be a godmother.

We were in a new phase of life—parents to three little ones. This was not too bad. I enjoyed being mom and homemaker, and Pelegrino was attentive to his role as daddy—or what he understood it to be. Annette and Karen enjoyed their little sister, and we started looking more like a real family.

Although we looked good together and I was able to keep up with Pelegrino, the girls' needs, and the upkeep of the apartment, Pelegrino still enjoyed going to the neighborhood and hanging out. In fact, between his job and outings to the neighborhood, I saw very little of him. When I brought it up, he didn't have much to say, until one day he spoke up and said, "You pay more attention to the baby than to me."

"Well, yes," I replied. "She is a baby and needs me to take care of her."

It was a battle making sense of his behavior that only took me back to old thoughts. *I should never have listened to my younger cousin's wife. I should never have accepted that date with the store owner or agreed for Angel and Pelegrino to come over that night, much less have sex with Pelegrino. I was better off waiting for Julio to come back, even if there was no sign of him doing so.* I was drowning in the lake of regrets. I did not want someone in my life who was not going to be present. For that, I could just stay alone with my girls, and I would not have to deal with the drama of it all. This was like living with Joey. I had a man in my life, but he was never around. I kept on trying and hoping.

I lived daily with great expectations of this man—hoping he would start growing with me and that we could build our relationship together and create a life as parents and partners. Not much was happening any time soon. Time was just passing by.

One day, I received a call from Rafy, my friend and Julio's brother. We had stayed in touch, and periodically he would call or stop by. A funny guy, he would laugh at his own jokes so hard it was contagious; you had no choice but to laugh along with him. He seemed to be in good spirits all the time. and there was never a dull moment around him.

Rafy's son Rafy Jr. had come to visit for the summer and wanted to stay in Chicago instead of returning home to his mom, who lived in Rochester, New York. That would be difficult for Rafy because his girlfriend's apartment was too small. Rafy was calling to ask if I could keep Rafy Jr. until he got a bigger place or a place of his own for him and Rafy Jr.

Rafy Jr. was a delightful young boy, very respectful and sweet. I told him I would run it by Pelegrino, but I was sure it was not a problem.

When I approached Pelegrino about Rafy Jr. staying with us, he said he did not think it was a good idea because it was a big responsibility. We went back and forth about it, but I kept insisting. So, Pelegrino said, "Do whatever you want."

I was very happy to be able to say yes. Rafy and Rafy Jr. were forever grateful.

When I told my younger cousin's wife about it, she was very against Rafy Jr. staying with me. She said it was not a wise thing to do because I did not know him, and I had the girls to think about. I didn't see any wrong in it. I said, "He is a little boy, and he wants to be near his dad. If I can help him be able to do that, why not?"

I followed Mami's saying. "Ha el que te pide dale, no le niegues de lo que tú tienes a nadie" (Give to him who ask of you. Don't deny anyone what you have). Without me knowing it, she was quoting scriptures:

- Then the King will say to those on his right, "Come, you who are blessed by my Father; take your inheritance, the kingdom prepared for you since the creation of the world. / For I was hungry and you gave me something to eat, I was thirsty and you gave me something to drink, I was a stranger and you invited me in, / I needed clothes and you clothed me, I was sick and you looked after me, I was in prison and you came to visit me." / Then the righteous will answer him, "Lord, when did we see you hungry and feed you, or thirsty and give you something to drink? / When did we see you a stranger and invite you in, or needing clothes and clothe you? / When did we see you sick or in prison and go to visit you?" / The King will reply, "Truly I tell you, whatever you did for one of the least of these brothers and sisters of mine, you did for me." (Matthew 25:34–40)
- There will always be poor people in the land. Therefore, I command you to be openhanded toward your fellow Israelites who are poor and needy in your land. (Deuteronomy 15:11)
- If one of you says to them, "Go in peace; keep warm and well fed," but does nothing about their physical needs, what good is it? (James 2:16)

- If anyone has material possessions and sees a brother or sister in need but has no pity on them, how can the love of God be in that person? / Dear children, let us not love with words or speech but with actions and in truth. (1 John 3:17–18)
- Share with the Lord's people who are in need. Practice hospitality. (Romans 12:13)

It was a joy having Rafy Jr. with us. The girls really enjoyed his company, and he was able to go spend time with his dad more frequently than once a year. The stories Rafy and the girls share today are warm and loving. He became part of our family.

CORRECTING MY SIN

One day, I went to visit Mami after church service, and she gave me a little envelope. In it was a little note that read, "Tienes que llevar las nenas a la iglesia. No les quites de que vallan contigo a la iglesia. Con mucho amor, Mami" (You must take the girls with you to church. Don't deny them from going to church with you. Lots of love, Mami).

Oh no, she was right. Sometimes I was running late, and it was easier to just go by myself. *I will talk to Pelegrino about it,* I thought to myself. I then kissed her and agreed to do what she asked.

Mami had shared her wisdom. I decided to talk to Pelegrino about attending church as a family. I explained that I should not be attending and leaving them all behind. To my surprise, he agreed to attend church. He told me about being a *monagillo* (altar boy) when he was a young boy and how much he'd enjoyed it. We both agreed that it was a great thing and started attending Sunday service regularly together at Our Lady of Grace, where some of our friends attended.

We started attending church that following Sunday and continued to attend. It was awesome. After service, we would often go to Gordi's home or her brother and sister-in-law's home for brunch. (This was being part of the church community.)

During one of our Sunday services, there was an announcement that the men's *cursillo* was coming up. Pelegrino signed up for the cursillo, a three-day retreat, which was new to me.

When the time for the retreat came, Pelegrino was excited. When he came back from the cursillo, he looked radiant. To my surprise, he had stopped smoking cigarettes and marijuana. He did not drink alcohol at the time. I was in awe. I asked him about it, but he said he could not share the details of what had taken place but that it had been a life-changing experience.

I asked if the church had retreats for women, and the answer was yes. I was excited. I told Mami about it, and she and Gordi signed up.

The time came. I was very excited. The retreat was held in downtown Chicago. The place felt holy, to say the least. It was the best three days of my life. I felt I'd had blindfolds on my whole life, and finally, they were taken off. I could see the wrong in my life, the sin I was living in, and how distant I was from Papa Dios (Abba God). Mami and I were not in the same groups, but we saw each other briefly between our classes and for picture taking.

Wow! I'd had this whole male/female relationship all wrong. I'd even had the whole act of sex wrong. There was a lot of clarity given during that three-day retreat. What stood out to me and convicted my heart was the ministry of marriage. I couldn't shake it off. The revelation about marriage was imprinted in my heart. It is the one ministry God uses to compare Himself and the church as His bride:

- "Return, faithless people," declares the Lord, "for I am your husband. I will choose you—one from a town and two from a clan—and bring you to Zion. (Jeremiah 3:14)
- For the husband is the head of the wife as Christ is the head of the church, his body, of which he is the Savior. (Ephesians 5:23)
- I am jealous for you with a Godly jealousy. I promised you to one husband, to Christ, so that I might present you as a pure virgin to him. (2 Corinthians 11:2)
- This is a profound mystery—but I am talking about Christ and the church. (Ephesians 5:32)
- Husbands, love your wives, just as Christ loved the church and gave himself up for her. (Ephesians 5:25)

When I got back home, I couldn't stop sharing how God had revealed truth to my heart. Pelegrino was now able to share what his experience was like. There was a rule not to share your experience with others so that everyone's experience would be a true encounter with Jesus Christ, not expecting this, that, or the other.

Pelegrino had asked me to marry him a few times during our time living together, but my answer had always been no. I did not want to remarry; it was just not in my heart to do so. We kept having issue with his lack of involvement in our day-to-day life. It had been three years since we'd started living together and had a baby together, and I had seen no growth on Pelegrino's part. That definitely made my answer to his marriage proposal a no.

But now, I'd heard from Jesus. I had come to realize I was in sin and to know it made a difference in a marriage if God was the head of the covenant. I was ready to make my sin right and make that commitment, that covenant with God and Pelegrino. As usual, I wanted to fix the situation.

I asked Pelegrino as we sat, sharing our experience at the cursillo, "Babe, you have asked me a few times to marry you. Do you still want to marry me?"

"Yes," he said, with no hesitation.

"OK, then that is what we will do. We can go to city hall and get married, and we will no longer be living in sin. God will be the head of our marriage, and we will grow together."

Pelegrino agreed.

The next time we visited with my younger cousin's wife, I shared our plans with her. She was so excited she called my cousin on the intercom and said, "Yayie has some great news to share. She and Pelegrino are getting married! Isn't that great?"

He congratulated us, and so did all the men in the shop. His wife hung up and started asking about our plans. I said, "We are going to city hall maybe next week."

"What? City hall? I know you have to get married in city hall either way, but Pelegrino has never been married, and you are a widow. You should be getting married in a church before God," she said, adding, "Isn't this the fair thing for Pelegrino, since it is his first time getting married?"

Pelegrino and I looked at each other and smiled.

"It's too expensive, and we don't have the finances for something like that," I said.

My younger cousin's wife replied, "Don't worry about a thing. You can have *padrinos* and *madrinas*" (Godfathers and Godmothers) "be sponsors to your wedding. Leave it to me. I will make a list of everything that is needed and a list of all friends and family members and let each person choose if they want to give you a gift. This will be their gift to you, being a godparent and choosing what they want to give you for your wedding. Mike, your godfather, should be able to sponsor your wedding dress. He is your godfather, right? OK. It is done. I will take care of everything. Your cousin and I will rent a small hall for the reception."

Pelegrino and I both smiled and said, "OK. We will get married in a church."

I thought this would be perfect. It had been revealed to me at the curcillo that I was in sin. Now, I could correct this wrong. If God was the head of our covenant, then we would have a great marriage. *De Colores! Santo!* This was my breakthrough—my way of correcting my wrong and doing something right that Mami and Papi could be proud of. I could not remove the stain from the family name, but I could show some growth—even if he thought I had gone from bad to worse. But I would not be in sin. That was my main focus.

We set the date for May 14, 1983. My younger cousin's wife was busy getting everything together. Pelegrino and I scheduled ourselves for premarital classes. This was something I hadn't known about when I'd married Joey. Pelegrino and I went through the classes and were ready for our big day.

My younger cousin's wife was getting all the details ready. Lou was my maid of honor. Annette and Karen, plus Carmen M., Pelegrino's sister, were our bridesmaids. Arisely was our flower girl. Carmen's husband at the time was the best men. Papi would walk me down the aisle. Mami made the *palomita capias*, Uncle Mike was buying me the wedding dress, Carmen M. and hubby were buying the cake, my younger cousin's wife bought us the wedding album and paid for the hall, and Lou's friend took pictures. Other items given by other family members and friends included champagne cups, a knife, pillow for the capias, the bride's bouquet of flowers, and invitations, to name a few.

I had never seen a wedding planned and come to pass quicker than ours (unless a couple was wealthy and had the means to get a team to put the wedding details together). I did the cursillo in March, and our wedding took place in May. My younger cousin's wife and everyone involved did a phenomenal job to help Pelegrino and me get married in a church, with all the trimmings, and celebrate our union with family and friends.

There may have been some difficulties, as with any function with such a short time notice. But overall, we were blessed, to say the least.

There was one especially important thing. I was running into a brick wall after the cursillo studying the Bible. There were no follow-up classes at a time or distance that worked for me. I was very protective about the girls. If Mami, my younger cousin's wife, or Carmen M. were not available to watch them, I would just stay home.

The classes were at the cathedral downtown, a distance from home, and the schedule was too late in the evening. I had very little comprehension skills. So, a self-study of the Bible seemed quite difficult for me. I got lost just thinking about it. Also, I did not have a Bible at the time. I depended solely on the reading from the pulpit on Sunday morning, which was not much at all.

Another dilemma was going through my mind and heart, one my younger cousin's wife brought up. Her question to me was, "Are you sure you want to marry Pelegrino?" She added, "You know, if Julio was to come back, you would no longer be free. You would be married, which would block the possibility of being with him." (Why even say that, when she was the one who'd told me I was selfish and wrong for not giving Pelegrino a chance and that I was waiting on a flying dove that was not coming back?) But I did not reflect on that fact then. I just became suddenly confused and fearful of the what–if.

After a few days, I went to see her and said "Yes, I have thought about it. It has been three plus years since Julio left, and I have not heard from him. I thought about what you had said about how Pelegrino is my age and how we can grow together. Remember you said he deserves a chance? He is Arisely's dad. I am going to go through with it by faith. With God being the head of our marriage covenant, our marriage will have a chance and be blessed."

I also spoke to Rafy, my dear friend and Julio's brother. Julio He said, "No sea que el brother no te de una sorpresa el día de tu boda aparezca en la iglesia y te la desbarate por su ira y celos" (May it not be that my brother appears on your wedding day and destroys your wedding due to his anger and jealousy).

Whoa. I hadn't thought of that. "Bueno el no me a llamado y no se nada de el" ("Well, he has not called me, and I know nothing of his whereabouts), I responded.

I mailed Maria Nelly and Julio an invitation to the wedding. My intention in sending Julio an invitation, in addition to actually inviting him, was to get a reaction. I thought maybe he would contact me. There was no response to the invitation. But if his brother had made that comment, it must be for a reason.

I had prayed to God about giving me the courage to call Julio and see where he was at in the whole matter of my marrying Pelegrino. Funny how I had not been able to get a number before, but at this point, one was supplied to me. I called, and to my surprise he answered the phone.

"Hola," I said in a soft voice.

He said, "Hello, Como estas? Que sorpresa tu llamada?" (Hello, how are you? What a surprise you called.)

I went straight to the point. "You know I am getting married. I sent you an invitation with your daughter. Did you get it?"

"Si, si. I did," he said.

I continued, "I changed my mind, and I am canceling the

wedding. I am flying to Puerto Rico tomorrow instead. Will you receive me?"

Julio said, "Espera, espera, mi amor. Las cosas no se hacen así. Tú tienes que hacer las cosas con calma y en orden. Tú no puedes cancelar la boda así, así namas" (Wait, wait, my love. Don't just go out of control like that. You must do things calmly and in order. You can't cancel the wedding like that, just like that.)

"Solo contestame una pregunta. Me recives mañana al yo llegar a tu puerta? Si o no?" (Only answer me one question. Will you receive me tomorrow when I arrive at your door? Yes or no?)

He went on to correct my actions—saying I must not cancel the wedding and fly to Puerto Rico and so on. I told him it was too late. I had already done it. He continued to try and help me understand that things were not done like that. It needed to be planned and carried out in the proper order.

I interrupted him and said, "Don't worry. I didn't cancel the wedding and will not be arriving at your door tomorrow morning. And yes, I will marry Pelegrino tomorrow. I just needed to be sure it was the right thing to do. And you have answered my question and doubt by refusing to receive me if I come to you."

He said, "It's not that I will not receive you. It's that those things must be done with order."

I was deeply hurt and refused to accept what he was trying to get me to understand. I continued to reassure him that I would marry Pelegrino.

He said, "Tu no puedes casarte porque acabas de comprobar que no le amas, porque me amas a mi y por eso no debes casarte con el. Dime que no me amas, anda, dime que no me amas y queda establecido que si te puedes casar porque ya no me amas" (You can't get married, because you just proved that you don't love him because you love me, and that's why you should not marry him. Tell me that you don't love me. Go ahead, tell me you don't love me, and it will be established that you can get married because you no longer love me.)

I could not tell him that I did not love him. That would have been a lie. I never stopped loving him, but there was no reason for me to do so.

I stood by my decision to marry Pelegrino and start a new life with him and said my goodbye. I was deeply hurt. But I knew, in order to have peace in marrying Pelegrino—after the comments of both my younger cousin's wife's and Julio's brother—I had to make the call. I knew it was a tough choice. But with Pelegrino being Arisely's dad and making the changes he had made after the cursillo, I found no other answer but to stay with him. And if I chose to do so, I would have to marry him, if I wanted to be right before God.

I did not trust myself to be single. I was too afraid of ending up with yet another relationship and probably another child. It was not something I felt I wanted or needed. But I had seen things happen in my life already that I didn't think would happen. Just out of nowhere, situations would arise, and I would end up making wrong choices that got me in trouble. I did not want to risk it.

Again, no Bible knowledge or godly counsel was available to me. I was acting too quickly—just wanting to fix the wrongs I had done in my life. It's very important to know that not everyone who is older, seems mature in the world's culture, or has read some of the Bible is qualified to counsel in these matters. Counsel should be straight from the Word of God. A person who is righteously mature and can back up what he or she shares with the Word of God confirms that the advice is coming from Him and not from his or her own opinion and will. It is God's truth and His good and perfect will.

May 14, 1983 came. The wedding was beautiful. I would never have imagined I would get married in a church. After all, I was not a virgin. I had ruined my chances back when I got pregnant at age thirteen. Like Papi said, I'd tarnished the family name. Thanks be to Jehovah-Tsidkenu, our Righteousness. God is a God of second chances:

- God has delivered me from going down to the pit, and I shall live to enjoy the light of life. / God does all these things to a person—twice, even three times. (Job 33:28–29)

- If we confess our sins, he is faithful and just and will forgive us our sins and purify us from all unrighteousness. (1 John 1:9)
- The Lord is not slow in keeping his promise, as some understand slowness. Instead, he is patient with you, not wanting anyone to perish, but everyone to come to repentance. (2 Peter 3:9)
- Forget the former things; do not dwell on the past. (Isaiah 43:18)
- But God demonstrates his own love for us in this: While we were still sinners, Christ died for us. (Romans 5:8)
- From inside the fish Jonah prayed to the Lord his God. / He said: "In my distress I called to the Lord, and he answered me. From deep in the realm of the dead I called for help, and you listened to my cry. / You hurled me into the depths, into the very heart of the seas, and the currents swirled about me; all your waves and breakers swept over me. / I said, 'I have been banished from your sight; yet I will look again toward your holy temple.' / The engulfing waters threatened me, the deep surrounded me; seaweed was wrapped around my head. / To the roots of the mountains I sank down; the earth beneath barred me in forever. But you, Lord my God, brought my life up from the pit. / "When my life was ebbing away, I remembered you, Lord, and my prayer rose to you, to your holy temple. / Those who cling to worthless idols turn away from God's love for them. / But I, with shouts of grateful praise, will sacrifice to you. What I have vowed I will make good. I will say, 'Salvation comes from the LORD.'" / And the Lord commanded the fish, and it vomited Jonah onto dry land. (Jonah 2:1–10)
- For God did not send his Son into the world to condemn the world, but to save the world through him. (John 3:17)
- Yet this I call to mind and therefore I have hope: / Because of the Lord's great love we are not consumed, for his compassions

never fail. / They are new every morning; great is your faithfulness. (Lamentations 3:21–23)

- For the wages of sin is death, but the gift of God is eternal life in Christ Jesus our Lord. (Romans 6:23)

This time it was my decision. Right or wrong, I was making the choice to marry Pelegrino and to correct my sin.

I stood in the back of the church, observing Pelegrino standing at the altar and looking back as the wedding party walked forward toward the front and took their places. His brother-in-law and Carmen walked ahead and then Annette and Karen. They were followed by Lou, my maid of honor, and Arisely, my flower girl dropping the rose petals and looking back for Mommy. Yes, I ended up carrying my flower girl down the aisle in my arms as I walked toward the biggest commitment of my life.

As I reached the altar and handed Arisely to someone to care for her, it was time to adorn the blessed Mary statue with a bouquet of flowers (a tradition). I used this time to address Papa Dios Almighty with my prayer and petition, as I aimed to make a covenant with Him, Pelegrino, and myself.

Father God of heaven, hallowed be Your name. Thank You, Father, for the honor and privilege to come before You. You know my heart, Lord; I want nothing more than to be right before You. I ask that You be the head of our marriage, that You give me what it takes to be that Psalms 31 woman You speak of in scripture. I ask that You give me the strength I will need to stand in our marriage in faith. May I have the strength to stay no matter what happens and not be convinced by those trying to help when our marriage faces problems, like with Joey. Put love in my heart for Pelegrino; teach me how to love him. Help me have wisdom when dealing with any issues. And remember that we are no longer two but one with you. Give me strength, Lord. Amen.

I slowly got up and walked toward Pelegrino and Reverend Lorenzo and felt secure that God was going to protect our marriage and be present always.

This was a bigger deal than I thought, especially since I believe Pelegrino was the first to marry in his family in the presence of

God, in a church with the blessing of God. And he was called to lead us. His grandmother Luisa had the joy and blessing to see her grandson get married and enter into a covenant between God, him, and his bride. She looked beautiful dancing with her grandson at our wedding reception. I'm sure his mom would have been proud of him as well.

We couldn't go on a honeymoon, but we did plan to stay out that night. We left the reception and drove to Lou Malnati's Pizzeria. We were still wearing our wedding clothes. I'm sure people must have thought, *Boy, they must love pizza.* When we were done, we drove to a local hotel, checked in, and called it a night. When we woke up, we noticed that Pelegrino's tuxedo pants were gone. My purse, holding all the wedding dance money was also gone. We were robbed while we slept. Thank God we had brought a change of clothing. We got dressed and went to the front desk and made our complaint. We could not pay the bill because the thieves had taken everything—his wallet and my purse.

What a way to start our marriage. Drama right from the start.

MORE SELF-DECEPTION

U pstairs from us lived Gordi's brother and his wife. They were the landlords of the building we lived in. She had a friend we called Conchi, who was living with them temporarily until she moved to Puerto Rico. When I would go upstairs, I would see her sitting at the kitchen table reading the Bible. I would always go to her and greet her with a hug and kiss, as it was the custom I was raised with.

One day, I paused and extended more than a hug and kiss. I asked her, "Why are you always sitting here reading the Bible whenever I come up stairs?"

She said, "It is by reading the Bible that you receive knowledge and get to know God." She asked me, "Don't you have a Bible?"

I said, "No."

"You should get one," she replied.

Of course, I did not tell her I was fearful of reading because I was extremely poor at reading period—much less understand what I had read, given my lack of comprehension. But I walked away with what she said lighting a light bulb in my head and heart.

Now, the next step was to get myself rooted in the word. My brother El had an Oxford Bible he had read thoroughly during his college years. In fact, it was part of one of his classes (Literature of the Bible). His study was just that, literature of the Bible, as teaching or speaking about the Bible in religious terms in a public school was not allowed. The Bible was still at Mami's apartment on his old bookshelf. I saw it one day while at Mami's and asked him if I could read it.

"Sure," he said. "I already read it. You can have it."

That was such a blessing. I had prayed that God would give me the ability to read the Bible and understand what I was reading. Though I was still not attending any organized Bible study group, I picked up that big book and started reading, fear and all.

It felt as if my life had just started again. Yet, there was so much I did not know or understand. The only thing I had going for me was those three days at the cursillo and what I heard God telling me through the teachings and roles played out there.

I did read the Bible during my alone time, mainly when the girls were sleeping. But I was not getting a whole lot from it. No revelations yet to how to move forward in my day-to-day life had come yet. I also did not read daily; it was more a matter of when I got a chance.

I kept an immaculate apartment and car (one of the reasons I did not read more). My girls were well fed and nurtured with affection. There was nothing I could deny Pelegrino if it was at my reach. Rafy was sheltered and nurtured with love and affection by both Pelegrino and me.

I was faithful at church and stayed attentive to Mami and Papi. I enjoyed my regular visits to my younger cousin's house, joining his wife as we cleaned, talked, laughed, danced, and got wet in the rain. I hung out at Carmen M.'s house every other weekend or as time permitted and practiced hospitality as often as I could at our place. It was a busy season for sure.

Pelegrino lost his job, due to layoffs. He collected unemployment for a short time until his brother-in-law told him the company he worked for was hiring. Pelegrino went in applied and was hired. A few months into them working together, Pelegrino started coming in really late. Sometimes, he was walking in when the girls were on their way out to school. And on the weekends, he would be gone all day and all night. He also started drinking alcohol and using cocaine.

Wow! What is this? I couldn't believe it, but it was as plain as day. I was once again married to someone who was addicted to drugs. He was acting differently. He was more active—but not at home, more like outside of the home with his friends. He was seeing other people. Every time I turned around, there was someone new.

What happen to that man who had come home from the cursillo and decided to live for God, cleansed from all substances? Why was this happening? I was filled with thoughts and questions. Hurt and anger filled my mind and heart. Feeling cluttered with so much to process, I went to my younger cousin's house, and I poured my heart out to his wife.

As she listened to me, she became so upset at what she was hearing. She said, "You should go out and come back later than him. See how he likes it."

I would have received different advice from the Bible:

- Do not repay evil with evil or insult with insult. On the contrary, repay evil with blessing, because to this you were called so that you may inherit a blessing. (1 Peter 3:9)
- Do not repay anyone evil for evil. Be careful to do what is right in the eyes of everyone. (Romans 12:17)
- Evil will never leave the house of one who pays back evil for good. (Proverbs 17:13)
- Make sure that nobody pays back wrong for wrong, but always strive to do what is good for each other and for everyone else. (1 Thessalonians 5:15)
- Do not be overcome by evil but overcome evil with good. (Romans 12:21)
- Do not say, "I'll pay you back for this wrong!" Wait for the Lord, and he will avenge you. (Proverbs 20:22)
- Do not take revenge, my dear friends, but leave room for God's wrath, for it is written: "It is mine to avenge; I will repay," says the Lord. (Romans 12:19)

She meant well, but it wasn't the right thing to say. I seriously would do most everything she would say, literally *most* of the time. It so happened that we were in the fall season. This was one of the seasons of the year where nightclub owners brought in performing attractions to boost their business at the beginning of the holidays. I heard that Julio was going to be performing at the Años 40 Night Club. I asked my sister-in-law if she wanted to accompany me, and she said yes.

Wow! I was extremely excited. They had put together a great show, about four artists in all. We had a great time listening to the musicians sing oldies and the new Spanish songs I was very fond of. But at the end, I failed big-time. I ended up going out with Julio and fell into sin. I definitely came home past 4:00 a.m. But guess what? Pelegrino was not even home. He didn't get the shock I had hoped he would at my late arrival. How could he notice what I was doing if he was preoccupied with himself? He was in his own world.

I felt badly. But I could not change what had happened. I had to let it go and just pretended it hadn't happened. Besides, I knew Julio would once again be gone. He was only in Chicago for that weekend. Sure, we talked about a lot of things, including why we didn't ever have a child together and so on, but this was not the time to open old stories and leap into a fairy-tale romance. I was married by God in the church. I had to let the dream of Julio go, start over, and get over the past. I was living out deception, not understanding what it was, just trying to have a solution for everything.

This brought me to my knees. "Heavenly Father, forgive me for my weakness. Forgive me for still having feelings for Julio. Forgive me for committing adultery. Forgive me for not holding on to what I learned in the cursillo. I do not understand this. How is it that I allowed myself to fail You? I asked You the day we got married to put love in my heart for him. But Pelegrino has made it so difficult to love him. The more I try to love him, the harder he makes it for me to do so. It is as if I am not important to him at all. And how is it that he turned back to the same things he was doing before? It is even worse now because he has started using alcohol and cocaine. I'm sorry, God. How can I talk about what he has done when I just failed You myself? I need help, God. Please help me. Amen."

A few weeks had passed. I was still feeling guilty over what had happened during my revenge night out, so I asked Pelegrino not to use protection. He asked, "Are you sure?"

"Yes, I'm sure," I responded.

He was thrilled to find out a couple weeks later we were expecting another baby. Funny that he was so thrilled to have children, yet he complained that I paid them more attention than to him.

We had a couple of good months. Pelegrino was a little more attentive, and of course, that put me on cloud nine. I was happy cooking, baking, cleaning, and enjoying my little family.

Then six months into the pregnancy, he started staying out more and being less attentive at home. One day, Pelegrino came to me with a phrase no woman wants to hear. "I have something to tell you." Pelegrino said he had been to see a doctor for a rash, and he'd tested positive for gonorrhea. He added that the doctor had advised him to have me go in and get tested, even if I don't have symptoms.

It added up. I had been feeling uncomfortable when I used the bathroom. I was so hurt I didn't have words to say to him. I just knew I'd better get to the doctor's office ASAP.

I tested positive. I also got educated on the disease and how it would affect the baby. I was fuming with anger and fear for the baby—especially when it was explained to me that the baby could be born with vision problems or even blind.

According to the Centers for Disease Control and Prevention 24/7), "Gonorrhea is a common STD in the United States. Untreated gonococcal infection in pregnancy has been linked to miscarriages, premature birth and low birth weight, premature rupture of membranes, and chorioamnionitis. Gonorrhea can also infect an infant during delivery as the infant passes through the birth canal. If untreated, infants can develop eye infections. Because gonorrhea can cause problems in both the mother and her baby, it is important for providers to accurately identify the infection, treat it with effective antibiotics, and closely follow up to make sure that the infection has been cured."

Pelegrino pleaded for forgiveness and said she meant nothing to him; she was not worth two cents to him. I asked him, "Why did you do this again?"

He said, "Babe, it's not that I don't love you. It's that it's not the same having sex with a pregnant woman as with a normal woman. Please forgive me. I love you, and I will never do this again."

Again, I was lost for words. But I did understand how a person could make foolish mistakes. After all, I had made mine too.

This, too, had to pass. I had to focus on being well for the baby. I did everything the doctors told me to, and I prayed.

On a regular day as I listened to music and cleaned the house, the phone rang. I answered it. "Hello," I said.

"Hi, Annie! Is Pelegrino there?"

I recognized the voice. It was Chiqui, Pelegrino's cousin. I said, "Chiqui?"

He responded, "Yes, is Pelegrino there?"

"Chiqui do you know who you are talking to?" I asked.

He replied, "Yes I do."

"Then why did you call me Annie?"

"Oh, I did?" he asked.

"Yes, you did, and you followed it by asking for Pelegrino."

He was caught and stuttered, trying to find an answer.

"Well, who is Annie? And why would you be asking her for Pelegrino?"

He ended up telling me who Annie was and about the relationship she had with Pelegrino.

He was having an affair, and even his cousin knew about it. I thought quickly. This is not just a one-night stand thing. She must know about this gonorrhea issue. "So, apparently you know this Annie very well. You must have her phone number, or you wouldn't be calling and asking for Pelegrino, addressing her by her name. You must have her address too. Can I please get her address? Don't bother with the number, because I have something I have to tell her, and I want to do it in person."

Chiqui would not give me her address, but he did tell me where they went to go get something to eat. It was a restaurant close to where she lived, about a block or two from her place.

I finished cleaning, took a shower, and got the girls and myself ready. I asked my younger cousin's wife if I could leave the girls with her briefly. I didn't tell her what it was about. I went to the corner Chiqui had told me about. I patiently waited until I saw Pelegrino and Annie come out and start walking back to her place. I followed them and waited for Pelegrino to come out.

As soon as he was on the street, I called him and beeped the horn. He was blown away. "What are you doing here?" he asked.

"I came to talk to your little girlfriend Annie. It is Annie?"

"You are delirious, babe. I told you it was over between her and me."

"Really? "That's why you are having lunch with her and you are at her place, because you ended it with her?"

"Yes, babe. You have to believe me," he pleaded with me.

"OK. Since this is true, you don't have a problem taking me to her and telling her in front of my face," I replied, adding, "Guess what? I'm not leaving here until you do."

"OK, OK," he said.

I got out of the car and said, "Well, come on. Start walking."

He walked ahead of me, and I followed closely behind. Opening a black gate, he made his way toward the front door. I stood by the gate as he knocked. Annie opened the door and Pelegrino said, "I have to talk to you. Can you come out?"

She looked over at me and decided not to walk completely out but stayed closer to the door.

I walked up closer and said, "Well, Pelegrino, don't you have something to tell her?"

He told her, "Annie, I just wanted to tell you that I am choosing to stay with my wife and will not see you again."

I said, "What else? Tell her everything you told me about her."

"Oh, yeah, you are not worth anything to me, not two cents. I love my wife, and I am going to make this right." Then he looked at me and asked, "Is that all, babe? I said it just like I told you."

I got closer and said, "I just wanted you to hear what he told me about his relationship with you. And I also wanted to tell you, in case you do not know, that he tested positive for gonorrhea. Just so you know. That's all. We are done here." I turned and extended my arm out, pointing to the exit. "Let's go." I directed him back to the gate door. I waited for him to be completely out before I continued walking out.

I was not about to let him lie to me and then come tell her something else and continue seeing her. I also wanted her to know that he was sick, and she may be as well.

The rest of the pregnancy was horrible. I kept thinking of our baby coming into the world blind or with other defects due to the gonorrhea and Pelegrino's betrayal and negligence.

About six weeks later, I received a surprise visit from Johnny, Julio's youngest brother. A couple months earlier, I had helped him while he was in prison. I'd allowed him to use my address as his place of residence in the hope he would be released. I was happy to see him but saddened at the same time.

Johnny looked a mess. It was clear he'd been in a fight of some kind. He started to tell me the story as I got the first aid kit to clean his wounds. I made him some *café colao* and asked him to stay for dinner.

I was preparing dinner when I felt a huge pool of hot water run down my legs through my clothes. I felt no pain, but the amount of water was an indication that my water had broken. "Babe!" I cried out loud. I did not want to move, but I started walking slowly toward the living room.

Pelegrino and Johnny came quickly.

I said, "I believe my water broke."

Pelegrino asked, "What do we do now?"

I said, "I need to go to the emergency room."

Johnny said, "Yep you do. I will be leaving so you two can get going."

I apologized.

He replied, "No problem. Just get going."

Pelegrino was nervous, and so was I. "We need to leave the girls with Olga until you get back home. Babe, don't forget the suitcase," I said as I went into the bathroom to dry myself.

Pelegrino and I drove to the hospital. I still didn't have any labor pains—just some discomfort and pressure. But because my water broke, the nurses rushed me in and started checking my vitals and preparing me for delivery.

I was having contractions, but I was not dilating. This was a problem. I was so hyper I started having cataplexy episodes, where my whole body loses all muscle tone, and I pass out. I don't lose consciousness, but I did stop breathing. The hospital staff didn't know about my cataplexy disease and thought I was dying. They kept saying, "We are losing her."

I couldn't speak to tell them what was going on because I kept passing out.

The house doctor said, "Emergency C-section."

The nurse started wheeling me to the surgery room. As they passed by Pelegrino, they told him they were losing me and were going to do a C-Section to save the baby. They took me to the surgery room. They tied me down. And as the anesthesiologist was about to put on the gas mask explaining it would make me sleepy, I felt the greatest urge to push. I started shrugging off the mask with my shoulder and moving my head, trying to stop the anesthesiologist from placing the mask.

She said, "I need to put this on to help you sleep so we can start. She had the right side on me and needed only the left side across my face to place it firm.

Again, I shrugged her hand off. "I need to push," I said.

The doctor said, "Let me check her again. Untie her legs."

As soon as my legs went up, I pushed, and the baby's head was seen. Wow! The doctor and nurses rushed to complete the delivery, and there came baby. Yes, the baby did come premature as predicted by the Centers for Disease Control and Prevention. And I was relieved when I heard her cry.

She was tiny and beautiful. The doctors reassured me she was fine, with one little problem. She had a hole in her heart (a heart murmur) that needed to be monitored. But she should be fine as her organs continued to grow.

Pelegrino was thrilled. "She is so cute and tiny. I am going to see her again," he said and left for the baby viewing room. Once again, he did not seem to mind that it was not a boy but, instead, another girl, four in total now. They had her in an incubator because of her heart and weight. She weighed only four pounds.

Now that I had peace of mind about the baby's health, there was something especially important I wanted to take care of before I was released from the hospital. I called the nurse and reminded her I had requested in my prenatal care to get a tubal ligation at the time of the delivery.

The nurse said she would confirm the order and get back to me when it was going to be done. The nurse left the forms for the baby's name to be filled out and left. I put them to the side to confirm with Pelegrino on the name of the baby.

A few minutes after the nurse left, another nurse came into the room and introduced herself. She explained she would be taking me to the operating room to get prepped for the tubal ligation. Wow! *That was fast*, I thought to myself. I'd just mentioned it to the nurse., and here they were, ready to take me to get the surgery done.

I returned to the room after surgery, and the document for the baby's name was gone. The nurses must have picked it up after taking me to surgery. I did not even remember it was there and needed to be filled out.

Everything was moving rapidly. I should be home with our healthy baby in a couple of days, and no more fears of becoming pregnant again—by Pelegrino or anyone else. It wasn't that I was planning anything in the near or far future. I did love children. But I wanted to feel free in the knowledge I would not conceive again in order to attend to the four I already had.

Children are not to be taken lightly. You are bringing life into the world, and that is a lot of responsibility. They depend on you to do right by them and be their provider, protector, and voice until they come of age. With all the struggles I was facing in this marriage, I did not want to add more to my plate than I could handle, I told myself, justifying my decision.

I also didn't know that my decision would be out of God's will and law, but it was. We read in Genesis 9:7, "As for you, be fruitful and increase in number; multiply on the earth and increase upon it."

It's incredible how far we are from the will of God, and most believers don't have the slightest idea or clue of this truth.

When the time to go home had arrived, I was ready. I packed my things, including a package from the hospital with the birth information in it. I took my baby and headed out to a new start again. Every time I had a baby, it felt like a brand-new start, filled with hope and tons of possibilities of good things to come. Pelegrino was right there waiting for us with the car in front of the hospital, that proud daddy picking up his bundle of joy and his jazzy lady (as he called me).

I was dying to see the girls and introduce them to their new baby sister. She was going to be like a little toy doll to them; she was so tiny. I still had Arisely's crib and a lot of her stuff. Mami had knitted a few items for this new little one, just as she had every time for each of the girls—a sweater, booties, hat, and blanket. She knew it was a girl and was excited to start making cute dresses. Each one of the girls had their crocheted dresses from Abuela. They dressed like little Puerto Rican princesses.

We had the names picked out, and I was happy about being able to name the baby Natalie Irene. If it was a boy, it would have been Steven (I loved the way the name sounded in Spanish, Estevan). This time, when deciding on a name I had shared my thoughts with Carmen Matos, and she had come up with the middle name Irene. Natalie was also the name of a beautiful song by Julio Iglesias that I was very fond of, and Carmen had added the middle name Irene. Perfect.

When unpacking, I came across the baby's birth certificate from the hospital and it read, "Baby Matos." "What! Baby Matos?" I could not believe it. They had not added the baby's name to her birth records. She had been recorded as Baby Matos. I called the hospital, and it was explained to me that I had not been in the room when they picked up the form, and it needed to be entered in their system. They added that I could go to the civic center and have her name added to her birth record for a small fee.

This just added another task for me. I could not believe that I hadn't completed the form and the nurse that picked up the form hadn't checked hadn't cared that it was incomplete. I truly dislike going to the civic center; reading and filling out forms is not one of my favorite things to do because I get fearful and doubtful about whether I'm doing it correctly. On top of it, people weren't very helpful. They seem to be bothered that they were being asked to do their job. Then again, that was my fault for not finishing school. Well, it was too much to do. I couldn't worry about it. The important thing was that Natalie was healthy.

All was falling into place—or so it seemed. I was back to feeling like myself and was busy as can be, which was a good thing. Pelegrino continued working at Chicago Press with his brother-in-law on the second shift. Annette and Karen were doing well in school, Arisely was enjoying being a big sister, and Baby Matos (Natalie) was precious as could be. I always made time for Mami and Papi. I was spending less time at my younger cousin's wife's home. But I was there at the drop of a call. Our time at the blue house (the girls' name for Titi Carmen M.'s house) was regular, at least every other Saturday.

I learned to make tacos like Bertha, Pelegrino's brother-in-law's *comai*, who was Mexican and married to his best friend, John. Carmen M. had shared Bertha's recipe at some point during our visits to the blue house. I have a lot of good memories from those visits, and I believe the girls' fondest memories would come from there, in addition to all the other great times they had as children. They seem to have forgotten most of their childhood as adults today, but that's a whole other story for another book perhaps.

I recall one day at the blue house, after we had cooked, and everyone had eaten. Pelegrino and his brother-in-law were in the backyard or garage. The kids were playing with Malissa across the street, and Carmen M. and I were sitting on the front stairs. She asked me, "*Cuña*" (Sister-in-law), "is this it? Is this what it's all about?"

I asked her, "What do you mean?"

She went on to say, "Well is this it? We are married, have children and a house, and that's it? What else is there?"

"I guess this is it, cuña," I responded.

I didn't know the answer back then, but I can answer it today. Our lives are not our own—as strange as that may sound. We were created with a reason and purpose, regardless of how unappealing it may sound to us because of the way we have lived. We were created in the image of God and given everything that has been created on earth for our good. Genesis 3:8 says, "The man and his wife heard the sound of the Lord God as He was walking in the garden in the cool of the day, and they hid from the Lord God among the trees of the garden." That means that they were able to walk and talk with God freely at any time.

This was the purpose for God creating humankind—to have fellowship with us in that perfect place He created the Garden of Eden. What turned things around was our sin:

- So God created mankind in his own image, in the image of God he created them; male and female he created them. / God blessed them and said to them, "Be fruitful and increase in number; fill the earth and subdue it. Rule over the fish in the sea and the birds in the sky and over every living creature that moves on the ground." (Genesis 1:27–28)
- For this is what the Lord says—he who created the heavens, he is God; he who fashioned and made the earth, he founded it; he did not create it to be empty, but formed it to be inhabited—he says: "I am the Lord, and there is no other. / I have not spoken in secret, from somewhere in a land of darkness; I have not said to Jacob's descendants, "Seek me in vain." I, the Lord, speak the truth; I declare what is right. (Isaiah 45:18–19)

- For You formed my inmost being; You knit me together in my mother's womb. / I praise You, for I am fearfully and wonderfully made. Marvelous are Your works, and I know this very well. / My frame was not hidden from You when I was made in secret, when I was woven together in the depths of the earth. / Your eyes saw my unformed body; all my days were written in Your book and ordained for me before one of them came to be. (Psalms 139:13–16)

- Now the serpent was more crafty than any beast of the field that the Lord God had made. And he said to the woman, "Did God really say, 'You must not eat from any tree in the garden?'" / The woman answered the serpent, "We may eat the fruit of the trees of the garden, / but about the fruit of the tree in the middle of the garden, God has said, 'You must not eat of it or touch it, or you will die.'" / "You will not surely die," the serpent told her. / "For God knows that in the day you eat of it, your eyes will be opened and you will be like God, knowing good and evil." / The woman saw that the tree was good for food and pleasing to the eyes, and that it was desirable for obtaining wisdom, she took the fruit and ate it. She also gave some to her husband who was with her, and he ate it. / And the eyes of both of them were opened, and they knew that they were naked; so they sewed together fig leaves and made coverings for themselves. (Genesis 3:1–7)

We normally made good of our time together. One day—I'm not sure where the men were—we piled up the kids in her car and drove to Wisconsin. It was a blast, to say the least. Other times, her little clan, along with Pelegrino and our little tribe, went to Lake Geneva, and together, we had other family outings during the summer months. We were not housebound all the time.

Then there was our St. Louis trip, a girl's weekend away with no hubbies and no kids. Lou lived in St. Louis at the time. I don't know what brought that trip on, but we packed up and headed South. That was such a fun trip, even though I kept thinking about the girls.

Carmen M., Lourdes, and I had lots of fun. We went to Six Flags, a comedy show, and a nightclub (where I got sick and ended up sitting outside just enjoying the sense of freedom.) One thing I can say, we truly enjoyed each other's company. Freddy, Lou's boyfriend, joined us for some of the activities, but it didn't even seem like he was around; it was just us girls.

This is how I imagined it would have been like with Lourdes and I as roommates, had I not made the poor choices when I was thirteen. As it was, my life had taken a whole different route.

I guess Pelegrino must have had that same question in his mind and heart. Is this it now that we are married? Was it a sign of boredom? I wonder because he tended to go out a lot. He got involved with life outside the home more than I thought a married man should. But I was just learning as I went along.

Because of the size of our family, we felt it was time to move into a bigger place, with more bedrooms for the girls, since now we had four. Wow, this would be a great opportunity to bring some separation between the neighborhood and Pelegrino. I decided to seek a place further north, which would make a difference in Pelegrino's travel time to the neighborhood. I figured it may keep him from staying out as much. I hoped it would.

We found an apartment way up north—it had third floor, a living room, a dining room, a kitchen, and three and a half bedrooms. How perfect was that? I thought that, since we currently lived 4.6 miles from the new place, and it already took twenty minutes driving and on the bus to get to the neighborhood, getting there would take even longer. He was sure to want to stay home more.

We were excited, to say the least. We even went shopping for furniture, beds for the girls, and a Zenith console color TV. We still have the TV today, and it works.

The day to move arrived, and the weather was bad. There was about two feet of snow on the ground, but we didn't let that stop us. Nope. Pelegrino, his brother-in-law, Angel, Carmen M., and I started loading everything into the U-Haul truck. We drove 4.6 miles in the slush and unloaded everything in the new place. It was actually a good time, with great memories of slipping and sliding, laughing, and getting the job done together.

I was completely done unpacking and setting everything up in forty-eight hours. It felt like a honeymoon. Yes, bigger is better, and the TV was amazing. I loved it. We got wall-to-wall carpeting, which I loved; the girls would not get cold feet, and I loved walking barefoot. Pelegrino and the girls were happy, and I was ecstatic, cooking up new dishes, baking cookies, and making homemade popcorn. There were always snacks and lots of TV time.

Rafy had been in Rochester, New Jersey, with his mom. He was back. And yes, he had his own room. We moved Annette to the other room that had an attached playroom and gave Rafy her room while he was with us. Rafy and the girls had some playful times in that huge apartment. So did dad and the girls. It was like a big playground when Mom was not home. Nowadays, I am blessed to hear them reminisce about those days when they played hide-and-go-seek, among other games while I was gone.

We also had a lot of other friends and family members live with us during the time we lived at the Troy Street apartment. We had Sonia, Tio Regino's daughter (a cousin); our old landlord's daughter; and Carmen Merino, my niece. They came at different times, of course, but our home was a haven for many during the time we lived there.

What it was not doing, however, was keeping Pelegrino at home more. Nope. That same pattern of him being away a lot started up again. Now that the new apartment honeymoon was over, Mr. Matos was at it again.

DOES ANYBODY HEAR HER?

Pelegrino's staying out was getting out of control again. I also notice blood on the pillow and bedsheets often. *This is not normal*, I thought. I asked him, and he claimed it was nothing. But I knew something was wrong. I saw blood in the bathroom and on the kitchen floor, and I'm sure I didn't see more only because we had the rugs. Otherwise, there would have been much more around.

On a Thursday, his regular payday, I waited until he walked in and confronted him. "Pelegrino, this has to stop. I am going to leave Chicago, and you will not be able to stop me or find me."

He gave me all the false promises again. "This is it, babe. I promise. You'll see this time for real."

I gave him my word that, one more mess up, and I was out for good. We ended the conversation, and he went to the bathroom to take a shower. While he showered, I checked all his clothes, shoes, and jacket and made sure he did not have any of that garbage in his belongings.

That next morning, Pelegrino got up and got ready for work. I was in the kitchen making him coffee and preparing his lunch. He stepped out but returned in a matter of minutes. He came into the dining room and sat down. I heard him as I finished preparing his lunch and café. I walked into the dining room, and I saw him about to snort a line of cocaine.

"What are you doing? Are you out of your mind?" I said in a loud, frantic voice.

He said, "What? Oh this? I just found this and was about to check and see if it is cocaine."

"That's a lie. Do you think I'm ignorant? Are you trying to make me go out of my mind? I checked all your clothes last night, and you had nothing in your belongings." I put down the items I had in my hand and picked up what he had in front of him and started walking toward the bathroom to throw it away.

"Go ahead. Throw it away. I told you I was just checking to see if it was cocaine. Yeah, throw that away," he said as I dumped the powder down the toilet.

"That does it, Pelegrino. I am going to pack up, take the girls, and get out of here. I am not doing this anymore. You need help. You are bleeding through your nose all the time and staying out all night. You don't even see the girls; they are leaving for school when you are walking in. You must get help! As for me, I am taking the girls and getting out of here!"

"OK, babe! OK. I'll get help! Go ahead. Find out where can I get help, and I will do whatever you say. It will be different. You'll see," Pelegrino proclaimed. He even had tears in his eyes.

"Oh, yeah?! Well, as a matter of fact, I do know where you can get help."

I became calm at his plea for help, and a light went on, regarding the help program I had just heard and inquired about earlier that week. I started looking for the information I knew I had written down just a couple days earlier.

I went on and explained to Pelegrino what to do. "The lady I spoke to gave me this number and said you just need to call and ask for help. The program is called Lifeline, and they have great success stories. Here, you call. And tell them you need help and want to enter the program."

"OK, babe," Pelegrino responded.

He made the call, and the program had space available.

He replied, "Can I go in tomorrow morning?"

"Sure," was the response.

"OK. I will see you tomorrow morning. Thank you!" Pelegrino responded and ended the phone call.

"What happened?" I asked.

"They said they do have a program, and I could come in and register for it. It's a thirty-day program, and they do have space. Oh, and they take my medical insurance. Isn't that great?"

"Why tomorrow? What's wrong with today?" I asked.

"I just wanted to start tomorrow early, so I can rest today," he replied.

"No! You go in today or forget it; I will leave. They said they have space, and they take your insurance, so you need to do this now—*right now*. Or I'm out. I mean it, Pelegrino," I told him.

"OK, babe. I will call them back," he said.

I could not let this slide. There was always something going on with Pelegrino. He was absent most of the time, and I couldn't ignore the many times I got those dreaded collect calls informing me he had arrested for this, that, or the other. He was arrested so often I had the number of every court agency recorded in my mind.

Pelegrino made the call and scheduled himself to be admitted that same day. We got the girls ready and drove to the hospital to enroll him into the Lifeline Recovery program at Wiess Memorial Hospital on Marine Drive in Chicago.

It was just as the woman had explained to me. The staff was all very nice and helpful. For Pelegrino, there was a negative aspect; visiting was limited to once a week from 2:00 p.m. to 6:00 p.m.

One day, Pelegrino called me and wanted me to bring him something to eat. He said he was tired of hospital food (as he called it). He wanted a home-cooked meal. But his request was on a no visiting day. By faith, I prepared him his meal and took it to him, and by the glory of God, they allowed me to give it to him. I was not allowed to stay, but I could give him the food.

Our car had broken down. The only way I had to get to Weiss Memorial Hospital was by CTA bus with a transfer. This meant I had to take two buses to get to the hospital. It was bitterly cold, and the wind in Chicago can be brutal, making it twice as cold. I would visit Pelegrino with the four girls on family visiting day and for counseling once a week. So, that was twice a week I would go to the hospital to partake in his recovery treatment.

This was during the month of November, and the Thanksgiving holiday had soon arrived. Pelegrino did not want to spend the holiday in the hospital. He requested a leave for that day, and it was granted to him, providing he could stay clean. He would be tested for substance on his return.

This made me uneasy because the individuals in our family he would normally like to be with all used one thing or another. I had to trust and fight the good fight of faith.

One of the family members we visited was my younger cousin and his wife. The time there was great, and Pelegrino felt like a free man again. At the end of our meal, my younger cousin and Pelegrino were sitting in the living room. My cousin asked Pelegrino to pull on a turkey wishbone with him to see who would get the winning end. To my cousin's surprise, Pelegrino got the winning end to that wishbone. They got a good laugh out of it.

We left shortly after because we had a curfew and needed to get back to Weiss Memorial Hospital. I was proud of Pelegrino. He did not use anything and got through the evening as clean as he was when he left the hospital.

I must say, I did not want Pelegrino near anyone who used alcohol, marijuana, cocaine, heroin, or any substance, period. I'd seen how he had been influenced by his brother after coming back from the cursillo, and I didn't want that happening again. But this time, I knew he had stayed clean because I hadn't left his sight. And if by chance it had happened, I would have known as soon as the hospital ran the drug test and released the results.

During the time he was in the hospital, I had conversations with the girls and explained to them that daddy was sick. His sickness was called addiction to drugs. We, as a family, needed to build him get through his treatment. I had them make cards as part of his recovery encouragement. They were adorable, expressing their love for him. They understood what it was all about—that it was a struggle to say no to substances that altered the mind. And they believed Dad was going to get better.

Once the thirty days were completed, it was time for Pelegrino to come home. The program had an exit session with all the other patients included. Pelegrino had his part of the session recorded onto a cassette tape. It was set up so that each person could share his or her testimony—how they'd become addicted, their behavior before and through the treatment, and how they felt at the time of exiting the Lifeline program.

It was harsh stuff to listen to, but I guess he wanted to use it for therapy at home, remembering lessons taught and the goal to stay clean. I still have the recording today, and I, too, have listened to it to try and understand him better.

I got to the hospital, picked him up, and took us home. The girls were thrilled Daddy was home, and Daddy was too. I was glad, but I knew it was a thin line between giving in to the cravings and simply saying no to it all, as some of the counselors explained to me.

That same week, he did it. He used. All of the work was thrown down the tubes. Wow! I still feel the shakiness all over my body I felt when I found out he'd used again. He made tons of promises that it was going to be the last time, and I wanted to believe him. I didn't want the girls to know, so my response was low-key. But now I was worried.

I recall praying. But every time I prayed, I was reminded of the covenant I'd made with God the day we were married. I had to stand and believe that God was going to get me through it.

I knew no man who Pelegrino respected who could talk to him. I was reminded repeatedly that his dad had left when he was twelve, and his mom had passed away when he was fourteen. He pretty much had no role model to follow or turn to. Well, he did. But it was the same person he'd started doing the cocaine with, so he was a dead end.

A couple months later, I received a call from *The Oprah Winfrey Show*. The caller explained there was an upcoming show on spouses who continue to live with their addicted spouse. The show was wondering if Pelegrino and I would like to be part of their panel. The caller explained it would help viewers who were going through the same situation. I was sold. If this would help other people, then absolutely. I spoke to Pelegrino, and we both agreed to be part of the panel. A couple days later, the show aired, and we were definitely one of the three panelists on *The Oprah Winfrey Show* (Spouses That Continue to Live with Their Addicted Spouse).

During the show, Pelegrino was calm, as usual. I, on the other hand, was nervous, especially because I was being attacked, and I didn't have the answers deep in my heart that were prompted by God verbally available or backed up by scriptures. I did not know much, and my time of prayer would have been the last thing I would have talked about. It was too personal. That is because I did not know Elohim. Nor did I know my role as His child as I know Him and my role today.

The two other couples described how the wives threw their addicted husbands out because they had hit rock bottom and how treatment and sobriety branched from that action. They went to a program and stayed sober after the treatment was over. We were the only couple where the wife had not thrown the addicted husband out (he didn't hit rock bottom) but had given him an alternative to get help and had the information handy at his disposal to get treatment.

Oprah asked Pelegrino, "Why do you think you continue to use?"

His answer was, "I did not enter the program because I wanted to. I did it so that I would not lose my wife and kids."

Further along in the interview, I shared, "I made the choice to leave my late husband, but I chose to stay in the marriage with Pelegrino this time around." I continued by quoting the doctors comment earlier. "Eighty-five percent of the population is addicted to one thing or another. So, I leave Pelegrino. I am young. And I can't promise myself to stay single and not wind up in another relationship. You don't know someone until you start living with them. So, what do I do then? Leave again and get into another relationship? How many relationships can a person have in a lifetime? I'd rather my children and I deal with their dad's addiction as a family and not wind up with some stranger in the future doing the same thing."

Did our presence on the show help other people? I want to say yes. There was a caller who identified with what I'd shared. A woman in the audience stood up to encourage me, sharing her story and her choice to stay with her husband despite his struggles. So, based on that, going on the air was a positive choice. I'm sure many people were able to identify with the problem and, if nothing else, they were given hope and were able to see that they are not a single case but that, rather, many were dealing with the same scenario.

I wish I'd had more time to prepare myself for the questions. In fact, I wish I'd had the spiritual knowledge and maturity I have today. My answers would have been very different. There were a couple of questions asked that I wanted to answer, but I did not have the answer to them myself. And what I did know, I did not know how to word correctly. So, on that note, I learned to continue to look for the answers and not give up.

We didn't get anything out of being on the panel, other than knowing I had to continue searching. We had to borrow the bus fare to get to and from the show. We met Oprah for about five minutes (maybe less), other than the airtime. There was a doctor on the program who was promoting his book. That was what the show was all about, promoting the book. We didn't even get a free book to take home.

What we did get was a lot of heat from friends and family members, criticizing us—me for saying yes and him for letting me talk him into it. We didn't get any help to follow up with after the show. Nor did we get any encouragement from anyone else. It was a cold, dry experience.

Time passed and Pelegrino's behavior did not improve. It just got worse. I was becoming fearful because he continued to bleed through his nose, and I didn't know what all that could lead to. But in my mind, it seemed like a serious illness, on top of the addiction or death.

I contacted my cousin in Puerto Rico, also named Carmen. I asked her to look for Pelegrino's dad's information so I could write to him and explain what was going on. I was able to get the information and contacted his dad, explaining, "Si quiere ver a su hijo con vida debe venir a Chicago" (If you want to see your son while he has life, you need to come to Chicago).

He hadn't seen his son since Pelegrino's last stay on the Island at age seventeen, shortly before he was given the sentence of four years in the penitentiary for burglary for the second time. He was not a teen anymore; he was twenty-six years old. But it was worth a try. Besides, he would get to meet his granddaughters, who he had never met.

Pelegrino Sr. did not delay; he was in Chicago in a week's time. It was beautiful seeing them get back together. Pelegrino loved his dad. And truth be told, he did respect him. His presence meant a lot. He did not use any drugs the whole time his dad was here in Chicago.

When he left, Pelegrino Sr. told me to let him know how his son was doing, and he made it clear to Pelegrino that he was there for him.

Well, once Dad was gone, Pelegrino was up to no good again. So, I called his dad and shared my heart. I just could not deal with him anymore; it was too much for me. I could no longer abide his staying out, spending his paycheck, and just not being there for me or the girls. I told my father-in-law how the situation was worsening. Pelegrino Sr. said he would send him a plane ticket. He could stay with him, in hopes he could help him kick the cocaine habit. I was all for it. Yes! I needed help with him. And who better than his father?

Pelegrino stayed there for three months, and he didn't seem to be in a hurry to come back home. He had stopped using cocaine, and apparently, he was physically doing great. He didn't have to work, and all his needs were met by his dad. Really, who wouldn't want to stay on the island? It is beautiful, with great weather all the time. But it was time for him to come home.

This was the beginning of a real test. It had been a battle of many years, a roller-coaster ride of drug abuse, alcohol addiction, jail time, and adultery with times in between of being a loving husband, dad, and buddy. Every time it looked like it was getting better, something would happen that would throw him off that wagon.

During his destructive behavior, I was dealing with inner anger that I did not understand how to manage. I became violent a few times. I stabbed him once out of the three attempts. Pelegrino would joke about it. He would talk about how he had to sleep with one eye open because of my bad temper.

My younger cousin was very talented in mechanical labor and had started a packaging business that had about fifteen employees; it was very prosperous. The family looked up to him and his wife because of their success in what looked like the American dream.

On one of those bad occasions, I went to him for help. He seemed to be wise, he did like Pelegrino, and Pelegrino was fond of him. So, he seemed like the right person to go to. I explained that the drug addiction was getting worse and that it was hurting us in many ways. I asked if he would be willing to talk to Pelegrino, in hopes he would stop using drugs and alcohol.

He chuckled and said, "Yayie, he just doesn't know how to do it. There is really nothing I can say to him. You just have to know how to do it."

I answered him quickly. "No one knows how to do it. It will control and even kill anyone who does use it. Thanks anyway." I went home, feeling despair, as I faced this beast of drug addiction. It seemed to be taking over our lives.

The girls were getting older, and of course there were greater fears for me. I only had a sixth grade education, and I knew my lack of education was against me when it came to pursuing a career. More than anything, I wanted my daughters to be protected, and I encouraged them to do well in school and have great careers like my siblings did. I recall how difficult it was for me to help them with homework. I would always need outside help because I did not understand most assignments. I did not know about tutoring. Nor could I have afforded to pay for it anyway. Thank God, I did have my younger cousin's wife; she was particularly good in that area. It was not often, but there were moments when my daughters would receive her help.

Annette was my all A's student. She was bright and did not seem to have any problems getting through assigned work. Karen was my C student. She did her work and felt that a C was passing, and that was good enough. Arisely had a learning disability and qualified for special education. She had a rough time in the very beginning but ended up with a gem for a special ed teacher, Mrs. Hershenhouse. She did wonders with her and truly made a difference in her academic progress in grammar school, which carried over into Arisely's high school career and later helped her in getting into Columbia College in Chicago.

I dreaded report card pickup day. It was worse than having my parents come in for me. I truly dreaded it. I guess I didn't want my children to struggle in school, and I didn't want to be the bad guy and discipline them if they were not meeting the standards in behavior or academics. Seriously, how do you correct misconduct and poor achievements if you did not do any better yourself? But it had to be done. And there was no one else to do it, since their dad had made it clear he wanted no part in that area of child-rearing (but that's a whole other book).

Annette was in high school and got there with great grammar school accomplishments, graduating with a high GPA. I did not think she would have any problem getting through her four years of high school. But that was not the case. During her freshman year, I went to the dreaded report card pickup and was disturbed to learn she was not doing as well as she normally did. I knew and understood there was a difference between grammar school and high school and believed the issue would iron itself out. She would pick it up in no time.

However, I found I could not brush it away like I wanted. I addressed her regarding the grade drop and the teacher's comment that she could do better but was not applying herself. I told her, "This is not you. You do very well in school. You have always been on the honor roll. Something does not seem right. What's wrong?"

Annette hesitated and seemed disturbed. She started by saying, "I will tell you, but I don't want you to say anything."

"Say anything to who?" I asked. Now, my heart was pounding a hundred miles per hour. I knew I was not going to like what I was about to hear.

She went on to say, "One day when I was twelve, we went to Madrina's house. You started helping her with what she was doing, and I went downstairs to look for Gladys. Gladys was not there but Al was. He called me to his room, and when I went in, he had me take off my pants, and he molested me. He had told me I'd better be quiet. I have been having nightmares, and I can't get it out of my mind. It just keeps coming up."

"What!? Why didn't you tell me right away?" I asked.

Annette answered, "I was scared to."

"You should never be scared to tell me when someone hurts you or threatens you. So, this was when you were twelve. Was it more than once?" I asked.

Annette said, "There was one other time. But just as he was about to start, you yelled out for me, and he stopped. That's why I don't go to the basement unless other people are there. I tried to forget about it, but I started having nightmares and stuff and really bad headaches afterward."

I hugged her and said, "He will never hurt you again. And we will make sure he doesn't hurt anyone else either."

Annette said, "He has done it to Mary too."

We ended the conversation, and I started trying to figure out how I was going to handle this. I could not believe my greatest fear had come true. One of my daughters had been sexually molested by a family member. Wow! I loved that kid like my own son! I treated him like a son. How could he?! How could he? Right under my nose. How ignorant of me to trust anyone after what had happened to me.

I remembered when I met Pelegrino. The one thing I'd felt confident about was that he was a big, husky, fearless, disciple of the street, and no one could get away with hurting the girls or me—or so I thought. I spoke to Pelegrino as soon as he got home. I asked him to go with me to my younger cousin's house to confront the situation, but he declined to do so. I was furious. But he declined, and I could not convince him to do otherwise. I guessed I would have to face my younger cousin and his wife by myself, but they needed to know.

As usual, I faced the situation on my own. Al's parents rejected the allegation that their son had hurt Annette. They decided it was best if we had a family meeting, where everyone in question could be present. They said they would let me know, and I agreed.

I went home and told Annette and started looking for a therapist I could schedule her with. Meanwhile, I was not having it easy. My thoughts were constantly racing, and there was no putting an end to it. I went to Queen of Angels church and kneeled for hours, praying to God. I asked over and over again how I could have been so ignorant and trusted anyone around the girls.

I was not getting a call back from my younger cousin and his wife. It seemed they were just going to brush it under the rug and make believe it didn't happen. Annette was told by Mary that she was not going to admit anything. So, it was just Annette's word against his. I also heard that my younger cousin's wife stated, "She's just like her mother." How could she even think those words about me, as loyal as I'd been to her, much less about Annette, who from birth had loved and worshiped her? As much as it hurts, I knew her negative, critical mind. I should not have expected any other reaction from her, especially if she was defending her son. She lived in denial about everything that went wrong in her life. How about my younger cousin? He knows he was a pedophile himself. How could he sit there and deny it happened? And to think that they were Annette and Karen's godparents. What happened with that picture of love and protection for them?

That family meeting never took place.

I got ahold of someone I thought would be able to help me get my vengeance taken care of. But the person declined. I guessed I would have to just take care of it myself. I asked Pelegrino one more time to help me take care of this, but he again declined. I took advantage of the fact that he was talking to his cousin Chiqui. I went into our bedroom, went into the closet, and took his gun. I would not let my daughter be neglected and not be vindicated. I made my way out the door.

As I was about to open the car door, Pelegrino came out and asked me where I was going. I replied, "To take care of what I have to for my daughter."

He knew I was up to no good and ran up to me. I took the gun out from under my armpit to get into the car. He yelled, "Oh no you don't. Give me that."

We started struggling for the gun, and Chiqui came to help Pelegrino. It took them a bit, but they managed to get the gun away from me.

I was furious. My only alternative was to drive to Queen of Angels and talk to God. I was crying and shaking, and it was not easy at all. Everything that had happened was going through my mind. I recalled asking God in the past, How could Mami know about what happened to Martita and still love and treat those who had hurt her like nothing ever happened? And then she'd died at age seventeen. Why God? Why?

As I recited the Lord's Prayer, I cried all the more. "Our Father in heaven, hallowed be your name, / your kingdom come, your will be done, on earth as it is in heaven. / Give us today our daily bread. / And forgive us our debts, as we also have forgiven our debtors. / And lead us not into temptation, but deliver us from the evil one." I paused and meditated on verse 12 before giving voice to it. "And forgive us our debts, as we also have forgiven our debtors" (Matthew 6:9–12, Bible Hub).

I cried and cried. "Help me, God! Help me! I can't. I want to, but I can't forgive them."

This was the biggest lesson in forgiving others as the Lord has forgiven me, since the cursillo retreat. Pelegrino's substance abuse and adulterous behavior paled in comparison. I pondered on what a poor child I had been to my Heavenly Father and how gracious He had been to me despite my disobedience. To forgive all my sins, even those I was not aware of. I did not want to leave the church; it was the only place I felt safe from the ugliness of this world. I slowly got up and walked out, looking back every couple of steps. I got in my car and reluctantly drove off, back to the apartment. My trips to Queen of Angels became a routine. It was the only way I could deal with the pain and stop myself from doing something drastic.

I asked God, "Is this why you took Joey home when you did? You knew he would have avenged his little queen. It would not have been a good outcome for sure. It would have been a tragedy. That's why you took him, right? I know it."

I thought of all Pelegrino's muscles and bad talk about the Disciples being the toughest gang out on the streets. It turned out that was all talk. I didn't see anyone coming to the rescue of my baby when she had been violated in such a dirty, painful way. I even thought that, maybe, the fact that Annette wasn't Pelegrino's biological daughter was to blame for his inaction. But that was Satan trying to poison my thoughts. Nevertheless, he didn't come through for us.

"God, help me. *Please* help me," I begged.

Time passed. Annette started doing much better in school. She did have problems when she started college and was seeing a therapist then. She did not want to continue after her first year. I did not want to make it more difficult for her by insisting that she finish.

I don't even recall when I started visiting my younger cousin's wife again. But it was in God's hands. I needed to accept what had happened to Annette, forgive, and move forward.

Karen started high school. I figured it would be easier for her since Annette was already there at the time. No, that turned out not to be the case. Karen came across a group of girls who, for reasons they could not identify, did not like Karen. I did not sit still. I went to the school and made all the complaints I could against the other students. I spoke to the principal and counselor and so on.

One day, Karen came home with her face cut by one of the girls. She'd used some object and cut across Karen's face. Again, that fury rose up within me. I took Pelegrino's pocketknife and headed to the girl's house. The school was not taking care of it, and I already knew I could not depend on Pelegrino. So, I figured I would take care of it myself.

I made it clear that the girl and her friends were not to even get close to Karen. In addition, I spoke to my sister Lou and her husband, Freddy, about the incident and how I was not comfortable sending her to school. Freddy wrote a letter to the senator, giving the details of the incident. He explained that, for Karen's safety, Chicago Public Schools needed to allow Karen to be transferred to a school out of her district.

The senator of Illinois, Carol Elizabeth Moseley Braun, wrote back and contacted the school as well, giving permission for Karen to be transferred to the school of her choice. Karen attended Mather High School, while Annette continued at Amundsen High School.

Those school years for the girls had me on pins and needles. But I knew it was extremely important for them to do well in school and get a complete education. I felt blessed every time one of them completed whatever they were working on—grammar school, high school, or just extra career choices they took on. For example, Annette worked at Jewel's food store part-time, and Arisely worked in the school office part-time while she attended Colombia College.

I wanted my girls to be nothing like me. I wanted them to be like Eliberto and Lou, who had been model children, the apples of Mami and Papi's eyes, great students, and career people. They were, today, living the American dream of success. I, on the other hand, had brought shame to my parents. I hadn't finished school. I had failed my two marriages. And it seemed I had even failed my children.

Regardless, I do have two great memories. One of my greatest memories was during one of my visits with my parents. I was helping them run some errands, and as I was driving, Mami said, "Me siento orgullosa de la manera que tu has criado las nena. Me hubiera gustado aberlos criado a ustedes asi" (I am proud of the way you have raised the girls. I wish I would have raised you all like you are raising the girls).

I may have only completed the sixth grade, but that compliment made me feel like I had a master's degree in child-rearing. What Mami thought meant the world to me.

Another memory that stands out was at my sister Lou's wedding reception party. I was asked to give the opening ceremonial greeting speech, and of course it would be bilingual, in English and Spanish. At the end of the speech, my dad said, "Serias una gran maestro de ceremonia. Tu discurso fue genial" (You would be a great master of ceremonies. Your speech was great). Those two memories are worth more than silver and gold to me, a true treasure.

Fast-forward a couple of years. All the girls were doing well. I was working full-time, and for the first time, Pelegrino and I were both working at the same time. This may just be that breakthrough we needed—the way we'd be able to save and get that house Mami kept praying for me to have.

Pelegrino was working as a material handler for a great company (Brush Wellman) with good benefits. I was blessed with a receptionist position at Family Dental Care. It offered no benefits, but it was a good job. The office manager was awesome. Her name was Jean, and she had a lot of great office skills. I called her Jeannie. We hit it off right from the start. Jeannie's husband worked for the dentist too. He was the custodian of the two-flat office building. He was a sketch artist by trade and had made good with his artwork. They did everything together—from evangelizing together to shopping together and everything in between. That was a couple anyone would admire. They were both fun, funny, and people oriented for sure. Sometimes, he would stop in, and the three of us would chitchat a bit, and there was always a funny story. Those were great times. They were an amazing couple. I admired their relationship with each other and admired them both as individuals.

There are so many great stories to share about working with Jean. I recall her wanting to get fit and lose a little weight, and of course she wanted me to get in on it with her. She said exercise was good for the mind and body and having a desk job could hurt our well-being. So, one day, she walked in all excited. "Look, at what I have for us," she said as she continued to take stuff out of her bag. She had a rolled-up vinyl runner and some footies. With a great big smile on her face, she said, "The object is to have fun while you exercise and get fit. So, on our lunch break, we can unroll this runner in the hallway. We run and slide on the runner and back again, trying to get a little further each time. Isn't that great? We can do it twice a week. The other three days, we can walk from the first busy street to the next busy street, which is eight blocks, and eight blocks back again."

"Sure, Jean, that sounds like fun!" I told her.

She was also a great listener and funny too. During one of my stories about Pelegrino getting caught cheating, she said, "I just don't understand why a man who has steak at home would want to go out for hamburger?"

Another time, we were talking about children, and she said, "Children are great until they hit age five. Then they become little lawyers."

Pelegrino called one afternoon to say the car had broken down, and he was "not about to take no bus to work." I was going back and forth, trying to come up with a solution. I told Pelegrino, "I can't talk about this right now. I am at work. We will talk later when I get home." I went to the back of the office to autoclave the instruments.

Shortly after, Dr. A. came by me and asked, "What's wrong?"

I explained to him, "Our car broke down, and it's not repairable. Pelegrino said he is not going to go to work on the bus; it's too far. Dr. A, he just got this job. I don't know what to do."

Dr. A, said, "Don't worry about it. Just get another car."

"No. It's not that easy, Dr. A. We do not have any savings to just go buy a car. We can't even get it on credit because we don't have credit."

"Don't worry, Carmen. You will get a new car," he assured me. "I will call my wife, and she will take you to buy a new car. I will pay for it, and you tell Pelegrino he can pay me back in monthly payments."

I declined again.

The doctor repeated his offer. "Go ahead. Call Pelegrino and ask him if that's something he would be willing to do. If he says yes, I will call my wife and set up for her to take you both car shopping tomorrow."

"No, Dr. A. I can't have you do that," I said.

"Don't delay. Call him. It's just like you're getting it from a car dealer on credit. Only, I will be your finance department."

I was lost for words; I could not believe it.

I did just as Dr. A told me to. I called Pelegrino and asked if that was something he would agree to. Pelegrino agreed. And before I knew, it Dr. A was on the phone setting up for his wife to take us car shopping. Dr. A advised, "Just don't fall in love with the first car you see. Look around and make sure it's a good car and that you both like it."

I agreed.

How about that? Pelegrino got a new car with no hassles or delays. He was a happy camper. We made our monthly payments and had worry-free transportation. It was a blessing for sure. I have to say that I have seen God work spontaneously many times, but I was not sure about this one. It was too, too easy. But I went along with it all to save the day and end Pelegrino's dilemma about getting to work.

One evening as we were getting ready for the next day, I sent the girls to bathe. Natalie was first to get in the tub. Natalie has always been a lover of the water, ever since she was a toddler. Getting her to bathe was never a problem. It was getting her out of the tub that was an issue. I knocked on the bathroom door and asked her to hurry up. "When you put on your pajamas, come on out so I can do your hair," I added.

Natalie normally combed her own hair, but I wanted to do curls on her hair before it got dry to ease the fuzziness in it. As I was stroking her long, beautiful hair, I couldn't help but notice that the right side of her back was elevated higher than the left side. I asked her to stand up, and I checked her back, up and down. Definitely, her right side was elevated a lot higher than her left side. She had a hump on her back. My heart started racing. I asked her how she felt and if she had noticed the hump on her back.

She said, "Not really."

"Does it hurt when I touch you here?" I asked.

"No, it doesn't," she replied.

I knew this was not a good sign. I sent her to bed and went in my room. Once I'd closed the door, I got on my knees and wailed to God. "How could I have missed that hump on her back? It is really big, God. I know I normally don't comb her hair, but it is so big I should have noticed it before."

The next day, I called and scheduled an appointment for her to see a doctor. I thanked God I was able to get her in to see a doctor right away. The doctor ordered some tests and gave us a referral to see Dr. Mardjetko, an orthopedic specialist.

When I got home, I told Pelegrino everything the doctors had said and that she needed to follow up with a specialist. I asked him to go with me, but he declined. He said he wanted no part of it at all until the day of the surgery.

I was devastated to hear him decline to be part of the pre-op process. But what could I do? I added, "I will be needing the car, because the orthopedic is in a north suburb, and the hospital is too."

He said no; he was not giving up the car. I could not believe it. Dr. A had been so quick to buy the car for us when he was having a tantrum over not having a car to drive to work, simply because he travels to the suburbs. His daughter had just been diagnosed with severe scoliosis of the spine that was threatening her health. How could he not let me take the car to get her to her appointments? He knew I would take him to work and pick him up. It was not like I was declining to do that. Wow! I was devastated.

I prayed that God would make it possible to get a car without compromising anyone but myself. By faith and faith alone, I got on the bus and headed to Cicero and Western Avenue in Chicago. I knew there were a lot of car dealerships on those two main streets. I trusted that God was going to come through. I was blinded by Natalie's need for the surgery and pre-op and trusted that God would lead me and make it happen.

Abba God Almighty surely did. I walked in and drove out. I drove up to the apartment in an eggshell white and beige four-door

Chrysler. I was determined to get my baby her treatment, and God was making it happen.

I took Natalie to get the test done. I was given confirmation of the diagnosis her pediatrician had made. Then we would meet with Dr. Mardjectko for the results and his diagnosis. It was not good. He showed me the X-rays. The shape of Natalie's spine was devastating. My baby's spine was the shape of a coat hanger hook. He went on to explain that her spine was pressing on her lungs and could cause her to stop breathing. He said she would need anterior/posterior spinal surgery. He told me her condition was correctable; they would use two of her ribs to tie the two steel rods, thus aligning her spine in order to straighten it and hold it up. I was heartbroken. He added that the cut would be across her left side by her rib cage, from the front to the center of her back and from the top of her back, at the tip of her neck, down to the bottom, right above her buttock. The incision would be a T shape.

He went on to explain the complexity of the surgery and the benefits. He said that, in the past, a person with this type of surgery would wear a cast from neck to bottom and would not walk until after the cast was removed. But with the advancement in medicine, she would not need to wear a cast. He said in fact, she would be encouraged to walk a few days after the surgery.

"Due to the complexity of the surgery, there is a chance that she could lose a lot of blood. It can be returned by using blood stored in the hospital's blood bank. Or she could donate her own blood, and it would be kept until her surgery to replace whatever blood she might lose. That is up to you."

Her pre-op would last for six to eight weeks, depending on how Natalie's body responded to the blood draw and how quickly her body built back the red blood cells that she would be losing. "Do you have any questions for me, Mrs. Matos?"

The more he explained, the faster my heart rate went up. "No, not at the time. I believe you covered everything. If I have any questions, I will call you."

"Absolutely. You can ask anything that comes up and speak to Dorinda my nurse." Dr. Mardjectko said.

"Thank you." I ended the conversation and headed out the door.

All of this was too much for me to handle on my own. I knew I could not rely on Pelegrino to support me through it all.

We came across an obstacle. I did not have insurance at work, and Pelegrino's insurance at work was not accepted by the hospital, as it was out of network. Pelegrino talked to his employer, and they changed his coverage to a PPO plan so it would cover Natalie no matter where she was treated.

It was a long process, but I didn't want them having to use the blood stored in their blood bank. The less chance of any complications, the more confident I felt in allowing Natalie to go through the surgery that I knew had to be done.

Every trip to the Life Source Facility for blood drawing was a challenge that involved keeping a joyful appearance and emotionally dying on the inside. I wanted so desperately to have Pelegrino's support emotionally, but I had to be strong for him too because he was not able to deal with it himself. That was the way he had always dealt with any painful situation since the beginning.

Natalie started with one good draw. But sometimes she was not able to give because her blood count was too low. So, we went back again in a couple of days. I was aware it would be like this, but it still took a toll on my emotional state. One thing Natalie looked forward to was her treat at the end of her visit, a trip to Mickey D's. Yep, to McDonald's we'd go for a cheeseburger or chicken nuggets, fries, and a milkshake or soda.

Finally, all the blood needed was collected, and the surgery was scheduled.

On the day of surgery, I took Natalie to the hospital, registered her, and handed her over to the nurse to start her off with vitals and so on. At the signing of the documents, there was a line of small print that I read repeatedly. "There is no guarantee that the surgery will be successful, and there is a possibility of not making it out of surgery." That was a true test of faith. I had to sign and agree that I may lose my baby in the process of trying to have her spine corrected in hopes that she could live a normal life. By faith, I signed the forms.

"See you later," I said and gave her lots of kisses.

I was sent to a waiting room, where I sat and prayed. With tears running down my face, I took a deep breath and exhaled. I said, "Jehovah God, I trust You just as Abraham trusted You when he was told to sacrifice Isaac his son. I trust that You have revealed to me what was wrong with Natalie's back in order that it can be corrected. And I trust that You will make the surgery a success and will heal her completely. And if by chance she does not make it out of the surgery, I trust that it is her time, and You are taking her home. You are her true father, and I thank you for her life and the time You have trusted me to love and rear her until now. Amen!"

A few hours later, the surgery was over, and I was able to see my baby again. It was a success, I was told. The first thing she asked me for when she woke up was Daddy. I reassured her that he would be in shortly. Pelegrino arrived a few hours later, glad that it was done and over. Natalie and I were in the hospital for a couple of weeks.

I was told that Natalie was the first patient in that hospital to walk after that type of surgery. In the past, patients had to wear a body cast and be bedridden for weeks before attempting to stand or walk.

In the discharge summary, I was given a list of things to keep an eye out for, and I did just as I was told. Unfortunately, about a week after Natalie was discharged, one of the signs to look for was present. There was lots of redness and swelling around the incision sight and heat. She also had a fever. I called the doctor, and he had me take her back to the hospital. They ran some tests. And sure enough, she had an infection, and it had spread throughout her body. They had to open her back up and flush her body with antibiotics. When discharged, she had to continue the antibiotics via IV for a few weeks.

When the IV treatment was over, she was tested, and all infection was gone. Her healing was lengthy, but the surgery was successful. Natalie was able to walk without becoming short of breath. Her spine was no longer pressing on her lungs. Thank you, Papa Dios! Our lives were pretty much back to normal. Natalie was able to return to school, I was able to return to work, and our lives continued.

Let's fast-forward. I lost my job at the dental office a few months after returning from my leave. I should mention that I was not compensated during my leave. I had no benefits, so I had no PTO or anything of the sort. Due to the reason for my leaving, I was not able to collect unemployment. (I would go into details, but it would be too long a story—maybe in another book.) We were going through a tough patch financially. We got behind two months' rent for the first time in fourteen years, and I honestly did not know how we would ever catch up. We had great landlords. They were very understanding.

Don and Classy were trying to start a church around that same time frame. They met at the park near our home on Sunday mornings at 10:00 a.m. One day, they extended an invitation to their Sunday service, and we accepted the invitation.

The service was led by a young pastor and his wife. They had a little boy and were humble and sweet and really easy to talk to. I enjoyed the service, and instead of attending Queen of Angels, I started attending their outdoor service. I'd been attending for about a month when I learned they were moving out of state and were stepping down from the position. Don and Classy did not want to close the Sunday service meetings. They felt a strong calling to keep the service going, and they did.

They came over one day and explained to us that it was getting cold out with fall beginning. They needed an indoor location to continue the Sunday service. They asked if we would be willing to open our home until they were able to get a permanent location for the church. Pelegrino and I agreed.

On Sunday mornings, instead of getting up and going to church, we were getting up and setting up to have church in our home. That was such an uplifting experience, to be able to serve God and others and receive from Him at the same time.

My younger cousin started getting ill. It was like night and day. He was fine, and then suddenly, he was terminally ill. God put in my heart to have Pastor Lysett Vega go to their home and pray for them. She did, and my younger cousin received Jesus Christ as Lord and Savior. About a week later, I bought him a Bible so he could start reading God's Word. My last visit with him was sad. I was trying to encourage him. And as I ended, he said, "Yayie, no one knows how to do it. You were right. No one knows how to do it." He said, "Look at me."

I looked straight into his eyes.

"Promise me you will stay in God's army and that you will fight," he said, "fight hard."

"I promise," I assured him.

Over the next couple of days, he was put in hospice, and he passed away shortly after that.

JESUS COMES AFTER ME

One day, I was at Jewel's grocery store. I'd just completed my shopping and was putting my groceries in the trunk of the car when a young woman came up to me. She said, "Excuse me."

I looked up.

"Hi," she said. "My name is Lori."

I stopped what I was doing to greet her and tell her my name was Carmen.

"Do you live in the area?" she asked.

"Yes, I do," I answered.

"That's great!" she said. "My husband and I lead a Bible talk group, and I was wondering if you would like to attend."

"Oh wow, that's funny. I have a church service on Sunday mornings and was about to ask you the same thing. Would you like to attend?"

Lori and I exchanged numbers and said goodbye. I hoped she would come to my home for Sunday service, and she hoped I would attend her Bible talk group.

I was excited and looking forward to seeing the Nerkies' church grow. During my prayer time, I asked God to lead and, as usual, asked Him to help the Sunday service prosper.

The next day, Lori called me and invited me to study the Bible with her. I was thrilled. I had never studied the Bible, except for one time with a Jehovah's Witness for about twenty minutes. I was about seventeen, and Joey was not having that; he put an end to the study. She explained that we would meet in a remote location to study the word and fellowship. I was on board for that, and we set up a date two days from the day of the phone call. Again, during my prayer time, I asked God to lead me.

The next day around 3:30 p.m., a knock came at the door. One of the girls answered the door and called out, "Mom there is a lady asking for you."

I walked to the door, and it was Lori. She was carrying two shopping bags. She said, "Hi," with a great big smile on her face. I invited her in, and as she was walking in, she said, "I brought you dinner." She went on to explain, "I wanted to give you a day off and bought you and your family dinner. Now you can enjoy a meal without having to go through all the fuss." She put the bags on one of the chairs in the dining room and started showing me the Items (rotisserie chicken, French bread, Caesar salad, and mashed potatoes). She said, "I hope you like my selection, and I got an apple pie for dessert. Ok, I have to run along now. Enjoy your meal. I will see you tomorrow, right?"

"Absolutely," I replied. "See you tomorrow."

When I first met Lori, I had started praying, saying that, if God wanted the Nerkies' church to grow, this would be the beginning of an increase in members. And if it was meant for me to attend Lori's Bible talk group, I asked Him to direct my steps to do just that. So far, her phone call promptly after our encounter at Jewel's, inviting me to study the Bible and her visit the day after with the meal for our family was a clear indication that God was directing my steps toward meeting with Lori.

I happily put everything in the kitchen. And when Pelegrino arrived from work, I shared with him and the girls who Lori was and how I'd met her. I served dinner faster than I ever had before (except for the times we'd gotten carryout on Friday's). I did the dishes and started getting ready for my date with Lori. Finally, I was able to use the Bible (the New Oxford Annotated Bible with the Apocrypha) Eliberto had given me years earlier. I did not realize it at the time, but Jesus set this divine appointment with me and Him through Lori.

The next day, I met Lori at a café not far from my apartment.

It was a beautiful, sunny but cool day at the beginning of spring. We placed our order, and Lori said, "Let's start with a prayer." She prayed, acknowledged God, and asked Him to lead us in the study. It was amazing.

As Jesus sat with us, Lori began the study. She said, "We will read out of the Bible. I will give a couple of points. And if you have any questions, feel free to ask." She started by saying, "Disciples, that's what God calls us to be, right?"

I remained quiet because, honestly, I did not know.

Lori would ask a question and then go straight into the Bible and read a scripture that would back it up. "The word *Christian* appears in the Bible three times," she said, explaining it was the name the world gave the disciples. "The word *disciple* occurs over 270 times in the New Testament. Jesus defines the term *disciple* throughout his ministry."

Wow. I was blown away. This first study was called "Discipleship."

We fellowshipped a bit and had a get-to-know-you kind of conversation. She explained that her husband, Mike, was the leading pastor at their church (CCOC). They had two children, a boy and a girl, and lived just a couple blocks away from us. The church service was on Sundays at 10:00 a.m. They had Bible talk on Tuesday at their home, and a group they called midweek on Wednesdays in the downtown area.

I, in turn, shared that my husband's name was Pelegrino and that we had four daughters—two adults who'd moved out and two teens at home—along with other such details of our lives. We scheduled our next Bible study and headed home.

The next study was called "The Word of God." I could not believe I had the instructions for living on earth in my hands and didn't even know it. Then again, I could barely read, and I didn't understand a lot of what was in there. Lori wanted me to attend the Bible talk group, but she wanted Pelegrino to join us. I could not promise but told her I would try to encourage him to come. We were still having service at our home on Sundays with the Nerkies. We scheduled our next study and headed home.

The next study was called "The Coming of the Kingdom." Wow—again, I was blown away. We scheduled our next study and headed home.

I was starting to have doubts about continuing with the Nerkies' Sunday service at our apartment. I prayed that God would make it clear to me what I should do about the services at home. I still was not sure. I talked to Pelegrino about it, and he agreed that I would have to make a choice. I could not attend two services on the same day and at the same time.

Pelegrino started his day really early. By 4:45 a.m., he was out the door, and I would cuddle in our room to watch Joyce Meyer's TV sermon that started at 5:00 a.m. She started that morning with a little speech. "I want to make something very clear to you." (I felt as if she was looking me straight in my eyes.) "You can read my books, listen to me on the radio, and watch my sermons on TV. But until you commit yourself to a Bible-based church, you are not doing anything, because you are missing a part."

Wow. I prayed to God and asked him to give me the words to talk to the Nerkies. I added, "May my heart be at peace and may their hearts also be at peace with our decision."

That following Sunday, I let them know that I wanted to continue attending service elsewhere. And yes, they were at peace with the decision. I, too, felt a great sense of peace, and so did Pelegrino.

I attended the first service at "1006" (as we called it) by myself. Pelegrino and the girls stayed home. I remember sitting in front with Lori. As everyone was getting settled, Lori leaned over and whispered, "You should take notes."

"Take notes? What is that?" I asked.

Lori said, "You listen to what Mike is saying. Whatever stands out to you, write it down in a journal."

"I don't have a journal," I answered her.

She took two sheets of paper from her notepad and pulled out a pen and handed them to me with a smile. Service was great, and I did manage to write a couple things down. I don't think I spelled them correctly, but it was just for me to read anyways. I did get myself a little notebook/journal and was ready for next time.

The next study was called "Light and Darkness 1, Light and Darkness 2, and the Cross." That's when Jesus captivated me. He just made it ever so clear and revealed his passion for me.

I just could not delay in saying, "I'm in. I want to be baptized."

Lori was fired up for me. Then she added a question, "How is that smoking doing?"

"Consider it done. I quit!"

She of course started planning for my baptism and added that they were having a men's game night / Bible talk at their place. She would come by and invite Pelegrino personally.

LIGHT AND DARKNESS, SIN AND FORGIVENESS

I learned that there are steps we must take to get close to the Lord:

- *Hear.* Consequently, faith comes from hearing the message, and the message is heard through the word about Christ. (Romans 10:17)
- *Believe.* And without faith it is impossible to please God, because anyone who comes to him must believe that he exists and that he rewards those who earnestly seek him. (Hebrews 11:6)
- *Repent.* I tell you, no! But unless you repent, you too will all perish. (Luke 13:3)
- *Confess.* If you declare with your mouth, "Jesus is Lord," and believe in your heart that God raised him from the dead, you will be saved. (Romans 10:9)
- *Be baptized.* Peter replied, "Repent and be baptized, every one of you, in the name of Jesus Christ for the forgiveness of your sins. And you will receive the gift of the Holy Spirit. (Acts 2:38)
- And this water symbolizes baptism that now saves you also—not the removal of dirt from the body but the pledge of a clear conscience toward God. It saves you by the resurrection of Jesus Christ. (1 Peter 3:21)
- This is the message we have heard from him and declare to you: God is light; in him there is no darkness at all. (1 Peter 1–5)

I was so excited I went home right away and shared with Pelegrino that I had just heard Jesus's invitation to follow Him. I was not going to put Him second in my life anymore. All Pelegrino's previous behaviors had to stop. He was going to be on board with me, or he had to get out of my life. I was going to live for Jesus moving forward. Pelegrino listened attentively and did not say a word. And truthfully, I did not care one way or another. My mind was made up.

Lori came by the following day. I introduced her to Pelegrino, and she joyfully invited him to the men's game night. Surprisingly, he agreed with no fuss. Or maybe, he just said, "OK. I look forward to it." That was totally the work of the Holy Spirit, as Pelegrino was normally very selfish with his time. It couldn't have been what I'd said the day before; my words normally had no power when it came to how he used his time.

Lori and I scheduled our next study session, and she headed home.

The Holy Spirit had just started a domino effect in me and my household. As in Acts 16:31, "They replied, 'Believe in the Lord Jesus, and you will be saved—you and your household.'"

Pelegrino and the girls joined me for service the following Sunday. Right after service, I ran to the restroom and changed into my baptismal clothes. The baptismal tank was ready. I walked up where Mike was standing with another brother. Pelegrino, the girls, and the rest of the congregation were surrounding the tank of water. Funny, I saw no one. I was nervous and excited. I knew this was a life change. I went into the tank of water; I was directed to hold my nose and close my eyes. Then I was asked a life-changing question. "What is your good confession?"

"Jesus is *Lord*!" I answered with true conviction.

And down I went and then back up again. That second as I took that first breath out of the water, I felt a peace and joy I had never felt before. I was a new creation in Christ Jesus. Everyone was singing, "I have decided to follow Jesus." They were clapping and yelling out, "Amen!" They helped me out of the tank and handed me a towel, and I made my way back to change. I did not want that moment to end.

After I was dry and dressed, Lori pulled me to the side and handed me an envelope that contained my membership document and the Bible talk group I would be added to moving forward. I was officially a CCOC member. More importantly, I was a disciple of Jesus Christ, a new creation in Christ Jesus. I would continue to attend service on Sundays and Wednesdays, and on Tuesdays, I would attend a Bible talk group. I was also assigned a disciple who would disciple me—someone I could call for any reason at any time. Wow. The fellowship was very encouraging, to say the least.

This was it. Pelegrino and the girls started attending Sunday service with me. The girls would start attending teen Bible study groups (which they were fighting me on). And Pelegrino started studying the Bible with Mike (Lori's husband, the pastor).

This was all new to us. We met incredible disciples of Jesus Christ who truly lived for God and served the advancement of God's kingdom.

I learned the essence of knowing the Word of God. This could and would only happen when a person was found. We were all lost from the time we entered our mother's womb. When we arrived into the world, we were spiritually separated from Almighty God. The amazing part was that Abba God knew the state we were in, and He knew exactly when we were going to be found and when we were going to respond to His invitation or not:

> How, then, can they call on the one they have not believed in? And how can they believe in the one of whom they have not heard? And how can they hear without someone preaching to them?
>
> And how can anyone preach unless they are sent? As it is written: "How beautiful are the feet of those who bring good news!"
>
> But not all the Israelites accepted the good news. For Isaiah says, "Lord, who has believed our message?" Consequently, faith comes from hearing

the message, and the message is heard through the word about Christ.

But I ask: Did they not hear? Of course they did:

"Their voice has gone out into all the earth, their words to the ends of the world."

Again I ask: Did Israel not understand? First, Moses says, "I will make you envious by those who are not a nation; I will make you angry by a nation that has no understanding."

And Isaiah boldly says, "I was found by those who did not seek me; I revealed myself to those who did not ask for me."

But concerning Israel he says, "All day long I have held out my hands to a disobedient and obstinate people." (Romans 10:14–21)

I was amazed by how much scripture everyone I met knew, especially Lori. She had a verse for everything we talked about. I asked her one day how it was that she knew which studies to study with me? She told me she was led by the Holy Spirit to use a combination of knowing a little about me and a book she used for discipling. This was a book that disciples normally used, which I should get for myself. It was called *Disciple's Handbook*. Here are some lessons found in the *Disciple's Handbook*:

- *Then we learn how to put on our new self.* Therefore, as God's chosen people, holy and dearly loved, clothe yourselves with compassion, kindness, humility, gentleness and patience. / Bear with each other and forgive one another if any of you has a grievance against someone. Forgive as the Lord forgave you. / And over all these virtues put on love, which binds them all together in perfect unity. (Colossians 3:12–14)
- *The fellowship of the believers.* They devoted themselves to the apostles' teaching and to fellowship, to the breaking of bread and to prayer. / Everyone was filled with awe at the

many wonders and signs performed by the apostles. / All the believers were together and had everything in common. / They sold property and possessions to give to anyone who had need. / Every day they continued to meet together in the temple courts. They broke bread in their homes and ate together with glad and sincere hearts, / praising God and enjoying the favor of all the people. And the Lord added to their number daily those who were being saved. (Acts 2:42–47)

- *How to activate devotion: Living as those made alive in Christ.* (Colossians 3) (Read the whole chapter.)

- *Why we should fellowship.* I pray that your partnership with us in the faith may be effective in deepening your understanding of every good thing we share for the sake of Christ. (Philemon 1:6)

- *How to discuss the expectation to tithe (10 percent).* "I the Lord do not change. So you, the descendants of Jacob, are not destroyed. / Ever since the time of your ancestors you have turned away from my decrees and have not kept them. Return to me, and I will return to you," says the Lord Almighty. But you ask, "How are we to return?" / "Will a mere mortal rob God? Yet you rob me." But you ask, "How are we robbing you?" "In tithes and offerings. / You are under a curse—your whole nation—because you are robbing me. / Bring the whole tithe into the storehouse, that there may be food in my house. Test me in this," says the Lord Almighty, "and see if I will not throw open the floodgates of heaven and pour out so much blessing that there will not be room enough to store it. / I will prevent pests from devouring your crops, and the vines in your fields will not drop their fruit before it is ripe," says the Lord Almighty. / "Then all the nations will call you blessed, for yours will be a delightful land," says the Lord Almighty. (Malachi 3:6–12)

- *The importance of prayer—it strengthens faith.* Do not be anxious about anything, but in every situation, by prayer and petition, with thanksgiving, present your requests to God. / And the peace of God, which transcends all understanding, will guard your hearts and your minds in Christ Jesus. (Philippians 4:6–7)

And I will do whatever you ask in my name, so that the Father may be glorified in the Son. (John 14:13)

- *Communion with God.* For I received from the Lord what I also passed on to you: The Lord Jesus, on the night he was betrayed, took bread, / and when he had given thanks, he broke it and said, "This is my body, which is for you; do this in remembrance of me." / In the same way, after supper he took the cup, saying, "This cup is the new covenant in my blood; do this, whenever you drink it, in remembrance of me." / For whenever you eat this bread and drink this cup, you proclaim the Lord's death until he comes.

  So then, whoever eats the bread or drinks the cup of the Lord in an unworthy manner will be guilty of sinning against the body and blood of the Lord. / Everyone ought to examine themselves before they eat of the bread and drink from the cup. / For those who eat and drink without discerning the body of Christ eat and drink judgment on themselves. / That is why many among you are weak and sick, and a number of you have fallen asleep. / But if we were more discerning with regard to ourselves, we would not come under such judgment. / Nevertheless, when we are judged in this way by the Lord, we are being disciplined so that we will not be finally condemned with the world. (1 Corinthians 11:23–32)

- *The conversion of Paul.* Immediately, something like scales fell from Saul's eyes, and he could see again. He got up and was baptized, / and after taking some food, he regained his strength. (Acts 9:18–22)

- *Saul in Damascus and Jerusalem.* Saul spent several days with the disciples in Damascus. / At once he began to preach in the synagogues that Jesus is the Son of God. / All those who heard him were astonished and asked, "Isn't he the man who raised havoc in Jerusalem among those who call on this name? And hasn't he come here to take them as prisoners to the chief priests?" / Yet Saul grew more and more powerful and baffled the Jews living in Damascus by proving that Jesus is the Messiah. (Acts 9:20–22)

He immediately began to preach. This is our calling too; we are to share what has been so gracefully given to us.

To think that I had been missing out on so much knowledge and wisdom for so long; it was heartbreaking.

Remember how the girls were fighting me on studying with the teen ministry? They came back fired up and could not thank me enough for making them attend. They, too, were hearing Jesus's voice. They met great teen disciples, and the teen leaders were great. We also learned that one of our neighbors who lived across the street was one of the teen leaders. How awesome is that?

Before long, Natalie, our youngest, decided to say yes to Jesus and was baptized. Shortly after Natalie's baptism, Pelegrino said yes to Jesus and was baptized. Then Arisely, our third daughter, said yes to Jesus and was baptized. Our oldest daughter, Annette, who did not live at home, started attending church and studying the Bible. She had been living out of wedlock and now married her baby, Josiah's, dad. She, too, said yes to Jesus and was baptized. Reggie, Josiah's dad, was next to begin Bible study and soon said yes to Jesus as well. Our second oldest, Karen, who did not live at home, also began to attend church and to study the Bible. Before long, she too said yes to Jesus and was baptized at the Living Word Church by Minister Winston.

"For me and my household will serve the Lord!" (Joshua 24:15, NIV). *Santo!* It was all exciting, encouraging, and uplifting to know—without question or doubt—that the God Who created heaven and earth and everything we see and everything unseen had called me and my family, just as scripture said.

• They replied, "Believe in the Lord Jesus, and you will be saved—you and your household." / Then they spoke the word of the Lord to him and to all the others in his house. / At that hour of the night the jailer took them and washed their wounds; then immediately he and all his household were baptized. / The jailer brought them into his house and set a meal before them; he was filled with joy because he had come to believe in God—he and his whole household. (Acts 16:31–34)

- For God so loved the world that he gave his one and only Son, that whoever believes in him shall not perish but have eternal life. (John 3:16)

It was more than just a Resurrection Sunday story, and it was coming in full force to life—in my life and in my children's lives. To see them all make radical changes was truly humbling to me.

All this great revelation was also adding extra responsibilities and a role change in the household. Pelegrino was learning from someone other than me that He was the head of household and what that meant. He could no longer refrain from hearing the message because it was coming straight from the creator Himself, Jehovah-Adoni (the God who owns and rules everything), and his study buddy was a God-fearing man.

Scripture is clear on this message:

- For the husband is the head of the wife as Christ is the head of the church, his body, of which he is the Savior. (Ephesians 5:23)
- One man from each tribe, each of them the head of his family, is to help you. (Numbers 1:4)
- But I want you to realize that the head of every man is Christ, and the head of the woman is man, and the head of Christ is God. (1 Corinthians 11:3)
- He must manage his own family well and see that his children obey him, and he must do so in a manner worthy of full respect. (1 Timothy 3:4)

- Husbands, in the same way be considerate as you live with your wives, and treat them with respect as the weaker partner and as heirs with you of the gracious gift of life, so that nothing will hinder your prayers. (1 Peter 3:7)
- To the woman he said, "I will make your pains in childbearing very severe; with painful labor you will give birth to children. Your desire will be for your husband, and he will rule over you." (Genesis 3:16)
- Husbands, love your wives, just as Christ loved the church and gave himself up for her. (Ephesian 5:25)

As much as I loved the idea, it was a challenge for me as well. It is said that you should be careful what you pray for because it will come to pass (sermon by Mike Kwasniewski). The girls, too, faced new challenges—both the adult girls living independently and the teens we still had at home. Guess who was the one faced with all the questions that needed answers and the pain that was borne from the challenges in question? That was me. In spite of Pelegrino being the head of household, the priest of our home, I was the one the girls would come to.

The sad part was that I didn't have the answers. The only thing I had true convictions of was that we had to be married. Otherwise, we were living in fornication/sin. And when we did get married it was a covenant between God, husband, and wife—one that should not be broken (divorce, separation) unless adultery was involved. And even then, we must stay single unless we are struggling; and if so, we are to reconcile with our spouse.

- Some Pharisees came to him to test him. They asked, "Is it lawful for a man to divorce his wife for any and every reason?" / "Haven't you read," he replied, "that at the beginning the Creator made them male and female, / and said, 'For this reason a man will leave his father and mother and be united to his wife, and the two will become one flesh'? / So they are no longer two, but one flesh. Therefore what God has joined together, let no one separate." / "Why then," they asked, "did Moses command that a man give his wife a certificate of divorce and send her away?" / Jesus replied, "Moses permitted you to divorce your wives because your hearts were hard. But it was not this way from the beginning. / I tell you that anyone who divorces his wife, except for sexual immorality, and marries another woman commits adultery." / The disciples said to him, "If this is the situation between a husband and wife, it is better not to marry." / Jesus replied, "Not everyone can accept this word, but only those to whom it has been given. (Matthew 19:3–11)

- To the married I give this command (not I, but the Lord): A wife must not separate from her husband. / But if she does, she must remain unmarried or else be reconciled to her husband. And a husband must not divorce his wife. (1 Corinthians 7:10–11)

I found myself in the school of life. I couldn't even identify what grade I was in by then; I had received the study book / Bible and instructions a bit late in the course. How I'd even gotten to this unknown grade was a guess to me. It was a reminder of Annette, my oldest, entering third grade and coming home with homework I could not help her with because I did not understand it myself. The brokenness I felt then I was feeling all over again.

The girls would talk to the disciples in their lives and come to me for confirmation. But I didn't know the scriptures that well, and I didn't know how to search for specific answers to their questions. So, I often found myself with no sure guidance to give them. Then, I became diligent about searching, reading, and listening to sermons from Dr. Charles Stanley and Joyce Meyers. And without failure, the Holy Spirit spoke through them daily. They were the vessels the Holy Spirit used to define scriptures and the daily challenges we all face in life. But of course, it was all a process, the sanctification process that I had yet to understand fully.

Yes, I was reading every day. And just as Lori had taught me,

I was writing out the scriptures and journaling. I was surprised at myself—surprised I was able to follow through with the reading and writing practice. The true joy was in spending time in the presence of God and hearing His voice in this intimate, special way. However, I wished He would speak to me as He had back then to the pioneers I read about before me.

Little did I know, I was starting to walk into storms that were also part of this wonderful new life. The sanctification process had begun. This was what I would be telling myself if I could go back:

> Be alert and of sober mind. Your enemy the devil prowls around like a roaring lion looking for someone to devour.
>
> Resist him, standing firm in the faith, because you know that the family of believers throughout the world is undergoing the same kind of sufferings.
>
> And the God of all grace, who called you to his eternal glory in Christ, after you have suffered a little while, will himself restore you and make you strong, firm and steadfast.
>
> To him be the power for ever and ever. Amen. (1 Peter 5:8–10)

God never promised believers would live an easy life, but He does promise our hardships are not in vain. As we read in 1 Corinthians 15:58, "Therefore, my dear brothers and sisters, stand firm. Let nothing move you. Always give yourselves fully to the work of the Lord, because you know that your labor in the Lord is not in vain."

Arisely and Natalie had a great time in their teen years and, later, with the campus group. But they were at that age when hormones also started nudging their flesh. They even learned how to play with their parents in order to get their way in some areas I would not have approved of. They would just go straight to Dad. For sure, he tended to give them what they wanted without seeing the trouble they could get into. But his word was the last word because he was the man/

priest of the home. This created a big conflict between us. We had two views on parenting at this point. Before, it wasn't as bad because he had given me complete control in the parenting area (really in all areas). But now he was acting out his role, and he felt no need to listen to my opinions on the matter.

I had a lot on my plate. I did all the domestic necessities, worked full-time, and took care of my parents' needs as well. My mother's health was declining, and her condition and the care required was becoming more difficult and sensitive emotionally for me.

I sought help from the church. They scheduled a meeting between the couple who oversaw the teen and campus ministry and Pelegrino and me. They were a lovely couple and had a couple children themselves (younger than the girls). We met at their home and spent the entire afternoon and evening with them (a get-to-know-you kind of day). The last part of the day we spent in discussion about our disagreement regarding the girls.

The next day while I was serving Kid's Kingdom, Robeca came to the class and called me aside. She said, "It was a pleasure having you and Pelegrino over. We think you are a lovely couple." Then she got closer to me and whispered in my ear, "You are a bit too passionate. You need to calm down." She pulled back and said in a regular tone, "You guys will be OK."

I almost fell back. Her comment kept repeating in my mind. I had to excuse myself. I ran to the bathroom and cried like a baby.

What! Too passionate? How can a person be too passionate? This was my kids' safety I was fighting for. This was about protecting them before they made mistakes they would regret for the rest of their lives. This was how a leader addressed the issue? How could this be? How could it be that you sought spiritual guidance, and all you got was, "You are a great couple, only you are too passionate. You just need to calm down." I felt that was a waste of time. I was in my flesh for sure.

I may not have gotten the answers I was hoping for. But going to someone who's spiritually knowledgeable is the right thing to do after going to God. "So Christ himself gave the apostles, the prophets, the evangelists, the pastors and teachers, / to equip his people for works of service, so that the body of Christ may be built up / until we all reach unity in the faith and in the knowledge of the Son of God and become mature, attaining to the whole measure of the fullness of Christ. (Ephesians 4:11–13)

Well, time went on, and I tried my best not to be so passionate about things.

Pelegrino had always enjoyed the media—indulging in movies and anything that was entertaining (at least for him). He told me there was a new movie out called *The Passion* about Jesus Christ, and he wanted to go see it.

"Are you asking me on a date?" I asked.

"Yes, this will be our date night activity."

This was part of the lifestyle we were taught at CCOC.

Our date night went well. We both loved the movie so much we bought the DVD when it came out on the market. The name was perfect for the movie. Our Lord Jesus Christ's life describes passion. I was blown away. I heard, "There is no greater passion than this, and there is nothing wrong with having great passion. In fact, it identifies with Me. Just be careful how you express it and where you apply it." Wow. There was nothing wrong with having great passion.

Fast-forward—Arisely (twenty-one at the time) had met a guy in the campus ministry, and they started dating. Sometime into their dating, they were discipled and disciplined by the church for slipping into sin. They started struggling with the issue and how it was handled. Arisely came to me and asked about getting married. I explained to her that it was better for her to grow spiritually and academically and just continue dating until she was a little more mature. I was keeping in mind that she had been born with disabilities, and it would be wiser to mature a bit more and gain confidence in herself before making such a great commitment that would take so much from her. She did not say whether she agreed or disagreed. But basically, I disagreed with her decision to get married at that time.

After some time had passed, one afternoon or early evening,

Arisely, her boyfriend, and his mom came over. I was in the kitchen and heard Pelegrino welcome them in. I was called over and was told that they had some news to tell me. Her boyfriend introduced me to him mom and then said, "I wanted to let you know that we were married yesterday. I have enlisted in the service, and I leave tomorrow morning. I just need to keep Arisely here with you until I get settled and set up a place for us to live out in Washington, DC."

I was blown away with all kinds of emotions. I could not believe that she would do such a thing behind our backs and just come so capriciously and tell us as if there was nothing wrong with what she had done. This was not like her. Oh, and he was expecting us to keep her until he was ready. This was our child. Who made him king to decide what was best for her?

Oh no, there came that passion; it was lit up and not in a good way. I repeated what he'd said and added, "Well, you made an adult decision by yourselves, and you should be ready to take on an adult responsibility. You married her; you take her with you. She is your responsibility now."

Pelegrino was infuriated. He did not delay in speaking up. "She is my daughter, and I say she stays here. That's fine. You can leave tomorrow in peace. She will be here until you send for her."

What? I thought to myself. I could not believe what had just happened.

Her new husband said, "OK. I will let you know when I am sending for her.

Arisely did not say a word. She just stood there. He left with his mom, and Arisely went to her room. Pelegrino told me he did not want to talk about it. It was settled. Then he continued watching his TV program.

I could not believe that, after all those years of special ed, meetings, and prayers, this was happening. We were just starting to see the fruit of all that hard work. She'd been accepted to Colombia College and had gotten a job at the school. She was participating in the campus ministry. And now that was all over simply because what? A young man who'd just walked into her life wanted his way. Not to mention, she had a father who would not seek true wisdom when dealing with his children in order to identify the true enemy that was out trying to devour them. Upset was not the word to describe how I was feeling. There was a whole lot of emotion there for sure.

Betrayal is a tactic of Satan. Satan comes to divide, kill, and destroy. And he was having a feast with this situation.

I continued to do what I was doing. I believe I'd been cooking at the time of the interruption. Of course, I had no say in important matters or anything else. But I still had to cook, clean, and manage all the details of our lives. I was not thinking of all the scriptures and righteousness that would bring me to a peaceful state. I did not understand that this was what Robeca really meant to say. I was letting my passion rule the hurt within me and giving Satan a foothold. I was just going over everything in my mind and drowning in my emotions.

Had I turned to scripture, I might have found Ephesians 4:26–27. "In your anger do not sin: Do not let the sun go down while you are still angry, / and do not give the devil a foothold."

I did not sleep all night. The thoughts were flying continuously, and the emotions that came with them were unbearable. *What's the hurry?* I asked myself. *Why could they not just date and listen to the church leaders? Why could she not concentrate on school and all the great things that were coming to pass for her?* There was proof of God's goodness; one school faculty said she was not college material, yet God had proved that statement wrong. She was twenty-one years old. This was not the time to throw it all away—not when she was getting so close to what God had in store for her.

The next morning, after Pelegrino left, I was still crying and emotionally unable to go to work. I didn't even get dressed that day. I stayed in my big T-shirt and moped all day. I was crushed.

When Pelegrino came home from work, I was still not dressed, just wearing my big T-shirt and moping and crying. I was still very emotional over the situation. Now, he wanted to clear things up, but I was too upset to talk about it. I felt he'd humiliated me in front of Ari's husband and his mom and literally told me I did not have a say in the matter—as if I was nobody. There was no way he could ever take that back. Those two individuals had left with a very poor image of me. Not to leave out how my uncontrolled passion had also made me look bad.

It was not long before he blew his top and told me to get out of his house. He said, "Get out."

I tried reaching for a pair of pants, and he snatched them out of my hand and told me I had nothing there. I guess I was taking a little too long in getting out of his apartment, so he grabbed me by my arm, opened the door, and started dragging me out.

He dragged me out of the building. It was about 4:15 p.m. on a weekday, around the time people start arriving from work. I remember it as if it was yesterday. It was April, and it had snowed the night before and that morning. There was snow on the ground, and it was freezing cold. I had no shoes and no clothes on other than a nighty T-shirt, not even under clothes. And as he pulled on my arm, it caused my T-shirt to rise up.

Boy, there was a free X-rated show for the whole neighborhood to see, and I was the one on display. He walked back into the apartment. I stood there, looking back and forth to determine the best route to take. I chose Fullerton Ave. I thought, *Oh well I guess I have to find a new place.*

As I was walking toward Fullerton Ave., I suddenly felt Pelegrino grab my arm again, pulling me back toward the building. Yup, he dragged me right back up the stairs and shut the door behind him, mumbling under his breath. I went to the bathroom, washed up, and started dinner.

I had a lot of soul searching to do. By this time in my life, I was exhausted. I felt burned out in more ways than one. One day, I was so bothered by Pelegrino's new way of using his leadership in a harsh way, I said to myself, "He was nicer when he used to get high." (Now, he was so mean.) I wish those words had never come out of my mouth. Again, I was still thinking and reacting in my flesh. Here again was that passion I didn't know how to control when getting angry.

Alcohol was not prohibited in the CCOC. The church believed that one glass of wine with a meal was OK. That was one of the beliefs I was against but the Catholic church I had come from also had similar beliefs, so I just prayed for answers. We need to be careful what comes out of our mouths; if you're not, you can give birth to something negative. As we're told in Proverbs 18:21, "The tongue has the power of life and death, and those who love it will eat its fruit."

A few weeks later, Pelegrino decided to have a beer while he barbequed outside. He had started that only a few weeks earlier. It happened every other weekend, but then it became a weekly thing. For a while, it was an exceptionally light intake, two beers at the most.

I was still pushing to be the servant God had created me to be, but it was not coming easy. I was always being stomped on. As usual, I stayed focused on what I knew my responsibilities to be. I could not just stop serving. That was part of my innermost being.

By some, I was taken advantage of for being so easy to forgive and criticized by others for it. I could not stay mad at anyone or stop serving. Nor did I want to. And when it was really challenging me, I would look at the cross, at Jesus. Or Abba God would send me a message via Dr. Stanley on my daily devotional. Or Joyce Meyers would come up with a new book or something else that would get me through the day. Even though I didn't know how to study the Bible for answers, Abba God made sure I was receiving what I needed to hear.

Some time passed. I continued working and taking care of the home. I continued attending church on Sundays and Wednesdays, Bible talk on Tuesdays, and having my quiet time with Abba God daily. I read the Bible on the bus ride to and from work and sometimes at the Starbucks for lunch, since my supervisor did not want me reading the Bible during the kids' nap time, which I used as my lunch. Since I was asked to stop, I would have to find other places to go. I was working at Cardinal Bernardin Montessori, which taught preschool to first grade, at the time. In addition, I took Mami and Papi grocery shopping and to run other errands as needed on a regular basis. I kept busy. That was a good thing, right?

One day as I was having my quiet time, I was reflecting on all the things I had done in my life before and after marriage. I truly felt broken and entered prayer. "I am so, so sorry, God. if I knew all that I know today spiritually, I would never have sinned against you as I have. Please forgive me."

I was like the author of Romans, who wrote:

What a wretched man I am! Who will rescue me from this body that is subject to death?
Thanks be to God, who delivers me through Jesus Christ our Lord! (Romans 7:24–25)

As I prayed, I remembered a saying Mami use to say. "No digas de este vaso de agua no tomo yo, porque un día tendrás que tomarte el vaso de agua completo" (Don't say I will not drink from this glass of water because you may one day wind up having to drink the whole glass). I didn't know the "why" then. But it's pretty clear to me today:

- So, if you think you are standing firm, be careful that you don't fall! (1 Corinthians 10:12)
- "But after I have risen, I will go ahead of you into Galilee." / Peter replied, "Even if all fall away on account of you, I never will." / "Truly I tell you," Jesus answered, "this very night, before the rooster crows, you will disown me three times." / But Peter declared, "Even if I have to die with you, I will never disown you." And all the other disciples said the same. (Matthew 26:32–35)

Papa Dios's Word is revealed further ahead.

PROPHECIES COME TO PASS

O ne day, I received a call from my nephew Rafy. He said, "I received a call from a family member informing me that my dad is in critical condition at a local hospital, and it is not looking good. Can you please go and find out what his status is? I need to know the truth and see how I can get out there."

Without hesitation, I said, "Sure. Absolutely."

We said our goodbyes, and I started the search. He was at Swedish Covenant Hospital, which was not too far. Unfortunately, the news was true. In fact, it was worse than the caller had explained it to be. So, I called Rafy back and gave him the information. He asked me to please keep close to his dad and keep him informed until he could get to Chicago. He was living in Rochester, New Jersey, at the time.

I did just as he asked me. I would go visit his dad daily and keep him informed of his status. Pelegrino accompanied me a few times and prayed over Rafy Sr.

On our last visit, Rafy Sr. asked me to bring him some *jugo de pera* (pear juice). I figured this was a good sign and was more than happy to do so. The next day, when I headed out to visit, I had his order with me. I walked in cheerfully, eager to see my brother from another set of parents, carrying his juice in one hand and my car keys in the other.

I pushed the revolving door and looked down. When I reached the exit point, I looked up and received the shock of my life. I was so stunned I dropped the cans of juice on the floor. As I bent to pick them up, I kept thinking, "No. Oh my goodness, no."

But yes, before me stood Julio, his mom, and his sister. They had just finished their visit with Rafy and were on their way out.

They all rushed over to help me, but I had managed to quickly pick the juice up. They all had big grins on their faces. I greeted his mom and sisters with a kiss and hug. Then Julio walked closer and greeted me with a hug. I was shaking all over. My knees felt like they were going to give out on me. He whispered, "It's OK. Come sit down."

His sister held my right arm, and Julio held my left as they guided me to a nearby seat.

His sister said, "How great to see you. How have you been?"

"I'm doing well, thank God. My husband and I were here yesterday, and Rafy asked me to bring him some jugo de pera. So here I am bringing him some jugo de pera."

"Nice. Thank you," his sister said. "They are cutting his visit time short so he can rest. We were just on our way out. You may want to get to his room before they end his visiting hour," his sister told me.

I replied, "Oh yes. Excuse me. Let me take this to Rafy."

"Are you OK?" Julio asked.

"Yes, I'm fine. Thank you."

I headed to Rafy's room. It was a short visit because he was getting overanxious, and the hospital staff wanted him to relax.

On my way back to the lobby, I kept thinking, *Oh my goodness, I can't believe I actually saw him.* I was still a little shook up, and some anxiety set in. To my surprise, when I got to the lobby, they were still there. They said they just wanted to make sure I was OK. After I assured them I was fine, we all made our way out the door.

When we got outside, they invited me over to his sister's home, since it had been so long since they had seen me. I agreed to a brief visit. His sister said to her mom, "You can drive with me, and Julio can drive with Carmen so he can direct her to my place."

Julio asked, "Is that OK that I drive with you?"

For a few seconds, I was lost for words but answered, "Sure."

Julio's mom and sister walked to their car, and Julio followed me to mine. I got in, started the car, and looked over to Julio and asked, "What's the address?"

There it was—Julio and me face-to-face after twenty-three years. Our eyes locked, our hearts beat rapidly, our hands were sweaty, and emotions so thick they could be cut with a knife hung in the air between us. I took a deep breath, wanting to be quiet. But I could not help it. The words just came out. "Why didn't you ever call me?" I asked.

He was the one shaking now. His eyelids were blinking rapidly, and his words could not come out. He was trying to say the right thing, but he was lost for words.

"What's wrong? Are you trying to think of the right way to say it? Or are you trying to think of a lie to cover up the truth? Just say the truth in plain, simple, non-fancy words. Just answer the question."

He finally answered. "Honestly, I don't have an answer. You are right. I should have called you. I'm sorry that I didn't."

I followed with a question. "What's the address?" I stayed focused on getting him to his sister's house. When we got there, I said, "I really should be going home. I will visit another time."

He handed me his phone number and asked me to call him.

I went home and told Pelegrino, "Rafy is not doing so good. Babe, you should have gone with me." I didn't mention the encounter with Julio. I don't know why; it just didn't come to mind.

So much was happening all at once. Annette was having problems with her husband (at the time). Karen was having problems with her baby Nia's dad. The choice Arisely had made prematurely against my wishes was still a tender spot for me. Natalie was struggling with school; this was her senior year, and she was wanting to start dating. At work, things were not going so well either. For whatever reason, the lead teacher was persecuting me for reading my Bible and gave me a hard time every chance she got. Pelegrino was attending Wednesday night's midweek service and Bible talk group less and less. By now, Rafy Sr. was terminally ill, and little Rafy was faced with the worst situation—a parent in near-death status while living in another state.

Rafy Sr. continued to decline. I called little Rafy and told him he really needed to get to Chicago. He replied, "On my way."

Sadly, Rafy Sr. was called home before little Rafy arrived. I guess the Lord was sparing him the pain of seeing his dad take his last breath (as is his belief today).

Wow. It was unbelievable but true. When turmoil comes, it tends to come hard and unexpectedly. There is so much we don't teach our children. And it is not always because we don't want to but, rather, because we do not know how to do so. Or perhaps it's that we just don't have the answers ourselves. This is especially true when your child is raised away from you for whatever reason, and you only have him or her part-time. There is one thing we can't explain because there is no way of keeping it from happening—how to avoid the pain of losing a loved one to death. Once they're gone, the child is left with so many unexplained facts of life and the pain of absence that he or she doesn't know how to deal with. This was difficult for me to witness, and I felt helpless in comforting Rafy.

On the day of the funeral, I was lost for words. I just kept close to Pelegrino and prayed for comfort for all of them. Julio seemed strong. He really held it together, considering that Rafy was his brother, and they were very close. He was able to say a few words and sing a song without breaking down. One of his sisters said to me, "See how strong he seems? That's a front. He will let it out when he is home alone."

When it was all over, Rafy Jr. went back to Rochester, New Jersey, and I was able to do just as Rafy Sr. had trusted me to do twenty-one years earlier—just love and be there for his son.

As I understood, Julio would be in town for a little while. Now that all was somewhat back to routine, I felt the need to talk to Julio and get closure. I shared with Pelegrino what I was feeling and asked him if I could do so.

He said, "Yes."

Wow! I couldn't believe it. Pelegrino had given me the OK to meet with Julio and get closure regarding our relationship.

I called Julio, and he agreed to meet with me, as he had asked me to do the day I drove him home to his sister's house after the hospital reencounter. He was ecstatic, to say the least. I could hear it in his voice. We set up a date to meet at a restaurant. It was a very emotional time. We talked for hours. It was as if we had never been apart. But I had to go home, and he had to go back to Indiana. What I had just done was given Satan a foothold in my walk with God—not that I saw or understood it to be so.

I started replaying our conversation in my mind. Although I believed it was closure, it was unshakeable. On Sunday after service, I shared with Lori. She asked me if we had kissed. I told her, "No, but I can't stop thinking about our meeting."

She prayed with me and asked me to keep praying and asking for peace.

I didn't realize it right away, but my Aunt Ana's prediction had come true. One day, I was hanging out at my younger cousin's home with his wife, and my aunt was also visiting. We were listening to music. I was sitting, singing along with one of Odilio Gonzalez songs that reminded me of Julio. As I sang, my eyes were closed and tears ran down my face. My aunt tapped me on the shoulder and said, "No llores, si todo es para lo mismo" (Don't cry. Everything is for the same outcome). With that, she walked to the kitchen.

When she came back, she asked, "¿Cuántos años tienes?" (How old are you?)

"Twenty three," I answered.

"¿Y Julio, cuántos años tiene?" (And how old is Julio?)

"Forty-three," I responded.

"Todas esas lágrimas son en vano. Recuerda mis palabras. Julio, en sus sesenta, volverá y tú cometerás adulterio, y Pelegrino lo aceptará. Recuerda mis palabras, porque pasara" (All those tears are in vain. Remember my words. Julio, in his sixties, will return, and you will commit adultery, and Pelegrino will accept it. Mark my words, because it will happen). She walked back to the kitchen.

Returning, she added one more thing. "De hecho, tendrás que lavar el cuelpo de Julio. Recuerda mis palabras" (In fact, you will have to bathe Julio. Remember my words).

This conversation happened shortly after we got married, and Pelegrino had already started drinking alcohol, using cocaine, and staying out, while my pastime was going to my younger cousin's house to hang out with his wife.

After I met Julio at the restaurant, Pelegrino started to drink more and more. He was still carrying that leadership power on his shoulders more often than I cared for, only because it was not done in a nice way. I felt the need to tell Pelegrino about my feelings, first to be open and honest with him and second to seek his help in getting rid of what I was feeling and to make him aware that I needed more from him in our relationship. I didn't want to go to someone else to hear me out or give me any counsel. I wanted to go to my husband to get the comfort I needed. I still had feelings (love) for Julio that had clearly never left my heart and mind.

Pelegrino listened and said, "That's OK. You'll get over it."

That was it. I felt brushed off, my emotions not acknowledged.

As I pondered all these emotions weighing heavy in my heart, I came to my regular outlet, writing. I wrote to Rafy Jr.:

August, 13, 2003

Dear sweetheart,
Hi. How are you today? I pray that at the time this letter lands in your hands you are in the best of health, high spirits, and prospering in finances and any goals. How is Dalie? I hope the same for her and that you may be growing in unity and love every day more as you walk closer to God and maturity in marriage.

Honey, I have a lot on my mind and in my heart. As the day unfolded and I proceed with my therapy (housework is therapeutic), I had you right there listening to my every thought. Walking through my memories and feeling my every emotion (I was writing to you in thought), I had so many things I wanted to share with you. It may be that now when I am done with the therapy, ready to sit and put it down on paper, I will be lost for words. However, here goes.

There was a pause, and I didn't return to finish the letter until the next evening:

August 14, 2003, 5:17 p.m.

Hi, I am back.

Sorry about that. It is ritual for me to be interrupted when I am trying to concentrate on writing, the telephone, or taking a shower; it's part of my role. The sad part is that I am not sure I will be able to retrieve the same words that crossed through my mind, expressing my emotions so precisely. It has to do with still being in shock and blown away with the latest challenge in my life. It leaves me breathless often in a day.

Wow, where do I begin? I can't even proceed with this sentence without breaking into tears. My heart beats at a hundred miles a minute (or so it feels), and my hands shake at every stroke. *My God, why?* Sorry. I have to stop for a minute. Oh, honey, now I have really messed up my life with such poor decisions.

As you may have read through me, I have had contact with Julio pretty often—more than I had planned to. So many questions have run through my mind. How could it be that, after twenty-three years (of no contact at all), I still want nothing more than to be the other half of him (his wife), part of his life (his partner) in everything.

In this time that we have reconnected, I have learned very plainly and clearly that he is nothing like what others told me but, rather, everything I believed him to be. It is as if I have known him all my life. And yet our romance (love affair) was actually very brief when I calculate the actual time we spent together. The twenty-five years I've known him mostly was spent waiting and hoping to one day make unity of this incredible love. Now I'm asking, otherwise, what was or is the reason for being in each other's lives and feeling the love I feel?

I can't believe the sleepless, endless nights of crying, praying, and writing letters that would never reach him. There's all the times of going over and over everything that he ever said to me. I recall using his positive words of wisdom to find encouragement in my life pursuits. Remembering that he would use Bible verses to explain certain topics gave me hunger to know more about what God really had to say to me. After all, I believed that God had taken him from me for His purpose, His Kingdom, and His glory. Had I known that it was a promotion for record sales, everything would have been so very different.

Why did I listen to those who said I was wasting my time on a person who would not be back and did not even think about me? Why didn't I just believe, trust, and follow my own instinct about a mutual love that was (is) so strong? All I needed was love and self-control.

- Love is *patient*, love is kind. It does not envy, it does not boast, it is not proud. (1 Corinthians 13:4, italics added)
- But the fruit of the Spirit is love, joy, peace, forbearance, kindness, goodness, faithfulness,

/ gentleness and *self-control*. Against such things there is no law. (Galatians 5:22–23; italics added)

And without a doubt, it would have changed so much the today and now.

Being young and doubtful of my own sense of truth, I did not know much truth (Word of God). My thoughts were very immature. I had no guidance or trustworthy people (who truly knew God). And all of this has led to a drastic, sad outcome of my life as it is today and has been for twenty-five years.

Funny how my tragically sad love story has a blessing. As in Romans 8:28, "And we know that in all things God works for the good of those who love him, who have been called according to his purpose."

It made me need God, desire to know Him, and hunger for His word. I have embraced the gift of God's grace (my salvation). I've been blessed to see a faithful prayer answered. A drug addict gangbanger and ex-convict is clean of drugs, off the streets, and far from the jail bars that once held him prisoner. Now, he has been saved by the grace of God and added to the book of life. And three of his four daughters have also been added to God's book of life.

As in Revelations 21:27, "Nothing impure will ever enter it, nor will anyone who does what is shameful or deceitful, but only those whose names are written in the Lamb's book of life."

A young man who had no real direction or financial support from his parents has gotten through school, holding in his hand a complete college education. He is the envy of many, especially those who, because of his background, did not find him to be worthy of their family or daughter. And I've received many other answered prayers.

There was one prayer I did not expect He would answer, and it turned out He did—the one where I met Julio once more. Moreover, I have been able to tell him how much he was (is) loved. I have shared my thoughts and faith in him over the years and how I did use the wisdom he shared with me. I hoped to be able to stand firm on solid ground and walk away without falling apart; this was my expectation of myself.

Boy, was I ever wrong. My heart aches for him desperately. I feel like I am falling totally apart. I can't think straight. My thoughts of him are endless. My heart feels like it has been ripped apart very slowly. I can feel every vein tearing, leaving me weak and putting pressure against my chest that causes enormous pain and often leaves me short of breath. My head pounds with pain, while the tears run down my face onto my pillow at night and in the mornings or when I'm riding on the bus as I attempt to continue forward in this life without him. I feel weak and brokenhearted and feel a loss of interest in my daily life.

The Word keeps me going: "But we have this treasure in jars of clay to show that this all-surpassing power is from God and not from us. / We are hard pressed on every side, but not crushed; perplexed, but not in despair; / persecuted, but not abandoned; struck down, but not destroyed. / We always carry around in our body the death of Jesus, so that the life of Jesus may also be revealed in our body. (2 Corinthians 4:7–10)

I am drawn in by his laughter, conversation, voice, and gentleness and, mostly, by the way he listens (so attentive) and knows me (even though he has not been in my life for the last twenty-three years) yet wants to know more. I'm drawn, too, to his readiness to meet my every need and desire to know my every desire. He puts me before his desires or needs. His humbleness is comforting and inviting, and his love for God is encouraging. His leadership just blows me away. He is just as I always thought him to be. He is my one desire in life that has been put on hold repeatedly, not totally removed but put on hold.

In Psalm 37:3–7 (italics added), we're told, "Trust in the Lord and do good; dwell in the land and enjoy safe pasture. / *Take delight in the Lord, and he will give you the desires of your heart.* / Commit your way to the Lord; trust in him and he will do this: / He will make your righteous reward shine like the dawn, your vindication like the noonday sun. / Be still before the Lord and wait patiently for him; do not fret when people succeed in their ways, when they carry out their wicked schemes."

How I love him so. However, I learned and understand now how I put him first before God just as I put Pelegrino and girls first, without realizing that's what I was doing. God has allowed Julio to walk back into my life at a time when I was feeling unloved, unappreciated, not understood, and with no desire to continue in this life setting. All the trials that have come—Pelegrino, the girls, you, illnesses, deaths, betrayals, poor friendships, and so on—do not measure up to this one. Julio walking back into my life precisely now does strike me hard. I was put through so much emotionally (Pelegrino and the girls) and was feeling defeated, weak, hurt, angry, and so many other emotions.

I was praying, talking to Abba God, and asking, Why have I not been loved in return and appreciated? Am I too passionate, as I was once told? Or am I just too sensitive and weak to trials? I prayed that the love I had given would be reciprocated one day, focused on the man in my life. If not, then please give me a why—some way, somehow.

Talk about answered prayers. This was somewhat quick. Not only did Julio walk back into my life, he has responded to my love. It has been exactly how it was and how I hoped it to be. And my heart aches for him just as it did twenty-five years ago when it all started.

We read in Jeremiah 29:11, "'For I know the plans I have for you,' declares the Lord, 'plans to prosper you and not to harm you, plans to give you hope and a future.'"

God has a plan for us, and 90 percent of the time, we tend to step in and mess with the original plan. We think it's our life and that we know no better. He lets us walk through the path we chose and works on bringing us back on track (His plan). All these falls, bumps, cuts, and wounds leave hard, ugly scars. But there's nothing God can't repair.

The many whys I asked as I talk with our Father gives me this: He could be asking, Who are you going to put first? What is the righteous decision here? Will you step into my plan and try to change it? You know the answer to that. *God Almighty and whatever His Word tells me is righteous.*

There is a saying that we all say. "If I could do it again, I would be obedient to God." So, here I am, wanting to run to the man I have always loved—who I've dreamed of spending my life with and living happily ever after (with a bump here and there). Here is the test, I have to deny myself. I must *put God first and deny myself.*

My goodness, is it ever painful and difficult. However, I know God would not allow it if He did not know I could handle it. So, on my knees I go, asking the Holy Spirit to give me the strength because I am nothing and can do nothing without Him. It has not been easy. Will you please pray for me?

Sweetheart, I don't know why, but I just had a strong urge to share this with you.

Let it be known—it is not that I don't love Pelegrino. It is totally different because I do love and care deeply about him. But that would be another topic altogether. Yes, I will be faithful and love him as God says I should. I know we married for the wrong reason. We should have already been in love and known each other well enough. Instead, it was that I wanted to love him and get to know him in the course of the marriage. Since he's been drug free, there is a whole different person here. I must remember to put others first and deny myself if it benefits them and not to do it with a personal gain in mind. I will do this because I have been given a Spirit of power, love, and self-discipline (2 Titus 1:7).

May God bless you and Dalie. Kisses, hugs, and lots of love. Bye for the moment, until I hear from you.

Love, Ma

Then I wrote to Jesus.

August 17, 2003
2:10 a.m.

Oh Lamb of God,
You who came to take away the sins of the world. Have mercy on me. You, who with pure joy, took

all my inequities upon Yourself for the sake of my salvation, please rescue me. For I am weak and feel faint at the thought of going on. I cannot sleep. My heart aches and beats rapidly as it pounds against my chest with such pressure that it causes a sharp pain. I am working hard to maintain a steady walk toward self-denial of my flesh that churns and desires to be on a wider road and not the narrow road I am called to walk on. It can be so easy to justify all of my desires. But I know that is a foolish thing, and there is no light in it. I would be only fooling myself and walking toward destruction.

I feel as if I am living in a completely different world constantly—having to adjust to every different setting as the day unfolds depending on the unexpected. I feel lost, not myself. In fact, I have lost myself. I have had to ask myself, Who am I? As I get confused in the many, so many, different phases of my life, searching for answers causes doubt. I walk away from the thought, continuing to the next agenda without ever resolving my dilemma: Whom am I? Really, who am I?

I know I am a child of God. But who is this child of God? I read God's word to find comfort. I seek a light to the darkness of the who, why, and how—the questions that run through my mind constantly. I am looking to find myself. I seek peace, a place where I can rest and find closure, a way to quiet this mind that never was a child yet really has not been able to grow up. This mind is still wanting to feel or know what it is like to be a child, innocent, protected, and without a load of responsibility that no one else wants to carry (or even help). Part of me feels dead without wanting to do anything about anything.

I turn to Psalms 23:1–6:

1. *The Lord is my shepherd, I shall not be in want.*

    (I do feel very often that I should not be in need of anything and feel guilty when I am.)

2. *He makes me lie down in green pastures, He leads me beside quiet waters.*

    (Green pastures I have seen. Quiet waters I'm not too sure of.)

3. *He restores my soul. He guides me in paths of righteousness for His name's sake.*

    (Thank You, for You have restored my soul repeatedly. And You do guide me in paths of righteousness for Your name's sake. Yet, too often the question/desire passes by me, and I slip.)

4. *Even though I walk through the valley of the shadow of death, I will fear no evil. For You are with me, Your rod and Your staff, they comfort me.*

    (I fear no evil. No one but You. And that can scare me at times, though I know You are with me. I don't want to become self-righteous. I can miss seeing Your rod and staff and become afraid of not being right by You.)

5. *You prepare a table before me in the presence of my enemies. You anoint my head with oil, my cup overflows.*

    (Thank You so much, for this is so evident in my life. Yet there seems to be a lot of drama most of the time and struggles to keep the cup full.)

6. *Surely goodness and love will follow me all the days of my life, and I will dwell in the house of the Lord forever.*

    (Oh, Father, how I would love to agree. But that is not how my life has felt. No, not at all. And how I wish I could say this, but only when in eternity will I feel this.)

I am speaking to Abba God while I pray this scripture out and express how I see it in my life.

I choose this prayer because it feels like I'm dying somehow. I'm numb. I don't know what to feel or if I even do feel or care. Could this be menopause? No way. I pray about hormones all the time. What is this?

I am tired now. It's 3:37 a.m. Good night. Thank You once again, Abba, for such a great gift, the Lamb of God, Jesus Christ.

Amen!

After all the battling with myself, I decided to get some professional help. I shared my decision with my nephew Rafy. And he said, "Ma, you are going to end up giving the psychiatrist advice before you are done with your session."

Sad to say, I met with a psychiatrist. I went through the whole procedure, telling him about my life from as far back as I could remember to the present time and what had driven me to seek professional help. I was diagnosed with bipolar disorder, depression, and some childhood traumatic stress that caused anxiety. He prescribed me some medication and asked me to schedule an appointment.

Rafy was right. I did not need that and could have told him a thing or two about dealing with X, Y, and Z. I never went back. I'm not saying that some people may benefit from the use of medication, but I knew in my mind and soul it was not for me. The therapy of having someone to talk to was very helpful. I just preferred someone who knew God, and the psychiatrist I had seen was not a Christian-affiliated doctor.

At work, I was working on a field trip for my class. Yes, despite the hard time Ms. T gave me, Sister BJ had given me the opportunity to teach the children Spanish. How about that? I had purchased my own supplies and had the honor to teach the children a second language. This was the end of the school year, and I was taking them on a field trip. We were scheduled to go for lunch to a Spanish restaurant, where they could each order their food in Spanish.

I was blessed when preparing the event. The owner of the restaurant had given me the kids' menu and I was able to teach them exactly what they would be seeing on the day of the field trip. The restaurant owners where really excited as well to be part of the children's experience.

The parents and grandparents were excited, and so was I. The children were even more excited. The day came, and we went out for lunch. Each child ordered what he or she wanted in Spanish. Both parents and grandparents were able to witness them apply what they had learned that year at school in a real-world situation. I was excited because they all did well and really enjoyed themselves in the process.

This summer break was no ordinary one. The kids left school with something exciting to practice during the summer break, speaking Spanish. Abba God truly got me through that one with flying colors.

Looking forward to the school summer break? Not so much. This meant that money was going to be tight. But God always made a way. I kept the positive attitude that I was going to do great things during the school break, such as house cleaning, tending to Mami and Papi, and spending more and more time with God. Little did I know what lay ahead of me.

Natalie graduated, and she also got a job. She and Annette were always productive in that area. She did start dating. Why couldn't they wait just a little longer? I pondered within. I also allowed her to use my van occasionally, which was a big deal for her.

The time started going by, and the bills were coming in. I just couldn't understand how to make this work. Pelegrino and I got into a few arguments during this time. One day, I was absolutely tired of it. I was overwhelmed, to say the least, in all areas—emotionally and physical—and the challenges seemed to have no end. Mami kept getting worst instead of better. So did Papi.

At my wit's end, I left the apartment. I just needed to get away. Pelegrino was not the same. He had changed so much it was unbearable. He was mean now. And I was being called by God to be submissive and loving. How did one do that? I drove away crying and trying to think. I wondered how I could get away. Suddenly, I remembered Julio had given me his number. I did not know what I would say. But I just wanted a way out.

I stopped the van and dialed the number—neither knowing the response nor caring. I just felt the impulse and needed to make the call. (This was definitely my flesh.) The phone was ringing, and I was getting more anxious. "Hola," Julio answered.

I paused.

He repeated, "Hola."

I said, "Hola. Como estas? Habla Carmen" (Hello. How are you? This is Carmen).

He sounded very excited to hear from me. I was moved deeply inside my tired heart. I said, "I just have one question I need to ask you. If I come to your doorstep right now, would you receive me?"

I remembered what he had told me once while he was staying with me. "I would never return to a woman who takes another man after being with me." I expected the answer to be no. But I had to know what he would say. Would it be, "I can't"? Would he make up an excuse, like he did the night before my wedding day? When I'd hoped he would say, "Come. Don't get married. I love you"? What would it be this time?

To my surprise, he said in a loud happy voice, "Claro que si. Si, si" (Of course, yes. yes, yes)!

I started crying.

He asked me what was wrong, and we talked for a while. At the end of our conversation, I said, "It isn't that coming to you is what I intended to do. But I wanted to know if it was an option available to me."

He reassured me that it was and that I could count on him.

That day, I felt a sense of relief. But it opened a whole new avenue in my already stressful life. And Satan was having a field day with my weakness.

Natalie had been seeing a lot of a young man she'd met at the college campus ministry. Not too long into their relationship, Natalie came to me saying she and her boyfriend wanted to get married. I was taken aback at how fast they were taking their relationship to the next level. We had a long talk about the pros and cons of marriage. She kept reassuring me that they had considered all of what I was presenting to her, and they knew there would be some challenges. I finally gave in. I told her that, if her dad was OK with it, we would talk to Mike and Lori, and she could get married. I did not want her to end up doing the same thing Arisely had done, eloping. She asked Pelegrino, and he was OK with it. So, I started the arrangements.

The wedding turned out really nice. I dressed a corner of the dining room like a wedding gazebo with guest chairs and lots of white lace and flowers. I sent out invitations and cooked. Pelegrino walked her down the little wedding aisle, and Mike performed the ceremony. The reception was sweet. After the greeting and thank you for coming, I had Pelegrino do the daddy-daughter dance with Natalie. They danced to "Butterfly Kisses" by Kenny Rogers. The tears were flowing all over the apartment.

It was done. The last of the four was on her way out to live her own adult life. And I had to let her go. None of this was sitting well with my emotions. But as I had learned to do, I took a deep breath, exhaled, prayed, and kept moving forward.

I found myself going to visit my younger cousin's wife. I shared about Julio, my battle with the thoughts of our closure meeting, and my desperate phone call to him that day when I was upset at Pelegrino.

She was excited and said, "Well, God wants you to be happy and you have lived a very challenging and painful life with Pelegrino. Maybe this is God's way of saying, It's time for you to be happy. You don't have any more children in the house. They are all married. And it's time for you to find some happiness. God says he wants His children to be happy."

I listened and told her it doesn't work that way. God hates divorce. And if you must divorce because of adultery, you must stay unmarried or reconcile with your husband.

She said, "Well, let's see how long you two will last now that you don't have any kids in the house."

I was crushed at her response. Now I knew going to her regarding any of my marital struggles was the wrong thing to do. I'm sure she meant well. But she was going by her opinion and worldly philosophy. In the past, I valued her opinion so greatly that I would go to her before I did things to get her approval. (I also recalled times I did not go to her on purpose because I had already made up my mind and felt she might disapprove. Yes, that was deceitful.) I was not clear on a lot of choices. I had a big mixture when it came to my understanding of what was right and wrong and the reason for it all.

Now that I was starting to know and understand things better in life and in myself, I had a different perspective on some things.

Funny, she was the one who had suggested I start accepting dates. She had explained how a woman needed a man in the home as a father figure for the children, during a time when I had no interest in getting involved with anyone. I had been stood up by the store owner, the person she suggested I get involved with. When I got involved with Pelegrino and found it was not working out and wanted to end our relationship, she said I was being selfish and should let the bird that was flying (Julio) go and give Pelegrino a chance. She had advised me not to do to him what had been done to me in the past—when I was left behind for being young and immature. I just couldn't trust her opinion anymore.

Meanwhile, I received a letter from Julio, which made it more difficult:

> Queries Amor Mio,
>
> Amada yo deseo que seas prosperada en todas las cosas, y que tengas salud, asi como prospera tu alma; que nunca falte el pan en tu mesa, y que El Espiritu Santo te guie a tierras de rectitud. Esos son mis deseos para ti y para todos aquellos a los que tu amas.
>
> Puedo escribir los versos mas tristes esta noche si pensara en el pasado viendo tu rostro hermozo entre tus manos, y tus lindos ojos llorando la amargura de mi desprecio, despiadado, sin ninguna misericordia de ti. O Dios mio! La perdi! La Perdi! Puedo escribir los

versos mas tristes esta noche. Tu tienes toda la razon, te ize sufrir te pido perdon, auque se que tu me amas y no me guardas renco. Esta noche he comprendido que te he perdido inrremediablemente. Tambien he compredido que te amo! Pero creo que he llegado trade a tu vida. Cuando te tube no te supe apreciar, no llegué a apreciar tus valores de mujer, tu dursura, tu ternura y tu amor tan grande que me tenias, y lo deje ir de entre mis manos. Ahora solo me queda contemplarte de lejos, cuando te tube tan cerca y toda mia, O Dios mio! Como se cobra la vida! Puedo escribir los versos mas triste esta noche! Te perdi, siento que te perdi! Siento un vacio tan grande en mi alma porque siento que te he perdido para siempre. Sabes algo? Lo mismo que tu pasaste por mi que perdiste toda esperanza, porque de que nos sirbe, o me sirbe que te ame, si ya tienes un hogar una familia, una vida organizada, mis esperanzas son tan pocas que aungue te amo con toda mi alma mis esperanzas se reducen a casi nada. Aunque por el amor que nos tenemos siempre se vislumbra un rayo de luz, un milagro! Ahora tu sufrimiento y tu Cruz la cargo yo. Puedo escribir los versos mas triste esta noche! Perdoname! Perdoname! No puedo seguir escribiendo te amo y ahora tu tormento es mio!

Te amo con toda mi alma
Siempre Tuyo.

Beloved, I wish that you prosper in all things, and that you have health, just as your soul prospers; May bread never be missing from your table, and may The Holy Spirit guide you to lands of righteousness. Those are my wishes for you and for all those you love. I can write the saddest verses tonight if I thought about the past, seeing your beautiful face in your hands, and your beautiful eyes crying the bitterness of my contempt, merciless, without any mercy from you. Oh my God! I lost her! I lost her! I can write the saddest verses tonight. You are absolutely right, I made you suffer, I apologize, although I know that you love me and do not hold a grudge against me. Tonight I realized that I have lost you irremediably. I have also understood that I love you! But I think I've come into your life. When I had you, I didn't know how to appreciate you, I didn't appreciate your values as a woman, your hardness, your tenderness and your great love for me, and I let it go from my hands. Now I only have to contemplate you from afar, when I had you so close and all mine, O my God! How life is claimed! I can write the saddest verses tonight! I lost you, I feel like I lost you! I feel such a big void in my soul because I feel like I have lost you forever. Do you know something? The same thing that you went through for me that you lost all hope, because what good does it do us, or does it help me that I love you, if you already have a home, a family, an organized life, my hopes are so little that even though I love you with all my soul My hopes are reduced to almost nothing. Although because of the love we have for each other, there is always a ray of light, a miracle! Now I carry your suffering and your Cross. I can write the saddest verses tonight!

Forgive me! Forgive me! I can't keep writing I

love you and now your torment is mine!

I love you with all my soul.

Always yours.

In my confusion I went into prayer. "Father God, Pelegrino is so selfish and detached from me. He is gone most of the time. And even when he is home, I have to beg and plead to get any attention. Maybe my younger cousin's wife is right. Maybe I was supposed to be with Julio all along, and I messed up by sinning with Pelegrino. And then wanting to fix my mistake I went ahead and got married. I'm a mess, Lord. I need help. Amen!

I think too much. But how do I stop this thinking? When I think about Pelegrino's shortcomings, it's so easy to give in to my thoughts of Julio and so difficult to refrain from doing so.

The struggle is depicted (explained) in scripture:

> We know that the law is spiritual; but I am unspiritual, sold as a slave to sin. / I do not understand what I do. For what I want to do I do not do, but what I hate I do. / And if I do what I do not want to do, I agree that the law is good. / As it is, it is no longer I myself who do it, but it is sin living in me. / For I know that good itself does not dwell in me, that is, in my sinful nature. For I have the desire to do what is good, but I cannot carry it out. / For I do not do the good I want to do, but the evil I do not want to do—this I keep on doing. / Now if I do what I do not want to do, it is no longer I who do it, but it is sin living in me that does it.
>
> So I find this law at work: Although I want to do good, evil is right there with me. / For in my inner being I delight in God's law; / but I see another law at work in me, waging war against the law of my mind and making me a prisoner of the law of sin at work within me. / What a wretched man I am! Who will rescue me from this body that is subject to death? / Thanks be to God, who delivers me through Jesus Christ our Lord! (Romans 7:14–25)

I was so quick to blame Pelegrino for my thought process, just like Eve did when God confronted her about what she had done. "Then the Lord God said to the woman, 'What is this you have done?' The woman said, 'The serpent deceived me, and I ate' (Genesis 3:13).

I didn't realize that all I needed to do was pray, read the Bible, and listen to sermons or anything that was related to God, especially worship music. This would be the way God spoke to me. I needed to trust God to give me the answers I was looking for. As we are told in Romans 12:2, "Do not conform to the pattern of this world but be transformed by the renewing of your mind. Then you will be able to test and approve what God's will is—his good, pleasing and perfect will."

Another blow came. I received a letter from Sister BJ informing me that my position had been removed. In other words, I was terminated. I had lost my job. Wow! I could not believe this or figure it out. Why? Why, Lord, why? *OK, it's not the first time I was facing an unexpected financial setback. We can get through this,* I thought to myself.

That evening when Pelegrino got home, I told him the news, and he was not a happy camper. We would not be able to afford this apartment, especially now that we were going into the winter season. Our gas bill alone was $300 plus a month. These were my thoughts as I listened to Pelegrino huff and puff. "Don't worry," I immediately interjected. "I will file for unemployment, and we should be OK. We can start looking for a smaller place now that the girls are all gone, and God will make a way."

I applied for unemployment and was approved. I started looking around and in the newspaper for a smaller, more affordable apartment. I knew that God would provide.

On Sunday, I shared with a couple at church, that we were looking for a smaller place now that the girls were all gone. The brother said, "We have a basement apartment we are looking to rent, if you want to look at it."

I told him I would mention it to Pelegrino. I did, and we agreed to look at it. That week, we stopped by and looked at the apartment. It was a lot smaller than I had hoped, but the rent was affordable, and it was heated, which eliminated the gas bill. It also had a washer and dryer, which was also a blessing. And the couple were nice people.

A couple months into us living at the new place, Pelegrino's ex-brother-in-law was also in need of a new place. Pelegrino had spotted a sign for rent down the street and told him about it. He stopped by and took the apartment. So, now we were neighbors, Pelegrino was walking distance from his best friend and lifelong idol.

He could do no wrong in Pelegrino's eyes; he worshipped the ground this man walked on. He was a happy camper.

During one of my quiet times during prayer, I asked God to direct me to what I should do with all the extra time on my hands. Although it was freeing up time for Mami and Papi, I knew I had to do something positive in addition to being there for and with them. I asked for Him to open the door He wanted me to walk through next. I paused in silence and heard, "Haven't you been wanting to go back to school? You can go back and get your GED."

Wow! I was blown away. *Yes! That's what I will do. I'll go back and get my GED.*

I looked up the information and found a program I could enroll in. I would be going back to school, and I couldn't wait. That evening, I mentioned my plan to Pelegrino. He said, "What! Go back to school? GED? That's a waste of time. You need to get a job. That's what you need to do."

I told him, "No, babe. I've been wanting to go back to school and get my GED, but there was always a problem with day care or something. Now that the girls are all gone, it's the perfect time for me to get my GED. Then I can get a job that pays more than five dollars an hour."

I went against Pelegrino's wishes and enrolled myself in the Wright College GED program. I was excited. I just had to share the news. I went to see my younger cousin's wife and told her the good news. She said, "That's good. I hope you finish it because you don't seem to finish what you start."

Yet another crushing comment from her. Yes, in the past, I had tried twice to go back. And during the course, I'd dropped out. But both times my leaving had been for good reasons. The first time, my aunt lied to my mother and told her I was staying out as if I was doing something wrong. This prompted Mami to tell me she was no longer going to babysit the girls. The second time I tried to take classes, the school had a day care, which was great. But when I brought the girls, Natalie was not accepted because she needed to be potty-trained. My children and their care came before anything. That did not make me a quitter. It was just an adversity I had to face in life.

Here it was—the tactic of Satan at work again.

I went to tell my parents about my enrollment. They did not have much of a reaction. I found myself going back to thoughts of the one person who always had something positive to say. Yes, I called Julio.

He was ecstatic. He said, "Que buena noticia! Como me alegro de tu decisión a volver a la escuela a terminar tu educación. Cuenta conmigo para cualquier cosa que necesites" (What great news! How glad I am for you in your decision to go back to school and finish your education. Count on me for anything you need). He added, "Sé que no puedo llamarte cuando quiero, pero ¿permiteme tener tu dirección para poder escribirte? (I know that I can't call you whenever I want, but can I have your address so I can write to you)? We exchanged addresses and said goodbye.

One day, Pelegrino asked me why a certain amount of money was gone from the account. I told him I had given the church tithes. He was upset. He said we did not have money for giving tithes. He asked me for the debit card and said he did not want me touching his income. I needed to get a job.

I couldn't get a job now. That would interrupt the GED course I was enrolled in, a regular class from Monday through Friday. I couldn't get a job and quit now. Besides, this was God's direction for me during this time in my life. He had revealed it in the secret place.

A friend told me about a DUI company that was looking for someone to lead the Thursday night class. I went to an interview and was hired. They even paid for a training for me to be certified as a DUI consultant. It was not much, but I was able to give a tithe at church and get gas for my car to get to my parents, school, and work. God made those fifty dollars stretch to cover my needs. More importantly, I was able to give a tithe to God.

I no longer was able to buy groceries on my own. Pelegrino had to go with me and approve what I bought, and he paid at checkout. I needed a textbook for school. I asked if he could give me the money for it and he said no. Another day, while we were out buying groceries, I remembered that I was nearly out of my medication (Synthroid, 125 mcg for my hypothyroidism disorder). I only had two doses left. I asked him if we could go to pick up a refill of my medication and he said, "No, that's not in the budget."

Wow. I was speechless.

Here was another tactic from Satan—to create division and to kill and destroy our marriage but, more importantly, my walk with God. As in John 10:10, "The thief comes only to steal and kill and destroy; I have come that they may have life and have it to the full."

Not that I understood it at the time. What I saw and heard was my husband, who had pledged to love me for better or worse, rejecting my dreams and denying me any financial help to do anything other than what he felt was needed for the home. I had never denied him anything in our twenty plus years together. In fact, I would put myself last for him all the time. Yet, I could not count on him to pay for my medication refill.

I needed someone to talk to, but I no longer felt confident discussing my problems with my younger cousin's wife. The last few times I had, I'd left feeling worse than when I'd walked in. I was filled with a lot of painful emotions. I cried and wrote and, yes, I journaled. What I didn't realize I was doing all along was what Lori had mentioned to me at church that first day I attended with her. I just didn't know it was called journaling. But writing my thoughts down was the way I would handle my emotions.

As I was writing, I thought of Julio. I called him. As we talked, he learned of my needs and directed me to pray and not lose faith. That was deeply comforting. A couple days later, I received a letter from Julio. In it was a money order that covered the cost of the textbook. I broke down in tears. I called him the first chance I got to thank him for the gift.

Time went on, and I followed my dream of finishing school or at least getting my GED. Pelegrino started spending more and more time with his ex-brother-in-law. I did not see much of him. I stayed focused on school and my homework.

The class seemed simple enough to understand. I was actually enjoying it a lot, but I came across a stumbling block. No matter how sure I felt about what I learned that week and how sure I felt when taking the test on Friday, when papers were returned, I had a low grade—60 or lower—and I couldn't understand why.

One day, I got my paper back. It was worse than the previous week's. I could not understand this for the life of me. It reminded me of Arisely and how she'd always come home with a sad face on her paper. I was ready to quit. *I guess Pelegrino was right*, I told myself. *I'm not going to pass this GED course.* I walked to the phone booth during break to call Julio and give him the news that I was thinking of dropping out. I was failing to meet the requirements of an average grade point level; I was at failure level. I couldn't hold back the tears as he counseled me with positive claims about me as a person, using scripture to back it up.

As I was walking out of the phone booth drying my tears, a classmate stopped me. He asked what was wrong. At first, I hesitated to answer him, and responded. "I'm OK."

He asked again, "Really, what is wrong?"

I explained that, no matter how sure I was of the material, when I got my test, back the grade was lower than the one from the previous week. He listened, and as I was finishing my sentence, he went in his pocket, pulled out a business card, and handed it to me. "I know what's wrong," he said. "Look. I can't explain it. But take this card and make an appointment to see this doctor. Explain to her what you are experiencing, and she will give you the answer as to why you are experiencing what you're experiencing."

"Thank you!" I replied. "I will call first thing Monday and schedule an appointment."

Wow. I recalled Julio saying God would make a way—that I just needed to trust Him. Sure enough, this must be it. I would not lose anything by trying. When Monday morning came, I scheduled myself to see Dr. Stahnke.

That night, I went home and prayed. I said, "God you said I was supposed to use this time off work to go back to school and follow my dream of completing my education. I'm trusting that I understood you correctly. May this appointment be the answer—paving the way for me to be able to finish school."

I met with Dr. Stahnke; I explained my struggles to her. She explained to me that it sounded like some disability. But for her to be sure, I would have to be tested. I was tested and told my results would be given to me at my next appointment.

At my next appointment, Dr. Stahnke said, "I have your results, Carmen. You tested positive for learning disabilities. You have severe learning disabilities. They're so great that I'm surprised you've had the jobs you've held over the years. The strangest thing is that one would not be able to tell by meeting and conversing with you. You speak and present yourself very well considering your disabilities, especially since you have never been taught or treated for them."

I was devastated, to say the least. Dr. Stahnke assured me that I would be able to continue my GED course. She said, "I will give you a letter to give your teacher, which will allow the program to meet your needs and accommodate you in ways that will work toward your success. By law, you are entitled to get accommodations that fit your disability needs at school and in any workplace."

I will be forever grateful to my classmate Robert. He was sent by God to meet my need at the right time; so was Dr. Stahnke. She had the patience and poise to help me through that time and set me up for success. Julio was right. God did find a way for me to continue with the assignment. I didn't have an earthly parent to get me through that ordeal, but my Heavenly Father, Elohim, sent angels to come to my aid. To God be the glory.

Julio and I started getting close, although just by mail and phone calls. Regardless, our relationship was growing.

As I mentioned earlier, Pelegrino had started spending more and more time with his ex-brother-in-law. His use of alcohol increased, and so did his use of other substances. One day, he came in from his time with his ex-brother-in-law. I tried talking to him about his behavior, and we got into a heated argument. He stated in a loud, angry voice on his way toward the door, "I'm just going to end it all!"

Knowing what that meant (he was going to commit suicide), I ran to him and got a hold of his arm. "No stop!" I yelled back.

At that point it became a wrestling match. I tried to keep him from leaving, and he tried to get himself out the door. He pushed me against the wall with such force that it created a huge hole in the wall and twisted my wrist to the point I could not move it.

So much for attempts to stop him. He left and went back to his brother-in-law's apartment, and I stayed home crying and praying. The next day, I could not move my hand. It was swollen, and the pain was constant. I went to the clinic to have it looked at; the diagnosis was a sprained wrist. Dr. Czajkowski asked me how it happened and wanted me to call the authorities, but I declined. I was given a hand brace, medication, and instructions on how to care for the injury.

Pelegrino was not a rowdy person by nature. He had a calm and collected personality. He seldom initiated an argument. He became harsh and sometimes could be aggressive when I questioned him about certain things, like his use of drugs, or when I complained about the amount of time he spent out of the home. At times, he could become defensive and get loud, but it didn't happen often. I learned not to question him as much besides he ignored me very well. There wasn't a routine of us getting into these types of conflicts. I did not see a need to press charges.

At our next Bible talk meeting (which he had stopped attending), the group asked about my hand. I explained that we had gotten into an argument, and in the struggle, I'd hurt my wrist. I believe our Bible talk leader felt the need to address the incident and, being that Pelegrino did not answer his calls and he was no longer attending the group, he took it to our pastor. (Mike and Lori were no longer with us; they had moved to another state and were leading a church there.)

The following weekend, Pelegrino received a visit from our Bible talk leader and our new pastor. They questioned him about his lack of attendance and about the incident that had caused my injury. They told him he had compromised his relationship with God and needed to reconcile with Him. That meant he would have to be attentive at midweek and Bible talk and have his personal discipleship meeting with the person disciplining him. Pelegrino would not submit to that. Pastor told him, "Unfortunately, because you are choosing not to reconcile with God, I am forced to remove you from the roster until you do want to reconcile with God. You can attend Church, but your name will not be on the roster until your reconciliation with the Lord."

Pelegrino was crushed. He stopped going to church completely and indulged even more in his activities outside the house. I knew he was using hard drugs in addition to the alcohol. I never meant for this to happen. But there was no hiding the truth of how I'd hurt my wrist or his lack of attendance at midweek and Bible talk. Yes, I was glad the Bible Talk (small group) leader and our pastor had reached out to him. But I would have preferred another method of discipline than to see them remove him from the roster of the church. I also knew that we were to be held accountable for our behavior as disciples of Jesus Christ. As in 1 Corinthians 5:11, "But now I am writing to you that you must not associate with anyone who claims to be a brother or sister but is sexually immoral or greedy, an idolater or slanderer, a drunkard or swindler. Do not even eat with such people."

I felt bad for Pelegrino, but I could do nothing other than encourage him to come back to church. What I did not know or understand then was that those who are strong ought to bear with those who are weak. While, I understood that Pelegrino was not being submissive, they should have used a different approach in handling the issue of Pelegrino's shortcomings—as Jesus would have—especially since it was the first time he had walked away from grace:

> We who are strong ought to bear with the failings of the weak and not to please ourselves. / Each of us should please our neighbors for their good, to build them up. / For even Christ did not please himself but, as it is written: "The insults of those who insult you have fallen on me." / For everything that was written in the past was written to teach us, so that

through the endurance taught in the Scriptures and the encouragement they provide we might have hope.

May the God who gives endurance and encouragement give you the same attitude of mind toward each other that Christ Jesus had, / so that with one mind and one voice you may glorify the God and Father of our Lord Jesus Christ.(Romans 15:1–6)

I was attending a women's group called, "12 Steps for the Spouse of an Alcoholic." The book we were reading had an assignment to write about your life as far back as you could remember and share it with the class. *Oh no. I can't do that*, I thought to myself. At home, when I tried to think about the assignment I broke into tears. I tried for three days, but to no avail. I kept crying and could not get myself to write it down.

We read in Jeremiah 31:28, "'Just as I watched over them to uproot and tear down, and to overthrow, destroy and bring disaster, so I will watch over them to build and to plant,' declares the Lord."

I kept asking God to help me do this, to help me get better and not tear me up. Finally, on the fourth day, I started writing and finished before the next meeting.

At the meeting, some of the women read their memories. When it was my turn, I took a deep breath and exhaled. *Lord, please help me get through this*, I prayed in silence. Just as I asked, Abba God got me through the reading without breaking down. The women all clapped, saying, "Wow." Some were even wiping away their tears. Several of the women told me I should write a book; they seemed deeply moved. My intention for being in the group was to help myself deal with Pelegrino and his addiction. I just did not know how to help him get where he needed to be with God. I didn't want to share my life in public, which was what writing a memoir was. It meant sharing with the world about your life—all of it, the good and the bad. Why? What good would that serve?

It wasn't the first time I'd had heard, "You should write a book." My younger cousin's wife would say it often. Every time I came with one of my deep stories, she would say, "Girl, you should write a book. I know you can't spell and have poor grammar, but you should write a book. Maybe you can get a ghostwriter."

I would laugh and not take her seriously.

I was doing well in class. My grades started going up, and I was enjoying it all very much. Unfortunately, Mami was declining more and more. I was able to take her to and from doctor visits and test schedules and ensure she was getting the proper care without worrying about having to take off from work. It had been the same way when I was raising the girls. Whenever I needed to give them more of me, I ended up without a job. The sad part was that I really enjoyed working, and the second income was needed. We tended to struggle financially 60 percent of the time.

Mami was declining rapidly. The most recent diagnose was kidney failure from the medication she was taking for high blood pressure and rheumatoid arthritis. Her doctors started her on dialysis once a week. She hated getting the dialysis, and I hated it just as much as she did. She would be terribly weak. As she declined, it seriously tagged at my emotions. Yet I knew I could only do so much. The rest was in God's hands.

I was struggling with the emotional part of dealing with my parents' declining health; it was heartbreaking. I wished so desperately that I had a house big enough to have them with me, but that was not the case. As much as I tried, all my attempts were in vain. It was one of those prayers and door knocks that were not answered. I would call Julio periodically, and he always found the words to encourage me, along with scriptures that backed up his words.

I would go back and forth a couple times a day while finishing my GED course. Dad's food had to be done by 3:00 p.m.; that was the house rule. It was challenging me to the core. But I prayed. I talked with their home caregiver, and she agreed to start later in the day and leave at 3:30 p.m. so I could finish my GED course. That was such a blessing. Abba God was looking out for me again.

The end of the course finally arrived. We took our finals. And to Abba God's glory, I passed. Yes! I couldn't wait to tell Pelegrino; he was in for a shock. Sure enough, when I showed him my test results, he opened his eyes and said, "Wow, you did pass it."

I told him with excitement about the graduation and pointed out my GPA of 3.5. *Not bad for having learning disabilities*, I thought to myself as he looked at the grade again. "It's going to be a real graduation, babe, with cap and gown and all that."

He grinned and said, "Congratulations!" And he gave me a kiss.

All my girls and grandbabies came to the graduation. Unfortunately, the ones I really wanted there—Mami and Papi—were not able to attend.

I prayed, thanking God and asking Him for direction and to guide my next step. In that secret place, I heard, "Didn't you say you wanted to be a nurse? This is the time to do it."

I replied, "Yes, Lord, I did. And I will. Amen!"

During that time, there was a new commercial on TV for Everest College Medical Program. How perfect was that? I enrolled and was able to keep the same schedule I had with my parents. This was beyond my imagination. I had not seen all these blessings coming. I literally felt like a schoolgirl facing the most exciting time of her life, with her dreams coming true.

When God has something for you, no one can prevent it from happening:

- -I know that you can do all things; no purpose of yours can be thwarted. (Job 42:2)
- Look at the nations and watch—and be utterly amazed. For I am going to do something in your days that you would not believe, even if you were told. (Habakkuk 1:5)
- Yes, and from ancient days I am he. No one can deliver out of my hand. When I act, who can reverse it? (Isaiah 43:13)

During one of my visits to Mami and Papi's, I told my dad I had enrolled in a medical course and should be certified that following year as a medical assistant, "like a nurse," I added. He was excited about that one. That made me feel so proud of what I was doing.

I called Julio next; he was so excited too. He reassured me that, if there was anything I needed, I should not hesitate to ask him. That was a blessing to hear.

The one who was not a happy camper was Pelegrino. He said, "What? You already got the GED. What do you need to do that for? A job. That's what you need to get."

I told him, "I prayed about it. This has been a lifelong dream for me, and this is the time to do it. It will not be that much longer."

Mami became ill with frequent vomiting and diarrhea. She was so weak I had to call the fire department to help me carry her down the stairs. This became a ritual moving forward in her care. She was treated at the emergency room of St. Mary's Hospital. After several tests and a medical examination, she was admitted. There wasn't a complete diagnosis. But because of her blood test result and her weakness, the doctors had to do further tests—so I was told.

Mami had been in the hospital a few days and was not getting any better. I would sit with her and watch her turn into this helpless being—so contrary to her character throughout her life. She had always been a go-getter, independent and a servant at heart. The heartbreaking part for me was when she would ask me, with tears running down her face, "Porque nadie me viene a ver? Solo tu me quieres" (Why doesn't anyone come visit me? Only you love me).

My heart would shatter as I tried to explain that everyone did love her. It was only circumstances, distance, and other such complications that kept people away.

One day, I left for an hour, and when I came back, she had the marks of a cross in black on her forehead and around her neck and chest. I asked her why she had those marks. What did they mean? And she did not know. She just said, "No se" (I don't know).

I was very upset and called the nurse. The nurses delayed in coming to the room, and that only enraged me. So, I walked to the nurses' station and questioned the markings in a harsh tone. They tried to calm me down, but I demanded to speak to the head supervisor. They reassured me that someone would come and talk with me.

It felt like forever. A young doctor walked in the room, and I got up immediately. He introduced himself, and I responded by introducing myself. I asked about the markings and why they were there. He blurted out, "They are the markings to start the radiation for the cancer treatment."

Mami jumped at that instantly. "Cancer? Yo, tengo cancer?" (Cancer? I have cancer?)

"No, Mami, no tiene cancer. Le explico ahora" (No, Mom, you do not have cancer. I will explain in a moment).

I made a gesture to indicate that the doctor shouldn't talk about it in front of her. We walked outside the room, and he explained to me that she had been diagnosed with stage 4 multiple myeloma, and they would start her on radiation to treat it. I was appalled that they had diagnosed her and decided on a treatment plan without notifying me, her power of attorney. Poor Mami was sitting there without a clue as to what was going on, and I let him know that in a stern voice. The doctor apologized and tried to give me words of comfort about what they were doing. I was not feeling it at all. But what could I do? Had I known what I know today—that the radiation would not help her in any way—I would not have agreed to this treatment.

Mami's doctors started her on the radiation. A few days later, she was discharged, with an order of ongoing radiation once a week. This was absurd. But I tried to think positively and tried to trust that the doctors knew what they were doing. Doing so was very hard, since it was the medication she'd been given that had caused her kidneys to fail in the first place. As a result, she was on dialysis. And now this radiation? I was speechless and heartbroken for Mami. Her greatest fear had come true. She had always feared cancer and kept her doctor visits regular to make sure she was doing what she could to prevent it, or at least get an early detection. This was not the case. Her cancer was in stage four.

One day, I arrived to pick her up for her appointment. She normally was ready at the door, but this time Papi answered it. She was in her room not fully dressed, and sweat was pouring down her forehead and neck. Her speech was very slow. The apartment was extremely hot; the temperature outside was a hundred degrees that day. I asked why it was so hot in the apartment. She said my dad would not let her turn on the air conditioner; he wanted to avoid the high electric bill. I started trying to help her get dressed and asked her what was wrong. Why wasn't she ready as usual? She couldn't explain it and suddenly fell on the bed. I called 9-1-1 immediately.

The paramedics arrived and took her to the nearest hospital. I went in with her. As I waited for her to be treated, I debated whether I should call El and Lou or wait. Mami was not looking good. I saw her struggling and moaning. I called the nurse twice before I got an answer from her, stating she would be there in a minute. Suddenly, Mami passed out. I yelled, and the staff came running. Checking her, they called out, "Code blue."

I became very nervous and anxious. I started dialing my siblings. I could not believe this was all happening. But it was. *I'm not prepared for this*, I kept thinking. All I could do at this point was cry and pray, pray and cry.

After a number of hours, the doctors finally came back with the diagnosis. She'd had a small stroke and mini heart attack. She was admitted to the hospital. She was there for a few days. El, Lou, Jose, and Elsa came by.

After some days, the doctors let us know there was nothing else they could do for her. They were going to release her. She would be going home. Hospice care was ordered, and she was sent home.

Wow. They placed the order and scheduled the hospice care team to go to the home and prepare the space before she was discharged. Mami was sent home, and Lou stayed for a few days. Then it was time for Lou to go home and pick up Freddy and the boys, hoping they would get back before the inevitable would happen. Pelegrino, too, decided to leave. I tried to get him to stay with me, but he declined. He said he would be back first thing in the morning. Sadly, I said, "OK." Papi called it a day and went to bed.

There I was, sitting next to Mami's bed, with soft worship music playing and the Bible on my lap. I started talking to her in a low, soft voice. "Mami, Lourdes tuvo que irse a la casa a recoger a Freddy y los nenes, Pelegrino fue a dormir un poco y Papi se fue a la cama. Le voy a leer algunos Salmos y espero que recibas Su paz. Pero no me voy, estaré aquí" (Mami, Lourdes had to go home to pick up Freddy and the boys, Pelegrino went to get some sleep, and Papi went to bed. I am going to read you some Psalms and I hope you receive His peace. But I am not leaving. I will be right here). I read Psalm 23 and others.

The nurse who was assigned to her care explained to me that, when I saw her fingernails turn completely white, it would mean she was gone.

I said, "OK. Thank you."

As I held her left hand and read to her, I paused and prayed, "Father God, here she is. Thank you for the time you have allowed her to stay with us, with me. She has suffered a lot. I don't want her to go, but if she is going to keep suffering, take her home. I cried silently and looked at her often and read the Psalms out loud to her. At one point, I stopped reading. I was admiring her face as she took her last breath. I felt she took part of my soul with her. I felt her hand become relaxed in mine. I looked at her fingernails, and for sure, they were all white on both hands. I called the nurse into the room. "She is gone."

The nurse examined her, looked at the time, and then confirmed that she had passed.

The nurse asked me to help get the tubes out of her nose and stomach and clean her around the waist. I did. When I was done, I sat next to her and started calling everyone, one by one. What truly broke my heart was walking into Papi's room, waking him up, and giving him the worst news ever. He was crushed. Pelegrino got there in no time. When I opened the door, he flew into her room and threw himself on her and wept like a baby.

I was stronger than I could have ever imagined. Eliberto and Lou paid for all the funeral and burial arrangements. It was a beautiful turn out. After it was all over at home, I wailed like a baby. And this was what came out after the wailing:

Felicita Cartagena Acevedo Seguinot
April 3, 1932 to August 25, 2007

*Cuando era una niña pequeña, la seguí
dondequiera que iba, no importa qué tan
lejos, la sorprendería mi corazón intrépido.
la capturé en mente, fotos,
canción y espíritu.
La compartí con los demás, estaba
seguro de que nunca me dejaría al
menos donde no pudiera alcanzarle.
Observé cada uno de sus pasos,
estudié su estado de ánimo.
Oré por su crecimiento e imité su fuerza
espiritual y pasión por Yahveh El Yo Soy.
Escuché su llanto y sentí el dolor
de sus lágrimas mientras le veía
alejarse lentamente y convertirse
en una niña pequeño sin saberlo.
La necesitaba desesperadamente,
nunca dije una palabra.
Miedo de herir su tierno y frágil
corazón que parecía estar sufriendo
eternamente sin restricciones.
Nunca pensé que me dejarías,
pero tuve que dejarla ir.
Quería curar tu dolor, no había
nada que pudiera hacer.*

Se llevo una parte de mí con usted,
senti mi alma tierna mientras
exhalas su último aliento.
Lamento no haberle dicho nunca
lo mucho que la necesitaba.
Necesitaba ser fuerte. Cómo la
extraño Mami Desearia poder
seguirte Anhelo ver tu cara.
Me dice que todavía no estoy lista.
¿Por qué no puedo pregunto?
Un día sé que la veré y me uniré a
usted una vez más mientras alabamos
y glorificamos Su nombre Aleluya,
Aleluya, Aleluya, al Rey de Reyes, nuestro
Señor y Salvador Jesús es su nombre.

This reads in English:

When I was a little girl, I followed you
wherever you would go, no matter how far;
you would be amazed at my fearless heart.
I captured you in mind, photos, song,
and spirit. I shared you with others.
I was sure you would never leave
me, at least not to go somewhere
I could not reach you.
I watched your every step,
studied your frame of mind.

*I prayed for your growth and
imitated your spiritual strength and
passion for Yahweh the I am.
I listened to you cry and felt the
pain of your tears as I watched you
slowly slip away and turn into a
little child, not knowing it to be so.
I needed you desperately. I
never said a word.
I was afraid to hurt your tender,
fragile heart that seemed to be
forever hurting without restrain.
I never thought you would leave
me, but I had to let you go.
I wanted to heal your pain. There
was nothing I could do.
You took a part of me with you. I felt my
soul tear as you breathed your last breath.
I am sorry I never told you how much I
needed you. I needed to be strong. How I
miss you, Mami. I wish I could follow you.
I long to see your face. He tells me, "Not
yet. You're not ready." Why not? may I ask.
One day, I know I will see you and join
you once again as we praise and glorify
His name. Hallelujah. Hallelujah.
Hallelujah to the King of Kings, our
Lord and Savior Jesus is his name.*

MOVING FORWARD
IN GRATITUDE

I took Mami's passing, this new stage of life, as all the more reason to focus on getting certified as a medical assistant. The experience I'd had with Mami had not been a good one. There were a lot of elderly people who needed people who truly cared about them and didn't see them as a number, especially if they were Hispanic and didn't know the language to defend themselves.

I had a list of books to purchase, and I knew Pelegrino was not going to give me the money to purchase them. I prayed for God to give me the resources to purchase the books. Sure enough, I received a letter from Julio, and in it was a money order that covered the cost of the books. I had not asked for it. I had not so much as mentioned my need. I knew this was God answering my prayer. But it also stirred up emotions that were difficult to handle.

In my gratefulness, I wrote:

No Se

*No sé por qué nuestro encuentro en
un tiempo tan tormentoso para mí.
No se como el amor que un día
me prometiste, lo pude perder.
Y luego llegar a mí 23 años después,
sin yo poder responder.*

No sé el porqué de mis desvelos,
por algo que sé que no debe ser.
¿Sera la espina que no puedo arrancar
Que me lleva de rodillas a Dios y
de su gracia sostener mi sed.
No sé cómo pensar ¿En qué? Si todo se
me va. Todo se me queda en blanco un
vacío, siento que voy a enloquecer.
No sé qué pasa con mi alma que pierde
la calma cuando pienso que te puedo
perder. ¿Sera mis temores, mi poca fe?
No sé porque tengo que escoger en una
situación que los tres vamos a perder.
No se. Parece que se hubieran secado mis
lágrimas, esto no puede ser después de
tanto tiempo y no me puedo contener.
El llanto oprima mi alma el
Corazón quisiera desvanecer.
Es cierto, todavía siento el dolor de
amarte y sé que no puede ser.
No se.
No sé.

I'll share the English translation:

I Don't Know

I don't know why our meeting came
at such a stormy time for me.

*I don't know how I could have lost
the love you promised me one day.
And now it has reached me
twenty-three years later, without
me being able to respond.
I don't know the reason for my
sleeplessness, over something
I know shouldn't be.
Is it the thorn that I can't pull
out, that brings me to my knees
before God quenches my thirst?
I don't know how to think. Of what?
Everything escapes me. Everything
leaves me blank, an emptiness.
I feel like I'm going insane.
I don't know what happens to my soul that
loses its calm at the thought that I may
lose you. Can it be my fears, my little faith?
I don't know why I must choose in a
situation where all three will lose.
I don't know. It seems by now my
tears would have dried up.
This can't be. After so long,
I can't contain myself.
Crying weighs down my soul. My
heart would like to fade away.
I still feel the pain of loving
you. Yet I know it can't be.
I do not know.
I do not know.*

MY CHURCH FAMILY

T ime went on. I was struggling a bit with the studies, and a bit of fear was trying to creep in. I kept praying and studying. At the same time, the strain of Pelegrino's selfishness and absence was pulling at me. I still had to submit to him and to serve him completely. But he was giving very little of himself to our relationship. He acted more like a roommate than a husband.

In the early part of spring, Annette came over with the boys. That was always a treat. Josiah asked me, "Are we going to Easter Sunday service together?"

I replied, "I don't know. Ask Grandpa."

Josiah addressed the question to Pelegrino. "Grandpa, are we going to Easter Sunday service together?"

"Yes, Josiah, we are," Pelegrino answered him.

Awesome! That was totally God. No one had mentioned the service to Josiah. It had come straight from his little heart.

Resurrection Sunday arrived. We all got together and went to church together as was custom. The service was being held at the UIC south building. When we arrived, we were told the building was at fully capacity, and no one else was allowed in. Pelegrino smiled, looked at me, and said, "See, but I did come."

I replied, "No. We are not missing service today. One of the nurses at St. Mary's Hospital told me her church had service across the street at the Roberto Clemente High School. We can go there."

All the kids said, "Yay!"

We headed to Roberto Clemente High School. When we got

215

there, Pelegrino went in to check to see if the service had started. There was a service running, but another one started in the next half hour. I looked at all the kids and said, "We are waiting for the next service."

They all yelled, "Yes."

The service ended, and the next one started shortly after. We took our seats, and I told Pelegrino, "See, babe. Jesus wanted us to have service today with the kids."

He replied, "Yeah, OK."

The service was amazing. From the pulpit, it was announced that a men's retreat was coming up. And Pelegrino said, "I'm going. Yup. I'm going to attend." As we were leaving, he ran into a few buddies from his childhood/neighborhood. All the kids enjoyed the service too.

Pelegrino added, "This is where we will be attending from now on."

That was taking it a bit too far. "What?" I said. "No. You can go to the men's retreat. But that doesn't mean we have to change our place of service. We will talk about it later at home."

When we got home, we went back and forth a bit. And then I took it to God. I could not understand why we had to change our place of worship. As I prayed about it, I was reminded that the important thing was that we had a place of worship, and I should respect Pelegrino's desire to start the process of reconciling with God, even if it meant going to a new church. After all, that was better than not attending at all. I also remembered a sermon—Mike's teaching on how we are not to follow a man but, rather, the Holy Spirit. If the service was out of the Bible, then the Holy Spirit was the one leading. I was also reminded about my prayers for Humboldt Park to have a church like CCOC. Could this be that church?

We started attending New Life Covenant. the Holy Spirit was definitely speaking through Pastor Wilfredo de Jesus, known as Pastor Choco.

Pelegrino attended the men's retreat and came back fired up. "Yes, this is our new place of worship. This is where I belong." He said it with certainty in his voice and joy in his eyes. We learned that his cousin, Pastor Lisette Vega, also attended New Life. Talk about a small world. (New Life was in the heart of Humboldt Park, where they'd both grown up.)

I was not a happy camper in total. I missed my church family and my regular Bible talk group and other forms of fellowship I'd enjoyed there. But I needed to be humble and submissive. The girls started attending sporadically, and I kept waiting for God's confirmation that this was where He wanted us to attend.

About six months into our attendance, our landlord told me, "Carmen, don't let Pelegrino distance you from God just because he is walking away from grace."

I responded, "Just because I'm no longer attending CCOC doesn't mean I am walking away from God. I am attending church and having my quiet time with God daily. But thank you."

Pelegrino's hanging out with Ralph did not cease. Instead, it increased. I was tired of it. About a year after that first encounter at the men's retreat and our attending New Life, Pelegrino stopped attending regularly. The girls, too, stopped attending regularly due to the distance and what they were all dealing with. They, too, had compromised their walk with God; it was different from what it used to be, at our encounter with Jesus in 1999.

I would arrive at church and wait for one of them to walk in with the kids. I ached that Pelegrino was not standing next to me. I would cry through worship and would ask God, *Why? Why have they all stop coming? Where is my family God?* For me and my household will serve the Lord. So, where were they?

Crying and feeling the deep pain of abandonment I heard, "Open your eyes and look around."

So, I opened my eyes and looked around.

"This is your family," I heard Him say.

I sobbed all the more, saying, *OK, Lord, because you say so.*

To this day, I can still feel the intense emotion of that moment. I had just died to my longing for my old church and my family. I understood this was where God wanted me to be. May it be Your will and not mine. I was unaware that there was so much more ahead I would have to endure—that I would have to die to myself—as I continued this walk of everlasting life.

I continued reading my *In Touch* daily devotional and viewing Dr. Stanley and Joyce Meyers on TV whenever possible. And I kept my commitment to reading the Word—at least a chapter a day or the guide in Dr. Stanley's devotional booklet. And I continued getting discipled from the pulpit weekly by Pastor Choco. The Holy Spirit was using him greatly to peel off those layers.

A JAIL CELL WITHOUT BARS:
THE PASSION OF THE PAST

I received the conviction to write to Julio:

Agusto 21, 2008

Querido Amor mío,
Dios quiera al llegar está a tus manos te encuentres
lleno de gozo, paz, amor, y gozando de perfecta salud
física, mental y espiritual. De mi te diré que gozando
en el Espíritu y permitiendo que se manifieste en mi
un día a la vez.

No te olvido, a lo contrario ha sido tu quien
Dios uso más que nada ni nadie para quebrantarme
y llevarme más cerca de Él. También creo que tenías
razón cuando dijiste un día que avías llegado para
ayudarme a cumplir con el estudio; con tu apoyo a
podido terminar la escuela, tener una carrera, una
profesión. 'También fuiste la persona necesaria para
estar durante el tiempo que tuve que luchar con Mami
y lo último de su vida. Dios lo ha designado así, El
sabrá el porqué.

Si te sigo amando. Si pienso en ciertas cosas, y si
me llegan a la mente cambio el pensamiento al Señor.
Ya sé que no quieres ser mi amigo. Y sinceramente
yo no podría tenerte como un amigo sin llegar a mi

mente otras maneras de tenerte. Así es que queda establecido que no seremos amigos almeno que Dios lo quiera así

Te deseo todo lo mejor del mundo y más. La otra noche te escribí una carta a puno y no te la e mandado, te la incluyo con esta. También te envió el CD de Sy Rogers el predicador que Dios cambio su vida de homosexual. Te lo compre en español para que tú también lo oigas y puedas comprender todo lo que dice sin dificultad, así puedes dialogar con J. Yo niego lo que J reclama y seguiré orando por él.

Julio, mi amor, te amo y sé que tú también me llegaste amar. Le doy gracias a Dios que, aunque me ha quebrantado en esto por lo menos me dio un deseo de mi corazón; que tú me amaras tal como yo te he amado. Perdóname, amor mío, pero si se lo pedí hace años y después de 23 años me lo concedió. Viví sintiendo tu amor por 5 años. Viví 5 años sintiéndome amada y valorada, Gracias amor mío por ser el ser que Dios ha usado en mi vida para tantas cosas hermosas y profundas. No en las condiciones que hubiese querido, porque emo sufridos tanto, pero sí, me lo concedió.

Que Dios te bendiga mucho y te prospere en todas tus cosas tal como prospera tu alma en Cristo Jesús. Amen!!!! Te amo.

August 21, 2008

My dear love,
God willing, when you receive this letter in your hands, may you find yourself full of joy, peace, and love and enjoying perfect physical, mental and spiritual health. As for myself, I'm joyfully in the Holy Spirit and allowing Him to manifest Himself in me one day at a time.

I do not forget you. On the contrary, it was you who God used more than anything or anyone to break me and bring me closer to Him. I also think you were right when you said one day that you had arrived to help me complete my education. With your support, I have been able to finish school and have a career, a profession. You were also the person I needed to be near me during the time I had to fight for Mami and the last of her life. God has designated it to be so. Only He knows the why.

Yes, I still love you. If I think about certain things, and if they come to mind, I change my thoughts toward the Lord. I know you don't want to be my friend. And honestly, I couldn't have you as a friend without thinking of other ways to have you. So, it is established that we will not be friends unless God wants it that way.

I wish you all the best in the world and more. The other night, I wrote you a handwritten letter, and I haven't sent it to you. I'm including it with this one. I'm also sending you the CD of Sy Rogers, the preacher whose homosexual life God changed. I bought it for you in Spanish so you can also hear it and understand everything he says without difficulty and so you can have a dialogue with J. I deny what J claims, and I will continue to pray for him.

Julio, my love, I love you. And I know you also came to love me. I thank God that, although he has broken me in this, at least he gave me a desire of my heart—that you would love me as I have loved you. Forgive me, my love, but I asked God years ago, and after twenty-three years He has granted my desire. I've lived feeling your love for five years. I've lived five years feeling loved and valued. Thank you, my love, for being the being God has used in my life for so many beautiful and profound things. It hasn't been in the conditions I would have wanted—because we have suffered so much—but yes, He granted my desire.

May God bless you very much and prosper you in all your things just as your soul prospers in Christ Jesus. Amen! Love you.

Then I was inspired to journal my emotions:

Una Cárcel Sin Rejas

Me hayo en una cárcel sin rejas. Vivo en el pasado con una pasión por vivir amar y ser amada.

Entregarme en total y recibir a cambio la misma entrega. Desde niña supe de Jesús, crei. Viviendo una vida de pruebas, maltrato, tomentos, torbellinos, ataduras que confunde a la realidad. Una verdad tan cerca y tan simple que se confunde fácilmente. Tan bella y calmante que invita a querer conocer. Pero me hayo en una cárcel sin rejas; que tu no quisieras conocer.

Me extendieron una invitación una tarde, acepte y hoy puedo decir; estoy empezando a conocer a Jesús. Cuando más joven creia en El, y hoy tengo la dicha de diariamente conocerle un poco más. No esperaba las tormentas, batallas, ni los tropiezos que he tenido que pelear; pues estoy en una cárcel sin rejas. ¡El enemigo detrás, y yo adelante llamando en El nombre del Señor "Jesús Ayudame!"

Cuanto no diera yo por poder estar donde estás. Con El Padre alabando y glorificando Su nombre. Haya donde no hay llanto y el cielo no necesita sol, ni luna que lo alumbre pues estas Tu y El; gozando de las alabanzas de los santos y los ángeles celestiales. Pero me dicen que no.

Que me sostenga de Su gracia y pelee la batalla de la 'Fe. O, como vivo en una cárcel sin rejas.

Como quisiera poder correr, te amo Señor y aquí me quedare. Denme fuerza, enciende el fuego del Espíritu Santo que vive en mí y ayúdame a sentir la libertad que me diste cuando me entregue y bauticé.

En El Nombre de Jesús,
Amen!

La cárcel es mi mente y cuerpo que combaten diariamente por alimentar sus deseos de los aperitivos que el mundo le ofrece. Colosenses 3:1-4 se dice, "Si pues, habéis resucitado con Cristo, buscadlas cosas de arriba, donde esta Cristo sentado a la mano derecha de Dios. Poned la mirada en las cosas del cielo, no en las de la tierra. Porque habéis muerto, y vuestra vida está escondida con Cristo en Dios. Cuando Cristo, se manifieste, entonces vosotros también seréis manifestados con El en gloria."

Here is the translation of my journal entry:

A Jail Cell without Bars

I find myself in a jail without bars. I'm living in the past, with a passion to love and be loved and to give myself totally and receive the same submission. At a very early age, I heard of Jesus and believed. Living a life of trial, abuse, thunderstorms, hurricanes, and entanglements can be confusing to reality. A truth so close and simple can be easily confused. So beautiful and relaxing, it invites you to get to know it. But I find myself in a jail cell without bars that you wouldn't want to be acquainted with.

I was extended an invitation. I accepted. And today, I can say I am starting to know Jesus. When I was young, I believed in Him. Today, I have the faith to know Him a little more daily. I didn't expect the storms, the struggles, or the stuff I've had to battle. Well, I'm in a jail cell without bars. The enemy is trailing behind, and I am running up ahead calling on the Lord, "Jesus, help me."

What would I not give to be where You are? With the Father, praising and glorifying His name? There, where there is no crying and the sky doesn't need the sun or the moon to give it light, for it has You and Him, rejoicing from the praises of the saints and angels?

But I hear no. I am told, "My grace is sufficient for you; fight the good battle of faith."

Oh, how I live in a jail cell without bars. How I would love to be able to run away and hide (there is nowhere to hide). I love You, Lord, and here I will stay. Give me strength. Light up the fire of the Holy Spirit that lives within me. And help me feel the freedom You gave me when I was baptized.

The jail cell is my mind and body in a daily battle as I deny my flesh the appetites the world generously offers throughout each moment of every day.

Colossians 3:1-4 says, "Since, then, you have been raised with Christ, set your hearts on things above, where Christ is seated at the right hand of the Father. Set your minds on things above not on earthly things. For you died, and your life is now hidden with Christ in God. When Christ, who is your life, appears, then you also will appear with Him in glory."

CONTEMPLATING OPPORTUNITIES, JOYS, AND LACK

It was getting closer to the completion of the medical assistant course. I needed to find a place to start my externship. I prayed, "Abba God Almighty, holy be your name. I need to do an externship in order to get certified. But I am clueless where at. Please reveal to me where I am to do my externship. And may it be the same place that hires me at my completion. Amen!"

I also needed to get all my vaccines in and a physical done. I scheduled myself for the physical with the clinic Pelegrino would attend and where I'd had the girls treated while they were at home. I was sent to the lab to get lab work done. As I was leaving, I felt a tug in my heart telling me to ask about the possibility of doing my externship at that location.

The young lady said, "Sure, people can do externships here." She handed me a business card and asked me to call and speak to Steve Pritt. "He is the manager and will explain the process to you."

"Thank you!" I said. I was so excited.

I did not waste any time. I called Steve. He gave me an appointment to meet with him. I met with Steve, and he explained everything to me and gave me a starting date. I called Julio to tell him the great news. He was so excited for me.

On the first day of my externship, they had me start in the lab. I recall the young lady I would be sitting with, said, "I'm going to let you know right now. You either know what you are doing, or you don't. Either way, you are not getting any instructions from me."

OK, that was strong and straightforward. It was abundantly clear that I was not going to get any type of assistance from her.

★★★

Two weeks into my externship, Steve asked to see me in his office. He said, "I have to level with you. I know it's not easy working with the staff here, but you are doing a great job. I wanted to ask if you would consider working here at the end of your externship?" He added, "I have to level with you. I didn't hire you because of your great achievements or the school you attend or because you're bilingual. I took you on because of what you have. I want what you have here in this clinic."

"I don't understand," I replied. "There is a glow about you. I want that loving nature to rub off here at Irving and Western. With that being said, will you accept my offer? You can take this time during your externship to think about it because, in fact, I don't have a position available. But if you say yes, I will call HR and get a spot open for you."

I didn't have to think about it. I knew this was from God, just as I had asked Him. "Yes," I said, "yes."

Wow. How good was God? Everything was going just as I'd prayed for. You are faithful Abba God, as You say in Your word: "This is the confidence we have in approaching God: that if we ask anything according to his will, he hears us. / And if we know that he hears us—whatever we ask—we know that we have what we asked of him" (1 John 5:14–15).

The Holy Spirit was talking through Pastor Choco on Sundays. I was in a battle. But I had Jesus right there holding me up. In the beginning of the new year, Pastor Choco would have a theme for that year. This next year was stand. We were called to stand. I understood that to mean stand in the new location of worship, stand in our marriage, and stand in the place I was at in all areas of my life. I was to stand on the Word of God to carry me through.

I was given the opportunity to do my externship at the first place I'd inquired about it, and I was hired at the same facility. This was totally God. The manager was very open and honest with me. He also gave me a piece of advice. "If you don't want something known about you, don't share the information with anyone here, because it will spread. You do what you've been doing so far. Triage the patients, treat them as if they were your parents just as you've been doing, and you will be fine."

There are so many stories I can share about the blessing of spiritual growth while working at this health care facility, but I will stop here for now. Sad to say Steve left the company about four to six months after my hired date.

Pelegrino was happy that he no longer had to carry the entire financial obligation. But I saw very little of him. I was working full-time. So was he. Other than sleeping and getting himself bathed and dressed, he spent little to no time at home.

This was not what I'd had in mind when I got married. I believed God's Word about marriage being the one ministry that is the reflection of God and His bride the church:

- That is why a man leaves his father and mother and is united to his wife, and they become one flesh. (Genesis 2:24)
- He who finds a wife finds what is good and receives favor from the Lord. Proverbs (18:22)
- Husbands, love your wives, just as Christ loved the church and gave himself up for her / to make her holy, cleansing her by the washing with water through the word, / and to present her to himself as a radiant church, without stain or wrinkle or any other blemish, but holy and blameless. / In this same way, husband's ought to love their wives as their own bodies. He who loves his wife loves himself. / After all, no one ever hated their own body, but they feed and care for their body, just as Christ does the church— / for we are members of

his body. / "For this reason a man will leave his father and mother and be united to his wife, and the two will become one flesh." / This is a profound mystery—but I am talking about Christ and the church. (Ephesians 5:25–32)

On a good note, which is very important, Pelegrino did help me take care of my parents. He took them to do their errands if I was at work, since I worked weekends. This was where it can get difficult. I knew Pelegrino had a good heart, but his priorities were all wrong. He needed to learn how to prioritize in the proper order—God, wife, others.

This weighed heavily on my heart. There was so much to process all the time. But the one thing that kept me struggling was Pelegrino's reluctance to spend time with me. We rarely did things together to build on our relationship. It seemed to be one-sided. It was all about what he wanted and when he wanted it. The way things were dealt with after a big blowup was by making up—which was not really dealing with the issue but, rather, more like sweeping it under the rug. He would say, "I'm sorry." We'd kiss and make up, and he'd refuse to hear me out about a solution. How could I help him see where he was lacking if he kept blocking me out when I tried to explain it to him?

He had no clue about what marriage was all about. Yet he did have the tools to having a healthy marriage, God's Word. Why do two people get together to begin with? It isn't just about the sex for sure; that's only one reason. Becoming one pertains to a lot more than just sex:

Two are better than one, because they have a good return for their labor:

If either of them falls down, one can help the other up. But pity anyone who falls and has no one to help them up.

Also, if two lie down together, they will keep warm. But how can one keep warm alone?

Though one may be overpowered, two can defend themselves. A cord of three strands is not quickly broken. (Ecclesiastes 4:9–12)

True, Pelegrino did not have a great role model to go by in his upbringing. But there were so many resources to get help on the topic nowadays. I thought that we would grow up together and learn to be that *one* we were called to be. But I was very wrong—I did not know his true thoughts. He had nothing in mind when he said I do but sex and a title; this was what he had demonstrated.

I often wrote to him when I had something of great importance pressing on my heart, since it was hard to get him to have a conversation with me about such things. Normally, he'd wave his hand at me, saying, "I don't want to hear it."

On one of those occasions when I felt utterly fed up, I wrote:

March 19, 1997

Pelegrino,
You want to know what is wrong? Well, I don't tell you because I know that we will start to argue, and I no longer want to play this little game of fight and make up.

You and I both know we see things in a completely different way when it comes to how to share our lives and the purpose of it. How things we do affect each other and the kids is something you don't seem to have any concern about, and I fear that you may never have it. If you do, you really have a negative way of showing it. So, I'd rather just leave you be and continue to look for my purpose in life. At the time, it doesn't look like you are part of it.

Ari and Nat are on the way, real close to that age where we don't have to play Mom and Dad, the family game. And that is all we really have in common, our kids. Even about that, we don't agree. We differ greatly on their upbringing. So, what is really left? Pleasures—socially, having fun or having sex. We do very well without each other, so that closes that.

I am not going to sit around and wait to find my purpose in life just to wake up one day too old or sick to do anything about it.

You don't have to do or say anything. Your ways and lifestyle are, after seventeen years, very clear. And that's OK for you.

Me, well my priority in life and goal has been to raise my children to the best of my ability, giving them a loving, safe, and nurturing parent and home. Well, I'm just about done, and I have to start setting other goals for myself. I have to find a purpose in life other than being a mom and then go after it.

So, there is really nothing to talk about. We do very well alone. You do your thing, and I do mine. When we are around the kids or other people, we act like we are really a happy couple. We do put on a good show. Don't we?

★★★

Sometime later, I wrote to myself, which I did periodically.

Hi thoughts!
Here I am, once again. Just why? I don't understand any more. I feel so far, so very far away. Could it be that I would like to be away, in a place I don't know, around people who are complete strangers to me and I to them?

I have a need I myself don't understand. I want to scream, but I can't. I want to run, but I don't have anywhere to go. I want to sleep and not wake up.

It's been so long since I gave myself any thought. I don't even know what I want or need. They need me. Why bother?

★★★

I was focusing on the things that hurt me. Yet there was so much I had that I did enjoy, and took pleasure in.

There was the whole concept of our home, the upkeeping of it, and the raising of our daughters. There was caring for my parents. And there were my several places of employment. I had worked in so many different fields, despite not having an education. That was a huge thing to be joyful about. So was serving others and spending time with my family members whenever that was possible. All of this was a joy for me. What plagued me was the severe lack of intimacy with my husband. It was an aspiration I treasured but simply didn't have.

This was how I'd felt and thought right before Jesus had come after me in that parking lot at Jewel's in 1999. Thinking back helped me understand the here and now. I did not know then that God already knew all of this. He knew all the adversity, storms, valleys, seasons, and trials—especially the lack of intimacy with my husband—all of which were part of the plan for my life, to get me where I needed to be.

What I did know at this point was that I had a new beginning. I was an empty nester. As painful as it was, it opened the doors for my childhood dreams of becoming a nurse. The dream I'd told Papi when I was nine had come true.

I continued working, caring for Papi as I'd promised Mami I would, and getting myself plugged in at church. I registered for the membership class and became a member. Shortly after that, I registered for the two-year School of Ministry course. And before the two years were up, I registered for the Deacon Ministry class.

LOSING PAPI

S adly, Papi's health was declining.

During a regular check-in on Papi, I arrived, and he told me he had been vomiting and had diarrhea all night, and his pain was ceaseless. He looked drained and fatigued. I asked if he had taken something, and he said he had taken some Pepto-Bismol. I put my things down and started getting his meal ready. I figured the Pepto-Bismol would take care of his diarrhea, and the food would take care of the fatigue.

After a few minutes, I came back into the living room, and he was out. It looked like when we pass out when having a cataplexy attack, but no one had made him laugh. I tried talking to him, but he was nonresponsive. I called 9-1-1. When the emergency responders arrived, they found his glucose level was critically low. They took him to the hospital, where he was treated to bring his glucose levels back up, and all kinds of test were started immediately.

The diagnosis was heart failure. Papi had a weak heart. His heart was working at 25 percent. In addition to diabetes and blood pressure issues, he was treated for heart failure. It shouldn't have come as a surprise, but it did. He was treated at the hospital for about a week and released.

By this time, I was already working at the clinic. The first thing I did when getting him home was schedule a follow-up appointment with Dr. Arana, a great Hispanic PCP we had on staff, who I worked with. The appointment was scheduled for a couple of days later that same week.

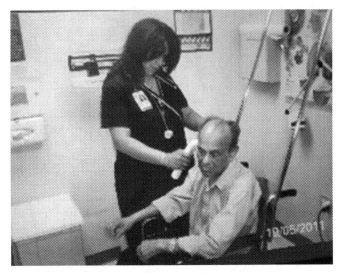

Here I am checking my dad's temperature.

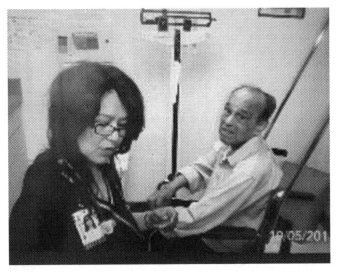

Here I am taking my dad's pulse.

On the appointment date, Pelegrino brought Papi in, and I had the honor to triage him before he saw Dr. Arana. I could not believe I was blessed to see my dream come true. I hadn't become an RN, but I was a great medical assistant. To God be the glory! I had the honor to triage Papi and put to practice my skills for him to witness.

When the day ended, I met with Dr. Arana. I told him about

Papi's cookies he kept on the kitchen counter and told him how many he had daily. I wanted to know if I should take away the cookies. Dr. Arana gave me the complete diagnoses of all the test the hospital had done and what he'd seen as he examined Papi. He ended by saying, "Let your dad have as many cookies as he wants. Give him a good quality of life while you still have him. His heart is not working. In fact, it is declining in function. Let him enjoy whatever he wants with what's left of his life."

Wow. This was a tough pill to swallow. I knew Papi would reach the end stages of life at some point, but I was not ready to hear the end was that near now.

About a month later, I graduated from the School of Ministry (SOM). Our class chanted, "SOM, Class of 2011," every time we saw each other. This was by far my greatest accomplishment; I was on fire for Abba God, and so many things were being revealed to me. A few months later, I completed the deacon class and was appointed a deacon at NLC. How could I be so fired up when Papi was so fragile? Yet, it was what got me through the heartache of Papi's health declining when it did. Pray, study, and pray some more.

A couple months passed. The caregiver called and told me Papi wasn't doing so good. The pain was back. I took him to the hospital, and his doctors kept him there for a couple of days. But there was nothing more they could do for him. Hospice was ordered, and I took him home. There I was, having to make that dreadful call to my siblings, children, and other family members.

A day or so later, I was informed by the hospice RN that Papi was declining. I called the church for someone to come and pray for Him. They were not able to at the time, so I called the priest at Mami's old parish. A priest came by and prayed. Later that evening, the prayer worriers came and prayed for Papi. He got double the portion. To God be the Glory! The following day I was sitting with him, and he said, "Me duele mucho" (It hurts a lot).

I told him to pray, to ask Jesus to take the pain away. Not too long after, I had half of my soul ripped out as he took his last breath.

I walked out of the room and collapsed on the floor. This time,

I was not able to hold my emotions back like I had with Mami. This was worst. When Mami passed, I felt that she was still with me because I had Papi. But this time, they both were gone. The pain was excruciating. I really don't have a word I can use because the pain was indescribable.

We will never be ready to lose a loved one. But we can surely stand strong and confident that we will see them again—providing that we have taken the steps to reconcile with God. To the day of this writing, my selfish heart yearns for Mami and Papi. I miss their physical presence. But my heart has learned to rejoice at the fact that they are no longer in pain and that God knows best. As Isaiah 57:1–2 promises, "The righteous perish, and no one takes it to heart; the devout are taken away, and no one understands that the righteous are taken away to be spared from evil. Amen!"

I was inspired to write, "It is finished. it is done. The genesis of my autobiography has come to an end. A book has been sealed and is now closed. Pain, reopened wounds, and unexplained threads of things said and done that built sorrow in my heart; fears, anxiety, and pressure; pain and anguish; and many tears have come to an end. Praise God for the honor, joy, pride, and strength that has kept me standing until this day. Thank God that the closing of one book means the beginning of what lies ahead.

And I was inspired to find God's voice:

- You can do all things through Christ who strengthens you. (Philippians 4:13)
- Fear not for I am with you; be not dismayed, for I am your God. I will strengthen you, yes, I will help you, I will uphold you with my righteous right hand. (Isaiah 41:10)

CHOSEN TO BECOME ONE

I needed a safety net, and Julio always met me with open arms and was always ready to listen to me and comfort me. Yet, this, too, was heavy on my heart because I knew in my spirit I shouldn't keep the relationship going, though it was platonic at this point. My flesh was weak, and all the harsh, painful afflictions were real and back-to-back, one right after another.

The enemy was busy with all his darts—temptations that might lead me away from faith, trials testing my faith, persecutions attempting to destroy my faith, and ideas and arguments attempting to undermine my faith.

One day, I came up with an idea. I thought of joining Pelegrino for a drink, in order to have him spend some time with me. I said, "Babe, let's get a bottle and listen to some music together, kind of a date at home. What do you think?"

"Sure, let's do it," he replied.

We did just that and had so much fun, just like the old days when we went to family gatherings. This new idea I thought of all on my own turned out great as far as spending time with Pelegrino. It was also confirmation of two things. First, if I did what Pelegrino liked to do, which was drinking and partying, he would spend more time with me. Second, I had just made a big mistake. I'd compromised my walk with Christ, which would lead me into a few unrighteous behaviors I ended up being broken for. I'd just made things more complicated for myself. I'd made a bad choice again. Fixing it myself, in my already troubled mind—this was warfare for sure.

Earlier, after my rebirth into Christ Jesus while I was praying and thanking God for rescuing me from the dead state I had been living in, I said, "Heavenly Father, had I known what I know today, I wouldn't have sinned against You. This is a new life dedicated to my Lord Jesus Christ. I will not sin against You as I did in the past."

Then came that moment in time moving forward where I was so sure of myself, yet I slipped. When I first realized that I had done just what I had said I would not do—realizing I still had feelings for Julio and giving into my flesh—I was so broken I couldn't stand it. I broke down and wailed to Abba God. "How could I have betrayed You, Abba God! I'm so sorry." I was so broken I was thinking of suicide. And attempting it, I failed. After pouring out all of my guilt and shame I got up, got my Bible, and started reading. And He said, "Simon, Simon, Satan has asked to sift all of you as wheat. / But I have prayed for you, Simon, that your faith may not fail. And when you have turned back, strengthen your brothers" (Luke 22:31–32, NIV, Bible Hub).

"I'm so sorry, Abba God! I'm so sorry." I continued crying and reading—receiving painful conviction. I recognized that Abba God new beforehand just what I was going to do back then when I was feeling so sure of myself. Just like Peter, I swore I wouldn't sin against Him, and yet, I did—by feeding myself what my flesh desired.

That day after I'd talked to Julio, my heart was heavy. I had found so much comfort in his presence, and then I felt all this guilt afterward. I fell to my knees, broken, and poured my heart out to Abba God. How can this be? Why has he come back in my path if it is sin to have a relationship with him? Why do I feel what I feel for him? Why is it so strong and difficult to deny myself? I can't help the way I feel. What am I supposed to do? Why do I love him so much? I thought this had all ended.

I was utterly broken. I cried and cried.

Then I heard a still voice say, "Love Me more than you love him."

"What?" I inhaled and exhaled deeply. "Love You more than I love Julio? Help me. I can't do this on my own. I don't understand why this love in my heart is so powerful. I don't know how to take it out. Help me, Abba God." Wailed from the bottom of my heart, I cried, "I will love You more, Abba God, just help me by taking all this from my heart. I can't do it on my own. I don't know how." I inhaled and exhaled a few more times, just like when I was having labor pains the first time and Mami said, "Just pray."

I got up and felt a great sense of peace. Yes, I felt that peace that transcends all understanding. I started reading, and He spoke again through an *In Touch* devotional:

- Do not conform to the pattern of this world but be transformed by the renewing of your mind. Then you will be able to test and approve what God's will is—his good, pleasing, and perfect will. (Romans 12:2)
- What good is it for someone to gain the whole world, yet forfeit their soul? (Mark 8:36)
- When He heard this, Jesus said, "This sickness will not end in death. No, it is for God's glory so that God's Son may be glorified through it." (John 11:4)

What God was telling me was to die to self and love Him with all my heart, mind, strength, and soul.

- Then Jesus said to his disciples, "Whoever wants to be my disciple must deny themselves and take up their cross and follow me. (Matthew 16:24)
- Hear O Israel: The LORD our God, the LORD is one. Love the LORD your God with all your heart and with all your soul and with all your strength. (Deuteronomy 6:4-5)

The transformation did not happening instantly. It wasn't all at once like many believe it would be when praying in faith to Abba God. It's not that He doesn't hear us or that he can't. Neither is He ignoring our plea. No, this was a process. I was being stripped, layer by layer, of all the impurities within me. And I needed to learn how to use the weapon God had given me, His word in the Bible, and how to embrace His indescribable peace.

All Christian soldiers need the same rigid training to know how to properly handle the Sword of the Spirit, "which is the word of God." The sword that Paul refers to here is the Holy Scriptures. We know from 2 Timothy 3:16 –17 that the word of God is from the Holy Spirit and written by men: "All Scripture is God-breathed and is useful for teaching, rebuking, correcting and training in righteousness, / so that the servant of God may be thoroughly equipped for every good work."

Since every Christian is in a spiritual battle with the satanic and evil forces of this world, we need to know how to handle the Word properly. Only then will it be an effective defense against evil. But it will also be an offensive weapon we use to "demolish strongholds" of error and falsehood. As 2 Corinthians 10:4–5 tells us, "The weapons we fight with are not the weapons of the world. On the contrary, they have divine power to demolish strongholds. / We demolish arguments and every pretension that sets itself up against the knowledge of God, and we take captive every thought to make it obedient to Christ." (Got Questions?)

★★★

Julio was a patient at AMG. That made him my patient. He was diagnosed with cancer and was scheduled for surgery. This would be the second time he'd had surgery. He asked if I could accompany him and his sister on that day. I brought it up to Pelegrino, and he approved of me going with Julio.

We arrived at the hospital and registered. The nurses escorted us to the surgery floor. Julio was asked to change while we waited in the waiting area. Then it was time.

We were brought to the patient preoperative area. A nurse walked in and gave Julio instructions on what to do. They would be taking him in a few minutes. She handed him a sanitary package and explained to him that he was to wash his body, starting from his neck down to his groin area. When he was done, he would be taken to surgery.

Julio looked at his sister and asked if she would please wipe him down as the nurse said. His sister said, "What? You want me to do what? No, not me."

Julio then looked at me and asked, "Would you please?"

I said, "Sure." I started wiping him down.

As I was finishing he said, "La profecia de tu Tia se a cumplido" (Your aunt's prophecy has been completed).

I was blown away. Wow.

And he was taken up for surgery.

The surgery went well, God being such a good Father. The recovery process was a painful, long one. God gave Julio the strength to push through as he received his healing. During this time, he asked me to find a pastor to come to the hospital. He wanted an old-school pastor who spoke Spanish. Even that God provided for him. There was a coworker I'd fellowshipped with, and she had shared about her church and pastor. I knew this pastor was just the person God wanted Julio to see. I contacted the pastor, and the date was made. Julio was able to reconcile with the Lord and receive that peace only Jesus can give. Praise God.

Every prophecy my aunt had told me back when I was twenty-three years old had come to pass. Even her request on her deathbed for me to tell Julio not to leave the church happened. I did not know I would ever see him again. Yet Titi Anna knew I would, and she had a word for him from God.

I'll include here the last two songs Julio composed:

¿Porque No Puede Ser?
By Julio Arzuaga

Como yo se señor
Que allá en la eternidad
No existe la pasión
Ni el deseo sensual

Ahora que estoy aquí
Permíteme vivir

Amando a la mujer
Que es todo para mi

Reconozco mi Dios
Que allá en la eternidad
Al entrar en tu reino
Nadie se casará

Por eso te suplico
Que entiendas nuestro amor
Y en nombre de tu hijo
Nos des tu bendición

Ella me dice
Que yo soy su único amor
Y yo la quiero
Con todo mi corazón

Si yo soy su hombre
Y ella mi mujer
Dime señor
¿porque no puede ser?

Me formaste de arena
Y me diste de ti
Ese soplo divino
La vida que hay en mi

Pusiste aquí en mi pecho
Un tierno corazón
Y me llamaste hombre
Haciéndome varón

Y así me hiciste libre
Libre para escoger

Todo cuanto yo quiera
Incluso una mujer

Y ahora que la encuentro
Tú me dices que no
Que no debo tomarla
Y te pregunto yo

Si ella me dice
Que yo soy su único amor
Y yo la quiero
Con todo mi corazón

Si yo soy su hombre
Y ella mi mujer

Dime señor
¿porque no puede ser?

Mi Ultima Canción
By Julio Arzuaga

Esta es la última canción
Que para ti voy a cantar
La escribí pensando en ti
Sintiendo ganas de llorar
Y para no llorar mordí
Mi boca hasta hacerla sangrar

Yo no sé guardar rencor
Tampoco sé lo que es odiar
Yo lo que se es hablar de dios
Hablar de amor y perdonar
Pero hasta aquí llego el amor
Llego la hora de llorar

Adiós, adiós, adiós, mi amor
Ya no te volveré a besar
Vuelvo a partir igual que ayer
Vuelvo otra vez a desandar
Presiento que no volveré
Y que este adiós será el final

Este es la última canción
Que mi guitarra sonara
La guardare en aquel rincón
Que acompaña mi soledad
Pues ella lo mismo que yo
Está cansada de llorar

Adiós, adiós, adiós, mi amor
Ya no te volveré a besar
Vuelvo a partir igual que ayer
Vuelvo otra vez a desandar
Presiento que no volveré
Y que este adiós será el final

★★★

Fast-forward once more. And yes, the struggles continued, as Pelegrino chose to return to the world and was not in a hurry to reconcile with God. I had double the task to stay sane and to stay faithful. Of course, we all think, just stay faithful by putting the kingdom of God first, and everything will be given to you (Matthew 6:33). I have evidence this is true. But it does not say you will have no battles. After all, untested faith is no faith at all.

In one of my battles, I sought the counsel of an elderly couple in the church. They spoke about enabling a person in his or her behavior of addiction (or whatever it be that takes the person from the Lord). I heard them out and went home, battling with what I had heard. I kept hearing the echoes of scriptures battling against what I had heard.

So, I went home, and to my knees I dropped. I cried out to God, "What do I do? What I heard today is not what You say in scripture. Help me, Lord!"

Then I got up and started to write what I heard God repeat to me—what He had already told me years before. I started a journal called "Becoming One."

Chosen to Become One

Sometimes, we make choices in life led by emotions, obligations, or profit. And in the long run, we reap the fruit of what we sow. But a covenant between God and two people means we have chosen to *become one*. And years later, after the hurricane, storms, hills, valleys, adversity, turmoil, and trials have been active and passed, we can taste the sweet, sweet taste of victory: You can't see the wounds or the brokenness that delivered a couple that has withstood this test. But you can see the joy and peace that continues to enable them to stand as one before God and men.

There is a beautiful quote that says, "The journey of a thousand miles begins with one step." Marriage, in becoming one, is just that—the first step toward a lifelong journey. That journey may have unpredictable weather, stumbling blocks, and long dark roads. But as long as you hear the whisper of the Lord, you know you are on the right path, and you are not alone. Yes, we are one until we come home and join Abba God.

The challenges are great. But greater is the reward of knowing we are being obedient to Abba God Almighty. Jesus tells us that, in this life, we will have trouble. But we must take heart, for He has overcome the world. This is what I keep in mind every time I want to run or throw in the towel with separation or divorce. It is that soft whisper of Almighty God, my Abba and my Lord Jesus Christ, through the Word and His Spirit that keeps me standing and being still.

Marriage

The Bible contains many scriptures to the sanctity and beauty of marriage. These Bible verses about marriage are the foundation you should set for your marriage before your wedding vows:

- Then the Lord God made a woman from the rib he had taken out of the man, and he brought her to the man. / The man said, "This is now bone of my bones and flesh of my flesh; she shall be called 'woman,' for she was taken out of man." / That is why a man leaves his father and mother and is united to his wife, and they become one flesh. (Genesis 2:22–24)

  The beauty of man and woman being one in the sense that woman came from the rib of the man was part of God's perfect creation. At the fall of Adam and Eve they not only face death—separation from God—but they also were punished for life by God for their disobedience, a punishment that follows all mankind.

- To the woman He said: "I will sharply increase your pain in childbirth; in pain you will bring forth children. Your desire will be for your husband, and he will rule over you." (Genesis 3:16, Bible Hub)

  This is the punishment of mankind. The New Living Translation more correctly translates this as you will desire to control your husband, but he will rule over you.

- To Adam he said, "Because you listened to your wife and ate fruit from the tree about which I commanded you, 'You must not eat from it,' cursed is the ground because of you; through painful toil you will eat food from it all the days of your life. / It will produce thorns and thistles for you, and you will eat the plants of the field. / By the sweat of your brow you will eat your food until you return to the ground, since from it you were taken; for dust you are and to dust you will return." (Genesis 3:17–20)

  For the woman, this scripture speaks of something that,

unlike many women, has been an innate desire of mine—to be led by my husband. Unfortunately, it is one of the roles Pelegrino has refrained from taking. He has—by choice or no choice—declined to lead, making me take the lead in the household and in our marriage (with the exception of that period when he was Mr. Leader). If not for God's Word, it would be a complete disaster for sure.

Now, let's consider a few more scriptures that tell us what we should be applying to our marriages:

- And this second thing you do. You cover the Lord's altar with tears, with weeping and groaning because he no longer regards the offering or accepts it with favor from your hand. / But you say, "Why does he not?" Because the Lord was witness between you and the wife of your youth, to whom you have been faithless, though she is your companion and your wife by covenant. / Did he not make them one, with a portion of the Spirit in their union? And what was the one God seeking? Godly offspring. So guard yourselves in your spirit, and let none of you be faithless to the wife of your youth. / "For I hate divorce!" says the Lord, the God of Israel. "To divorce your wife is to overwhelm her with cruelty," says the Lord of Heaven's Armies. "So guard your heart; do not be unfaithful to your wife." The Messenger of the Lover. (Malachi 2:13–17)
- For your Maker is your husband, the Lord of hosts is his name; and the Holy One of Israel is your Redeemer, the God of the whole earth he is called. (Isaiah 54:5)
- Wives, submit yourselves to your own husbands as you do to the Lord. / For the husband is the head of the wife as Christ is the head of the church, his body, of which he is the Savior. / Now as the church submits to Christ, so also wives should submit to their husbands in everything. / Husbands, love your wives, just as Christ loved the church and gave himself

up for her to make her holy, / cleansing her by the washing with water through the word, / and to present her to himself as a radiant church, without stain or wrinkle or any other blemish, but holy and blameless. / In this same way, husbands ought to love their wives as their own bodies. He who loves his wife loves himself.

After all, no one ever hated their own body, but they feed and care for their body, just as Christ does the church— / "For this reason a man will leave his father and mother and be united to his wife, and the two will become one flesh." / This is a profound mystery—but I am talking about Christ and the church. / However, each one of you also must love his wife as he loves himself, and the wife must respect her husband. (Ephesians 5:22–29, 31–33)

- When Jesus had finished saying these things, he left Galilee and went into the region of Judea to the other side of the Jordan. / Large crowds followed him, and he healed them there.

Some Pharisees came to him to test him. They asked, "Is it lawful for a man to divorce his wife for any and every reason?"

"Haven't you read," he replied, "that at the beginning the Creator 'made them male and female,' / and said, 'For this reason a man will leave his father and mother and be united to his wife, and the two will become one flesh'? / So they are no longer two, but one flesh. Therefore what God has joined together, let no one separate."

"Why then," they asked, "did Moses command that a man give his wife a certificate of divorce and send her away?"

Jesus replied, "Moses permitted you to divorce your wives because your hearts were hard. But it was not this way from the beginning. / I tell you that anyone who divorces his wife, except for sexual immorality, and marries another woman commits adultery."

The disciples said to him, "If this is the situation between a husband and wife, it is better not to marry."

Jesus replied, "Not everyone can accept this word, but only those to whom it has been given. / For there are eunuchs who were born that way, and there are eunuchs who have been made eunuchs by others—and there are those who choose to live like eunuchs for the sake of the kingdom of heaven. The one who can accept this should accept it." (Matthew 19:1–12)

Too many married couples fail when it comes to obedience to these verses. And then we wonder why we are going through such hard times. If you doubt that you can keep this covenant. don't get married. God will be your husband, and you will not be in need of anything. Live to serve Him, and your rewards will be endless.

Being in an unhealthy marriage can feel like being in a jail cell with no bars, yet you are confined to stay put. If you're in a troubled marriage, your complete submission to Abba God Almighty will carry you through, giving you joy, peace, and the hope that God works all things for the good of those who love and trust him.

Marriage is a blessing, but it also is a covenant that should not be broken. We should study it out and get to know the law of the covenant, weighing the pros and cons before making such a great commitment:

- A woman is bound to her husband as long as he lives. But if her husband dies, she is free to marry anyone she wishes, but he must belong to the Lord. In my judgment, she is happier if she stays as she is—and I think that I too have the Spirit of God. (1 Corinthians 7:39–40)
- Set me as a seal upon your heart, as a seal upon your arm, for love is strong as death, jealousy is fierce as the grave. Its flashes are flashes of fire, the very flame of the Lord. Many waters cannot quench love, neither can floods drown it. If a

man offered for love all the wealth of his house, he would be utterly despised. (Song of Solomon 8:6–7)

- Two are better than one, because they have a good return for their labor: If either of them falls down, one can help the other up. But pity anyone who falls and has no one to help them up. Also, if two lie down together, they will keep warm. But how can one keep warm alone? (Ecclesiastes 4:9)
- With all humility and gentleness, with patience, bearing with one another in love, eager to maintain the unity of the Spirit in the bond of peace. (Ephesians 4:2–3)
- And over all these virtues put on love, which binds them all together in perfect unity. (Colossians 3:14)
- Though one may be overpowered, two can defend themselves. A cord of three strands is not quickly broken. (Ecclesiastes 4:12)
- Therefore what God has joined together, let no one separate. (Mark 10:9)

In a marriage, we are called to follow God's Word and not justify our own interpretation that sooths our flesh. When physical abuse is present, we should seek help as instructed in the Word of God and the legal system of the land, which is governed by God. If it is bad, call and get help for an emergency exit. Continue to pray, and God will work all things out.

Marriage is a physical picture of the spiritual relationship that exists between Christ, the bridegroom, and the church, His bride. A marriage is referred to in the Bible as a man knowing his wife, just as, we can know Christ, our bridegroom. A husband and wife are one flesh—just as we are one spirit with the Lord (1 Corinthians 6:17).

My Prayer

Heavenly Father God, I am asking you to be the head in this marriage. Put true love in my heart for Pelegrino, the kind that is real, not pretense but sincere. Give me the strength to stay married and handle the obstacles that come. Don't let me make the same mistake I did in my first marriage. Don't allow me to be influenced by other people's opinions, even those who are trying to help; rather, help me to listen to Your voice only. I want to be the wife described in scripture and the Proverbs 31 woman You talk about in Your Word. Teach me and guide me.

And this Abba God Almighty has done. He has been faithful to the date—although I have failed to live up to the scripture's standards. I have slipped, engaged in sin, and been disobedient to God. Yet Abba God has been right there, forgiving me, teaching me as I tripped on each stumbling stone, and supporting me through all the adversity. Every time I cry out, He has reminded me of my prayer. His whispered voice would ask, "Do you love me?"

"Yes, Lord, You know I love You."

"Do you trust me?"

"Yes, Lord, I trust You."

On one occasion, He asked, "Have I not given you the strength you asked me for?"

I have, indeed, been lifted; dusted off; and, layer by layer, peeled away to look a little more like that woman Abba talks about:

> If I speak in the tongues of men or of angels, but do not have love, I am only a resounding gong or a clanging cymbal. / If I have the gift of prophecy and can fathom all mysteries and all knowledge, and if I have a faith that can move mountains, but do not have love, I am nothing. / If I give all I possess to the poor and give over my body to hardship that I may boast but do not have love, I gain nothing.
>
> Love is patient, love is kind. It does not envy, it does not boast, it is not proud. / It does not dishonor others, it is not self-seeking, it is not easily angered, it keeps no record of wrongs. / Love does not delight in

evil but rejoices with the truth. / It always protects, always trusts, always hopes, always perseveres.

Love never fails. But where there are prophecies, they will cease; where there are tongues, they will be stilled; where there is knowledge, it will pass away. / For we know in part and we prophesy in part, / but when completeness comes, what is in part disappears. (1 Corinthians 13:4–10)

What I failed to do to make my prayer complete was pray for my husband. In my eagerness to be that wife described in the Bible, I failed to ask God to strengthen Pelegrino's walk with Him, empower him, and prepare him to be that man and husband who is spoken of in the Bible. He needed to become that God-fearing man who would put God first and, in doing so, would love his wife the same way Christ loved his bride, the church.

Christ was willing to lay His life down for His bride, the church. I forgot to ask Abba to empower Pelegrino daily with the desire and ability to say no to the world and yes to Almighty God Jehovah and our Lord Jesus Christ. This was spiritual immaturity. It was about me not knowing how to pray and what I should have been looking for in a marriage and a man. My focus was on God helping me not to fail in our marriage. And I left out the key to seeing my prayer answered that would benefit us as one. What we ask for we will receive when we believe and trust God with all our hearts.

Abba God Almighty is awesome. He is true to his Word and faithful in every way. He gave me the desires of my heart. I grew to love Pelegrino, not only with a phileo love but also with an agape love as well. He has taught me to love him as Christ loves him, unconditionally. He has taught me to look at Pelegrino with Christ eyes and not my own. He has taught me not to depend on Pelegrino to change or make me happy but, rather, to depend on the Holy Spirit to move in me and through me. He has taught me to let Abba fill me with His joy, while praying for Pelegrino and being patient with him. He's taught me to expect God's "mighty hand to move and make all things work for the good of those who seek and love him" (Romans 8:28).

There is so much that can be told about the seasons, storms, valleys, obstacles, adversity, turmoil, and self-afflicted wounds (sin) that lead to some of the consequences we still live with today. But getting through it would not have been possible without Abba's mercy and grace and His son Jesus Christ. I have a new focus today—peace, joy, hope and a daily relationship with Abba God Almighty, El Shaddai.

I know these truths promised us in scripture:

- For our struggle is not against flesh and blood, but against the rulers, against the authorities, against the powers of this dark world and against the spiritual forces of evil in the heavenly realms. (Ephesians 6:12)
- And God Blessed them, and God said to them, Be fruitful, and multiply, and replenish the earth, and subdue it: and have dominion over the fish of the sea, and over the fowl of the air, and over every living thing that moves on the earth. (Genesis 1:28)

I read, study, and apply:

Therefore put on the full armor of God, so that when the day of evil comes, you may be able to stand your ground, and after you have done everything, to stand. / Stand firm then, with the belt of truth buckled around your waist, with the breastplate of righteousness in place, / and with your feet fitted with the readiness that comes from the gospel of peace. / In addition to all this, take up the shield of faith, with which you can extinguish all the flaming arrows of the evil one. / Take the helmet of salvation and the sword of the Spirit, which is the word of God. / And Pray in the Spirit at all times, with every kind of prayer and petition. To this end, stay alert with all perseverance in your prayers for all the saints. (Ephesian 6:13–18)

We saw blessing come when facing challenges when our four daughters and I prayed. I started praying and fasting and would have a conference call prayer meeting including Lourdes and Eliberto. All praise and glory to You, my King, my All, my Abba God!

Marriage comes with written instructions. Unfortunately, not many people know this. It's the Bible. If we open the Bible, we are able to learn what is required before making that big covenant. Then we can receive these instructions and apply them. In some cases, it takes a lifetime of work to see it come together the right way. In others, it may come to pass rapidly. The timing depends on each person's response to the Word of God. Most of us jump into marriage without carefully reading the instructions, being confident we can figure it out. But we quickly get into struggles and find ourselves having to read the Bible again and again. Most of the problems we get into in marriage can be traced to our neglect of reading and obeying God's instructions.

A lot has happened since I last wrote in my Becoming One journal.

Today, as I was organizing our new one room, a card fell from Pelegrino's nightstand, where I'd placed it the day we moved in. I picked it up and felt the need to read it again. It has been a while since I got this for him. I didn't even remember what the occasion was. Ironically it was for Valentine's Day, and we were in the month of February now as I reread the card. And yes, I needed to add it to this journal. It just confirms that it's not the position a man holds. Nor is it his yearly income. And, yes, he is still struggling with his man cave and addictions. So, it is not his sober status either or his righteousness level. This card helped me recall what becoming one truly is. It is so much more than what the world has categorized it to be—meaning that, sometimes, we have to sacrifice.

The card reads, "It's not the million little ways we're different.

It's the handful of big ways we're the same. It's not long, deep conversations. It's a soft kiss that says it all. It's not a dream come true. It's better. *It's real. It's love. It's us.* It's that God strengthens and teaches how to become one."

Let me enlighten you about why we moved into one room. The battles had been challenging for some time now. A lot of issues at work came up—clearly related to my need to take time off and use FMLA and coming in later than I was scheduled due to my illness. This was the opposite of when I had once been the first one at work and the last one out. I also got written up for saying, "Amen. Hallelujah." This caused me to lose my place of employment. Unemployment was over more quickly than expected. I used up my pension while I was off of work to keep up with our living expenses. Before I knew it, all the income was gone. My brother's help also had ceased.

Government help was available with the landlord's agreement, which he declined to do. Pelegrino's employer had a hardship fund. But again that would require the landlord's agreement, which he declined. And before we realized what had happened, we were asked to leave our apartment of ten years. He put it like this: "Your problems are not my concern."

We were blessed, to say the least, to have family take us in. But putting thirty-nine years in one room was quite difficult. For me, it had been forty-four years of being independent and the one to give shelter to others. Such a change is a big tester of one's faith (and relationship if you're married).

During our stay, I have heard Abba God's voice. I've been given the Word, through scripture, sermons, devotionals, other believers who are struggling, the homeless, worship, and even the stillness of the night when I can't sleep. It all points to the quiet whispers of Almighty God and what makes a married couple one. It's something as simple as history, faith, and those small things that go on ignored or overlooked—like the card said.

I also recalled writing a poem called "Como No Amarte?" (I will add the poem at the end of the book, as well as its replacement.)

When reading it, one would ask, How can a person give up someone who sounds so perfect for what seems unlovable? We read in Luke 6:32, "If you love those who love you, what credit is that to you? Even sinners love those who love them."

It's all about God. He makes things happen and opens the eyes of the blind. He enlightens the eyes of the heart so that we can see when we are wrong. He gives us hearts of flesh so we can understand what love is really all about. He makes all things work for the good of those who seek Him and *love* Him—because He is *love*. It is so true that, if we abide in Him, He will abide in us. This is the only way we can truly become one when we have true *love*. Abba God Almighty—that's what we have that makes us one—Abba God, our Lord Jesus Christ, and the Holy Spirit.

THE WORD "MANIFESTATION"
IN MY LIFE

"If you are insulted for the name of Christ, you are blessed, because the Spirit of glory and of God rests on you."

—1 Peter 4:16

Typically, when you feel God's manifest presence, something shifts, something changes, or something happens. God doesn't just show up for no reason or purpose. When He manifests His presence, there is something He wants to do in your life. This could be to encourage, convict, strengthen, heal, or save you—whatever He desires to do (Christianity.com).

Being born with severe learning disabilities can take a toll on a person's life, especially when you live with the thorn in your flesh and aren't aware it's there until age forty-six. But God's grace gets you through the courses needed to bring to pass a childhood dream to be a medical assistant.

Nine years of persecution were not easy to endure. I'd arrive an hour early in order to keep up for the first few years, until I became physically challenged. Being the last one to leave gave me the opportunity to walk through hallways and stairways covering both floors, praying and thanking God for getting me through yet another day.

My health began to fail. I was having to use FMLA pretty frequently. A second thorn developed; now there was more against me. I stood in joy and love, knowing God's grace was sufficient for me.

I underwent a third surgery, in addition to the last four hospital ER visits and two other surgeries during nine years at AMG. This added a third thorn to my flesh. But I stood in faith, filled with love, and embraced the joy of knowing that God's grace is sufficient for me.

When I was written up at work for saying "Praise God, Hallelujah," I received it as just what the scripture says, a blessing. "Blessed are you when people insult you, persecute you and falsely say all kinds of evil against you because of me. / Rejoice and be glad, because great is your reward in heaven, for in the same way they persecuted the prophets who were before you." (Matthew 5:11–12)

When I was terminated for being sick, I received it as a blessing— and it truly was for the same reason. As time passed and things did not look particularly good, I took it as a blessing. When we lost our apartment, as absurd as it may be, I stood in faith and received it as a blessing. When I ended up where I least expected to be for shelter— where my daughter had been violated at the tender age of twelve—I stood in faith and took it as a blessing. When Pelegrino lost his job, I received it as a blessing. I learned to love those who had afflicted my daughter. I learned that my stay there was not only so I could learn how to forgive and love them more but also for the sake of others. One day in a conversation with my cousin Jessica (RIP), I said, "I really don't know how or why I ended up here."

She answered, "You're here for me. I needed you during this time in my life." This moves me to share about my sweet Jessica, the youngest daughter of my younger cousin. On July 8th of 2018 I texted her for her birthday. She texted me back wanting to talk to me. I said, "Of course." When she called me, she shared that she had been diagnosed with lung cancer stage four. I was blown away. She asked if I could pray for her, and I responded by praying for her at that moment. When I was done with the prayer she asked me, "Yayie if I die today will I go to heaven or not?" I said, "Sweetheart lets let God answer that for you. If you can come by, we can hear what God tells us." She agreed and came over. We started with prayer and then we studied the discipleship and the light and darkness study in the Disciple's Handbook book. She was convicted and broke out in tears saying, "I want to be baptized when can I get baptized?" We made the necessary steps and not long after she was baptized ant the Mother Church by Pastor Paul Chicol. To God Be the Glory! Jessica battled for four years with the lung cancer and May 11, 2022, took her last breath.

When Pelegrino's choice was not to seek employment until his return from Puerto Rico (after months), I stood in faith and received it as a blessing, against everything inside of me, for the sake of peace.

During this time of trials, a couple of days after Pelegrino had lost his job, we received devastating news from our Natalie. Apparently, she was playing with Shawn, her husband, and suffered an accident where her neck was broken, completely broken. Again, I went into prayer, crying before God. Again, I stood in faith and received it as a blessing.

Due to Pelegrino's unemployment (which meant free time), we were able to visit her in Little Rock, Arkansas, which was a blessing.

I had felt completely rejected by Pelegrino's trip to Puerto Rico (and not being included again). I stood in faith and received it as a blessing.

On September 2, we were out driving around just to see our options when I got a call from my brother Eliberto. He said, "Hi." But he didn't sound right.

"Hi," I said. "Can you hear me?"

He said, "We are here with the state troopers." And there was a pause.

"Hello," I said. "Hello. El, are you OK? Where is Lou?"

That's when he said, in a low voice, "Jose died in an accident."

It was a dramatic moment as we went back and forth. I screamed loudly, unable or, perhaps, unwilling to believe what I was hearing. Immediately, I recalled Jose's request for me to pray for him a couple weeks earlier. He was very fearful of pain and had been diagnosed with cirrhosis of the liver. He feared the declining of his health and the pain that would come with it. I'd prayed that, whenever God was ready to take him home, He would take him instantly, not allowing him to undergo any pain. But I did not expect what I was just hearing. Still, I stood in faith that it was God's will, an answered prayer despite the pain. I embraced it and received it, choosing to see it as a blessing.

As for staying in the very room where I least would have wanted to be for an entire year, as I mentioned earlier, gave me revelation in many areas. I will add, one Sunday as I served at church, I was in the VIP room when the service came to an end. I looked up and saw Al walking from the sanctuary toward the VIP room, crying profoundly. He came straight to me and threw himself on me, holding me tightly and sobbing. I felt his brokenness for what he had done to my baby and released that forgiveness I didn't realize I was holding back.

Time passed, and no light had been on our situation. I was starting to feel crushed in my spirit. So, in the car, during my alone time, I poured myself out to Abba God. I wanted Him to speak. I just wanted to hear from Him.

I was listening to the Word on my app while driving alone (not by choice again). And suddenly I heard this message from Ezekiel 12:3–4:

> Therefore, son of man, pack your bags for exile. In broad daylight, set out from your place and go to another as they watch. Perhaps they will understand, though they are a rebellious house.
>
> Bring out your baggage for exile by day, as they watch. Then in the evening, as they watch, go out like those who go into exile.

I couldn't believe what I had just heard. But I knew I had heard it. Still, I questioned it. Then I heard, "Didn't you just ask Me to speak?"

I kept crying and praying. *If this is what you truly want, Abba, give me confirmation. Show me the key to our new place of residence.*

I also set up an appointment with one of the leaders at church, Alicia. I wanted her to hear what had just happened and help me pray about it all. She said, "Yes, I will pray for God to give you clarity."

I told Pelegrino, "We need to start looking for an apartment, even if we didn't have enough money saved up."

We started looking a week or two later, on a Sunday. About fifteen to twenty minutes into our search, I saw a big key sign on the lawn that read, "For Rent." I asked Pelegrino to pull over, and he did. I entered the phone number on the sign into my phone and called to inquire about the apartment. The manager was willing to meet us in one hour. I told Pelegrino, "This is it. I asked God to show me the key, and there is a key on the lawn."

We met with the manager. He gave us the price and ran a few more things by us. The rent and deposit together came up to, $2,400. We had $600. The manager told us he would have to run a background and credit check. He asked if we minded. We told him that was fine and agreed to meet later that day so he could give us the application to fill out. After we'd completed the application, he told us he would let us know as soon as he got the response back.

We waited two days, and there was no call. Pelegrino asked me to call him and inquire about it. But I said, "If this is from God, he will contact us. If not, it's not for us."

Shortly after that, I got the call. The manager apologized for not getting back to us sooner and added that he had not received word back from the company that does his background search. He would meet with us meanwhile and give us the lease.

We still did not have the money needed to move out by November 1. I prayed and prayed without ceasing. During this time, I was going through the Intercessory Prayer Class #9 and going into #10, Prayers for Increase, at Living Word Community Center. After the exit prayer one night, Pastor Steve Keys, pulled me to the side and said, "God just told me during our prayer to tell you that a financial blessing is being released, so you and your husband can get what you need."

I could not imagine what had been held back. We had no pending financial transactions being held back anywhere. But I was not going to doubt the Word from God. I gave Steve a high five and hug and stood in agreement with him.

The manager called again, wanting to meet with us. He wanted to know if we would be moving in on November 1. I prayed and then texted him back. I asked if it would be possible to wait until December. To my surprise he said yes. He added, "Does this mean I can have the sign removed?"

"Yes, I said.

This was confirmation from God. It gave me a peace of mind. Not that I was doubting God. I just wanted to receive clarity like Pastor Alicia and I were *praying* for. I didn't want it to be one of those cases where I was rushing the process and doing things on my own, like I'd done for years. There would still be the moving cost and so on.

On Sunday, Pastor David, in his closing before the altar call, said, "Now move. Get up and go." This was another confirmation that God wanted us to move.

The last conversation with the manager was on Tuesday. Pelegrino kept asking me about the apartment and sounding worried—wondering what we should do. I told him, "I'm trusting God. If it's for us, He will make it happen."

I kept praying and added to the prayer, "I believe this is from You, Abba. You will pay the rent now and after we are moved in so that we will not become homeless again. In Jesus's name. Amen!"

On Thursday, October 31, 2019, I went on my regular medication pickup and post office errand. There it was—a financial blessing and just what we needed to sign the lease in peace. It had come two days before our meeting with the manager to sign the lease and give him our deposit. This was the confirmation that this was from God Almighty.

We signed our least. God willing we would move into our new place of residence soon. To God be the Glory. Santo!

Natalie's doctors removed her neck brace, which she'd worn since the beginning of April. The doctors said she was a miracle. Anyone with her injury would have been dead or completely paralyzed from the neck down.

But God was there.

Natalie was healed. *To God be the glory!*

NEW BEGINNINGS

"These words I am commanding you today are to be upon your hearts. / 7And you shall teach them diligently to your children and speak of them when you sit at home and when you walk along the road, when you lie down and when you get up. / Tie them as reminders on your hands and bind them on your foreheads. / Write them on the doorposts of your houses and on your gates."

—Deuteronomy 6:6–9

Today after service, I was given a mezuzah from my dear sister Esperanza, who had just returned from Israel. It would go on the post of our new door. In Jesus's name, everyone who came in and walked out would be blessed. Amen!

I got a call from Eliberto letting me know that though Jose had a life insurance policy we did not know about. He wasn't married and had no children. His siblings would be the next of kin. Another financial blessing had come. And yes, there was a financial blessing held back that I did not even know about, just as God had told me through Pastor Steve. Amen. Hallelujah! Santo Jehovah!

During the wait, I continued praying. Pelegrino was blessed with a job. It was so on time.

Pelegrino was on his way to work when he was pulled over by a police officer. It was 4:45 a.m. There was no violation for which he had been pulled over. The officer had merely run his plates, and it came back showing his driver's license had been revoked.

I heard my phone ring but did not get to it fast enough. I looked at the time and could not believe it was 4:55 a.m. As I was trying to get back to sleep, the phone rang again. It was Pelegrino telling me he had gotten pulled over and that he was being taken to jail for driving on a revoked license. He wanted me to meet him at the courthouse, where he would go in front of the judge for bail. He asked the officer for the location.

"It's 1500 Maybrook Drive, Maywood, Illinois," the officer responded.

"You have to be there by 8:00 a.m. That's where they'll have me," Pelegrino stated.

"OK," I said. "I'm on my way."

Oh my, where is this at? "Lord, I need a little help on this one. I have no clue where I'm going. In Jesus's name, amen," I prayed. I got myself up and ready, had my quiet time, and out the door I went. Oh, by the way, Pelegrino was driving a car given to him by his friend. I had told him not to drive it. But of course he knew better. And we suffered the consequences.

This was definitely an undesired adventure. Putting the address into my phone's GPS app, which I wasn't fond of using, I headed out. I arrived at the location given to me and inquired about upcoming court cases, giving the information I had been given. They had no record of any inmates with Pelegrino's name and no new cases on the way to the courthouse. I asked if they would check again, and they did. Unfortunately, Pelegrino was not in their system. One officer suggested I try checking the 26th and California district. I may be able to find him there, it being the holiday week and all.

I called the number for the 26th and California district while I was there and was told I would have to come in person and check the list of upcoming cases displayed on the wall. It was already passed 8:00 a.m., and I was about an hour away from 26th and California. "Heavenly Father God Almighty, I really need You to give me traveling mercy and get me to the courthouse safe and on time. In Jesus's name, amen!"

I worshiped the whole ride there. I was totally blessed. Traffic was great. The list I was instructed to look at had Pelegrino's name on it, and the hearing wouldn't start until 11:00 a.m. "Yes! Thank You, Jesus! Santo! Santo! Santo! Are You, my LORD!" I praised.

I went into the court room and waited and waited and waited. I heard every case presented that day. Court was almost done, close to closing, and no Pelegrino. I continued to pray and worship in my inner self. Finally, he was called. He was the last case called that day. I stood up so he could see me and then sat back down. God is so good that he was granted an I bond. He was to return on Monday for his hearing. I asked the bailer what was next, and he informed me I would need to wait outside the building, which was where Pelegrino would be released. I would see him come out. It was already 4:30 p.m. I assumed it could not be much longer.

I was relieved that there was no bond to be paid. We could not afford another cost with the move and all. I waited outside for as long as I could. In that time, I met a few people. I would go to the car and warm up and come back to the waiting spot again.

I drove the car around, getting as close as I could to the entrance. I started texting everyone I knew who could pray for us. I texted our girls, Rafy, and our spiritual leaders. And I felt I should let his friend Christian know, too.

I prayed, "Abba God, hallowed be Your name. In the name of Jesus, may this not affect Pelegrino's new job. May he be able to continue working. In Jesus's name, amen!"

I walked back and forth between the waiting area across the street, the facility, and my car to warm up. All the while I kept my eyes peeled on the building in hopes of seeing Pelegrino walk out.

As I waited in the car, I saw a young lady walking back and forth as if she was anxious or cold. At one point, it seemed like she was walking toward the car, but she turned around and walked back to the area where she had been pacing back and forth. I pulled down the window and called out to her. "Did you need something?" She seemed hesitant to answer, so I asked again, "Did you need something?"

"I'm not familiar with the area. It's cold, and I was wondering if you know of a place where I can go inside, like a store or something?" she said.

I responded, "I don't know the area either. But you are welcome to sit in my car and keep warm."

She said. "Sure, if that's OK. Thank you."

We introduced ourselves to each other, and I learned that Ashley was also waiting for her partner. In fact, this was the cased that had been called right before Pelegrino's.

Once Ashley was settled, she called a family member. I didn't mean to listen, but it was kind of unavoidable. When she was done, I said, "Excuse me, I couldn't help hearing your conversation. Are you a believer?"

She responded that she was, and I shared what the Lord had put in my heart regarding the topic she was talking about, using scriptures to back up what I was sharing. When I asked if she was currently attending a church, she said, "Not really."

I ministered to her during the time she was sitting in the car. Ashley, in turn, shared her spiritual experience. She was on the phone with her family member on and off during this time. After one phone call, she asked if I would be willing to drive her to 44th Street. She was going home. She also asked me if I could keep an eye out for her boyfriend and ask him to call her. And would I let him use my phone to make the call?

I said, "Sure, if I am still here when he gets out."

I drove Ashley to 44th Street, where her family member was going to meet her, and headed back to the courthouse building—praying the whole time I would not miss Pelegrino's exit from the building.

Some more time passed, and no sign of Pelegrino. I parked the car as close as I could to the courthouse building and walked back to the waiting area by the building. A Hispanic man came out and was looking back and forth from side to side. Then he approached me, asking if I knew how to get to 22nd street. I explained to him the best I knew how. He walked away and started walking toward the bus stop. But he returned to ask for a ride. He said, "Don't be afraid. I don't want to hurt you. I just want to get home. I don't have anyone who can pick me up, and I don't feel too sure of how to get there."

"I'm not afraid. I'm not alone. Jesus is with me. Sure, I will take you home."

I introduced myself and guided him to my car. During the ride, I gave him some words of encouragement, telling him God was giving him a second chance at a new beginning. "If you trust in Him," I added. I shared some scriptures with him:

- But seek first his kingdom and his righteousness, and all these things will be given to you as well. (Matthew 6:33)
- Take delight in the Lord, and he will give you the desires of your heart. (Psalm 37:4)
- Trust in him at all times, you people; pour out your hearts to him, for God is our refuge. (Psalm 62:8)
- But those who hope in the Lord will renew their strength. They will soar on wings like eagles; they will run and not grow weary, they will walk and not be faint. (Isaiah 40:31)
- So do not fear, for I am with you; do not be dismayed, for I am your God. I will strengthen you and help you; I will uphold you with my righteous right hand. (Isaiah 41:10)

He was grateful. I invited him to church and gave him some scripture prints I had in the car.

After dropping him off, I headed back to 26th Street and California. It was getting late, and still no sign of Pelegrino. I prayed and worshiped for the rest of the time I waited. Finally, Pelegrino walked out of the building. The waiting area was empty. It was 3:00 a.m. But he was out. Amen! Praise God! Hallelujah!

He was eager to get back to the house. I asked him to wait a few minutes because I was supposed to give someone a message. (I don't recall Ashley's boyfriend's name at the moment.) At the time I did recall the young men's name, and Pelegrino had met him inside and knew who I was referring to. As we were talking about him, Pelegrino spotted him walking out. He called out to him and introduced him to me. I shared what his wife had said and gave him my phone so he could call her.

He called her, and it ended up that he wanted us to give him a ride to the train station because she was not coming back out again.

The station he needed to go to was on 44th Street. Pelegrino really wanted to get home, but I couldn't see myself not giving him a ride, at least to the train station. I wanted to take him home. Pelegrino disagreed. He agreed to take him to the station, and we did.

Wow! That was some night—more like twenty-four hours, minus two. What seemed to be a horrible night, the Lord had used to evangelize and aid His people. Everyone He put in my path that night needed to hear from the Lord in word and deeds.

To God be *all* the glory!

Heavenly Father Elohim, God Almighty, I don't know anything. All my life I have been making all kinds of poor choices that were easy for me to make. But You, Abba God, knew me before the earth was created. You formed me in that secret place and have known my every mistake—before even one of them came to be. Yet You love me so much. You loved me enough to send Your one and only Begotten Son Jesus Christ to die for me. I'm in awe of You twenty-four-seven. I humble myself before You and lay my life down that You, Heavenly Father, can have Your way in my life. In Jesus's name, amen!

- Then the Lord said, "Go out and stand on the mountain before the Lord. Behold, Lord is about to pass by." And a great and mighty wind tore into the mountains and shattered the rocks before the Lord, but the Lord was not in the wind. After the wind there was an earthquake, but the Lord was not in the earthquake.

  After the earthquake there was a fire, but the Lord was not in the fire. And after the fire came a still, small voice.

  When Elijah heard it, he wrapped his face in his cloak and went out and stood at the mouth of the cave. Suddenly a voice came to him and said, "What are you doing here, Elijah?" (1 Kings 19:11–13)

- If my people, who are called by my name, will humble themselves and pray and seek my face and turn from their wicked ways, then I will hear from heaven, and I will forgive their sin and will heal their land. (2 Chronicles 7:14)

- For I have given rest to the weary and joy to the sorrowing. (Jeremiah 31:25, NLT)
- Commandments that I give you today are to be on your hearts. Impress them on your children. Talk about them when you sit at home and when you walk along the road, when you lie down and when you get up. (Deuteronomy 6:6–7)
- *Personal concerns.* Make every effort to come to me quickly, / because Demas, in his love of this world, has deserted me and gone to Thessalonica. Crescens has gone to Galatia, and Titus to Dalmatia. / Only Luke is with me. Get Mark and bring him with you, because he is useful to me in the ministry. / Tychicus, however, I have sent to Ephesus. / When you come, bring the cloak that I left with Carpus at Troas, and my scrolls, especially the parchments.

  Alexander the coppersmith did great harm to me. The Lord will repay him according to his deeds. / You too should beware of him, for he has vigorously opposed our message. (Timothy 4:9–15)
- *The Lord remains faithful.* At my first defense, no one stood with me, but everyone deserted me. May it not be charged against them. / But the Lord stood by me and strengthened me, so that through me the message would be fully proclaimed, and all the Gentiles would hear it. So, I was delivered from the mouth of the lion. / And the Lord will rescue me from every evil action and bring me safely into His heavenly kingdom. To Him be the glory forever and ever. Amen. (2 Timothy 4:16–18)

The apostle Paul knew the value of having good friends. Barnabas encouraged him in his ministry, Silas partnered with him in building up churches, and Timothy and Titus became like sons to him. But, as we see in the passage, Paul also knew the heartache of co-laborers turning away from him when times got tough. We may experience something similar in our lives.

I have lived a life of pain and suffering. All kind of adversities have found me. I have been persecuted, betrayed, and frequently misjudged. But when Jesus came after me in that parking lot at Jewel's, my life and my priorities all started to have a different meaning of truth. It has been a bumpy ride, and the seasons have been stormy for sure. But there has been a big difference since that day.

It wasn't that I started walking a perfect life and that everything was perfect and I had no needs. It wasn't that at all. I had known of Jesus all my life. My first three years of school were at a private Catholic school. In my life, I had completed all my religious sacraments, and I'd had my children do the same. But now, today, I know Jesus. Like Job (42:5), "My ears had heard of you but now my eyes have seen you." He has revealed Himself to me in such a beautiful clear way as described in scripture:

- So the Lord will make himself known to the Egyptians, and in that day, they will acknowledge the Lord. They will worship with sacrifices and grain offerings; they will make vows to the Lord and keep them. (Isaiah 19:21)
- He made known to us the mystery of His will according to His good pleasure, which he purposed in Christ. (Ephesians 1:9)
- I have made you known to them, and will continue to make you known in order that the love you have for me may be in them and that I myself may be in them. (John 17:26)

I did not know who I was. Now, I know I am the daughter of the Most High God Elohim, who teaches us all what we need to know about life:

- But love your enemies, do good to them, and lend to them without expecting to get anything back. Then your reward will be great, and you will be children of the Most High, because he is kind to the ungrateful and wicked. / Be merciful, just as your Father is merciful. (Luke 6:35–36)
- Blessed are the peacemakers, for they will be called children of God. (Matthew 5:9)

- And, I will be a Father to you, and you will be my sons and daughters. (2 Corinthians 6:18)
- Dear friends, now we are children of God, and what we will be has not yet been made known. But we know that when Christ appears, we shall be like him, for we shall see him as he is. (1 John 3:2)

Elohim—this is the very first name given to God, found in the very first verse of Genesis. This name shows that God is the majestic ruler over all. Elohim is a plural word. Used as the first name of God, it sets Him high above all other gods. It also foreshadows the later revelation of the triune Godhead—Father, Son, and Holy Spirit (newchristians.org).

When I asked God to teach me how to love Pelegrino, He also taught me how to love mankind. It's not that difficult to love people at a distance. But when you have to see them every day, and they act unloving toward you, that is a task for sure. God used my husband, my place of employment, my family members, even a couple spiritual family members to teach me how to love the unlovable. Just as I was starting to question what I was doing wrong, God did it again. The most recent lessen/reminder came through a book, *Love Them Anyway* by Pastor Wilfredo De Jesus.

I have been blessed to have in my life the influence of great men and women. Dr. Charles Stanley would meet me daily with his daily devotional and sermons on TV and through his books *First Principles, When the Enemy Strikes*, and *Emotions: Confront the Lies. Conquer with Truth*. The Holy Spirit always speaks to me through his work and never misses the key point I need for the day.

Mike and Lori Kwasniewski came to me in the parking lot at Jewel's. From there, I did the light and darkness study with Lori, through whom Jesus took hold of me and gave me a new identity. I learned from their Bible talk meetings and from Mike at the pulpit for nine years.

Joyce Meyers spoke powerfully to me with her book *Battle of the Mind: Do it Afraid*, among many others, and her sermons on TV. She was the first woman who helped me be able to identify the incest in my life without seeing myself as an outcast. The Holy Spirit spoke to me through her one morning at 5:00 a.m. She said, "You can read my books, watch me on TV, and follow me on any other platform. But until you plug yourself into a church and start following God, you are doing nothing." This was during my hesitation to join CCOC, where Mike and Lori pastored.

Lissette Vega aided me in bringing the gospel to several family members and walking them through the sinner's prayer outside the walls of the church to their conversion at a crucial time in their lives.

Karen Wheaton invites me to meet her, on her front porch or the millhouse daily via YouTube. I listen to Collins Smith on the Moody Radio station. Alister Begg blew me away with *Lasting Love*. I have it on audio and in paperback, and I listen to his sermons on the app and *Turning Point*. Jimmy Evans gives great sermons on marriage on YouTube. I listen to Tony Evans's sermons on YouTube. Reinhard Hirtler, who wrote *The Heart*, has been another great blessing.

Our dear Pastor Wilfredo De Jesus discipled me for twelve crucial years from the pulpit and through his books, *Amazing Faith*, *In the Gap*, *Stay the Course*, and *Love Them Anyway*. His messages were just perfect for this era.

Jarixon Medina gave a message at the School of Ministry graduation in 2022. Just as I was having thought of not publishing *Open Book* although it was finished, I heard the Holy Spirit speak directly to me. Every word was incredibly on point to what I was feeling. When he said, "Stop saying no to God!" I felt as if the Holy Spirit grabbed me and shook me. At the end of the ceremony, as Pastor Jarixon was about to pray for the graduates, he said, "If anyone has been moved by this message, join them."

I hesitated, but I did go up. At the very end, at his last word, I felt a touch on my right shoulder that squeezed me gently. It was the same way I'd felt the Holy Spirit shake me when he'd said, "Stop saying no to God!" But this time it was a physical hand, the hand of Pastor Jaro (as we call him). Wow—powerful to say the least. And so is his book *Shift Change Your Mind, Change Your Walk*.

Pastor Steven A. Keys gave me a prophetic word unexpectedly when I needed to hear from God and continues to encourage me when he delivers a sermon.

Pastor Efrain Muñoz started a discipleship class I had been praying about for years and it came to pass. And when ever he delivers a sermon.

Just writing about the great impact these men and women have had in my life brings me to tears. It reveals how amazing Abba God is and how He keeps His every promise. He will never leave us nor forsake us:

- Be strong and courageous. Do not be afraid or terrified because of them, for the Lord your God goes with you; he will never leave you nor forsake you. (Deuteronomy 31:6)
- Paul said, "How, then, can they call on the one they have not believed in? And how can they believe in the one of whom they have not heard? And how can they hear without someone preaching to them?" (Romans 10:14)
- Jesus said, "Remain in me, as I also remain in you. No branch can bear fruit by itself; it must remain in the vine. Neither can you bear fruit unless you remain in me." (John 15:4)

Each one of the spiritual guides I have listed here has played a big role in rearing me spiritually. The Holy Spirit has been mighty busy working in them and through them. Mike Kwasniewski said in one of his sermons, "Keep in mind that you do not follow men. They may not always be there or may fail you in some way. Be mindful to follow the Holy Spirit, who will never fail you or leave you."

I have my time with God daily in His Word. My time with Him has increased over time greatly as God has permitted. To God be all the glory.

My life is a living testimony. I will quote Reinhard Williams, who said, "Everything that we experience today is, in simple words, what our heart believed yesterday. Your life today is not a result of what people did to you, the traumas you lived through, your upbringing or your past, but rather the beliefs engraved on the tablets of your heart.

From scripture, we are told, "Above all else, guard your heart, for everything you do flows from it" (Proverbs 4:23).

Everything in life that we go through will leave an impression in our heart. What we do with that impression is up to us. There is an invitation extended to us that makes all the difference in the world: "Here I am! I stand at the door and knock. If anyone hears my voice and opens the door, I will come in and eat with that person, and they with me" (Revelation 3:20).

I see how some of what happened in my life was the consequence of my own poor choices (sin). I have repented in a broken and contrite heart and surrendered completely to our Heavenly Father Elohim. I have experienced what Solomon's says in Ecclesiastes 12:13–14. "Now all has been heard; here is the conclusion of the matter: Fear God and keep his commandments, for this is the duty of all mankind. / For God will bring every deed into judgment, including every hidden thing, whether it is good or evil."

I did not realize how valuable my life was. I did not see that it did have a reason and purpose that outweighs all the world's values. I walk in peace and with the reassurance that I am protected by Almighty God. He will never leave me or forsake me. I am covered with the blood of Jesus, my Lord and Savior. And to Him be all the glory and honor forever and ever—all because I accepted the invitation and opened the door with a completely surrendered will and heart. Amen! I have accepted the invitation in Revelation 3:20. "Here I am! I stand at the door and knock. If anyone hears my voice and opens the door, I will come in and eat with that person, and they with me."

As I was writing out Abba's task for me, this *Open Book*, doubt tried to creep in. So, I prayed. "Abba, it has been so rocky with Pelegrino's shortcomings, and I'm still facing the same challenges in our relationship. What good am I sharing, other than my spiritual maturity? What do You want them to know? Is this all You want me to share? Is it all about standing in the storm and being resilient? My marriage is still facing some of the same struggles. How do I end this

Open Book? Will I be writing a part two or will I just keep standing in the storm?" And I stopped writing.

About two weeks later as I was sitting in the living room, Pelegrino approached me. He stood in front of me as if something serious was happening, and said, "Babe, this is it."

"What?" I asked.

"I'm not going to drink anymore."

"OK" I responded. (I recalled him saying this before.)

"This is it. I'm not going to drink anymore, and I'm not going to smoke weed either. The Holy Spirit told me that I must stop." There was a seriousness about him that I had not seen before.

I sat quietly, listening to his serious proclamation that he would be alcohol and drug free. But inside I was screaming, *Amen! Hallelujah! Santo!* I think I even did a summersault.

"Yeah, babe, this is it. I'm done." He walked back to his man cave (where he likes to spend most of his time with just him and his digital toys—the TV, radio, tablet, and phone.)

That Sunday, we sang "He's Not Finished Yet." I was standing as a testimony of that truth, claiming it at the top of my lungs for Pelegrino and myself. Pelegrino's last drink was December 30, 2021. To Abba God be all the glory. We should live expecting God to move suddenly, whether it takes two weeks or forty-three years—because He does.

Pelegrino reconciled with our Heavenly Father Elohim and is serving Him, just as it was meant to be. Our four daughters are all well, living life one day at a time and trusting Jehovah God to walk them through their journey. We have eleven grandchildren, and our hope is that they too will accept Jesus Christ as Lord and Savior of their lives and walk a life worthy of Him. In Jesus's name, amen!

One day about a year into Pelegrino's recovery and reconciliation with God, we stopped by to visit my younger cousin's wife. After our visit, as we were saying our goodbyes, Pelegrino gave her a hug and kiss and started walking toward the exit door.

My younger cousin's wife called out, "Palo" (which is what she calls him). "Palo."

He walked over to her, and she grabbed his hand and said through tears, "I am sorry. You have no idea how many times I told her to leave you. I am so sorry."

Pelegrino gave her a kiss and said, "That's OK. I forgive you."

She then looked up at me and said, "I'm sorry," as tears rolled down her face.

I pointed to heaven and said, "God's plan, not mine, will prevail." But God chose the foolish things of the world to same the wise; God chose the weak things of the world to shame the strong. 1 Corinthians 1:27

I had crossed through a number of different valleys, making it possible for me to share on a number of topics over time. Many individuals have told me I should write a book. Two stood out to me. Mis Helen (LPN at MG), a coworker who I shared my journal with, returned it with a sticky note on the first page that read, "The making of a million." The last person was Juliza Robledo. (May she rest in peace.) She led the One2One Ministry I was in. During our second to last meeting together, we were speaking on the topic of love, relationships, sacrifice, and so on. I was sharing a couple stories, and she ended by saying, "Girl, you should write a book."

Mis Helen explained to me why she put the sticker on my journal. She said, "When I met you, my first impression of you would have never matched what you have lived. Normally, a person who has gone through what you have would show some signs of anger, bitterness, or withdrawnness. What I saw was peace, joy, and love." Mis Helen was seventy-five at the time and had lived through and seen plenty in her days.

Juliza said she could not believe a person could sacrifice as much as I had and be so full of joy. Also because of her experience in life.

It was the Holy Spirit, not me at all. He carried me, strengthened me, taught me, disciplined me, and protected me while I went through the wilderness, and He always would as I continued walking through my sanctification journey. Otherwise, I wouldn't have been able to live through any of it without carrying a heavy heart, filled with bitterness and resentment.

Here I was, completing my assignment from God—in hopes that

whoever read my story may be able to identify with the adversity, struggles and imperfection in my life and, in comparing it with their own, may know that there is hope. Nothing we go through in life is wasted. Abba God will use all of it to His praise and glory. We have an amazing God Who has given us much:

- For God so loved the world that He gave His one and only Son, that whoever believes in Him shall not perish but have eternal life. (John 3:16)
- If you declare with your mouth, "Jesus is Lord," and believe in your heart that God raised him from the dead, you will be saved. / For it is with your heart that you believe and are justified, and it is with your mouth that you profess your faith and are saved. (Romans 10:9–10)

Papa Dios has been with me through every single season, storm, valley, adversity, turmoil, persecution, failure, and victory. Yes, in every single episode, I have not been alone. He has made things possible and given me a resilient heart through it all. He has shown us the way to attain his promises:

- We can do all things through Christ Jesus who strengthens us. (Philippians 4:13)
- No one has ever seen God; but if we love one another, God lives in us and his love is made complete in us. (1 John 4:12)
- Trust in the Lord with all your heart and lean not on your own understanding; / in all your ways submit to him, and he will make your paths straight. (Proverbs 3:5–6)
- This is what the Lord says: "Cursed is the one who trusts in man, who draws strength from mere flesh and whose heart turns away from the Lord." (Jeremiah 17:5)
- Be joyful in hope, patient in affliction, faithful in prayer. (Romans 12:12)
- But in that coming day no weapon turned against you will succeed. You will silence every voice raised up to accuse you.

These benefits are enjoyed by the servants of the Lord; their vindication will come from me. I, the Lord, have spoken! (Isaiah 54:17, NLT)

When the scriptures report that David was a man after God's own heart, the implication is not that he was perfect or without sin. David proved himself to be sinful in many shocking ways. God had high regards for David because he was humble and approachable, merciful and just in his rulings, repentant in spirit, and faithful to God. He had a deep confidence in God's grace and mercy. He was assured that God's good plans included both himself and the nation of Israel (The Care and Counsel Bible).

The most beautiful part of my story is that God will do it for you too. All you have to do is say yes to His invitation, surrender yourself completely, and watch Him work.

To God Be All Glory! Amen!

"God is not a man that He should lie nor son of man that He should repent. We can trust every word that He has promised us in His Word the Bible" (Numbers 23:19).

If Abba God has touched your Heart and you want to receive His gift of Salvation repeat this prayer:

> Lord Jesus, I admit I am a sinner. I have been living my life according to my will. I understand now that I have sinned against You. I believe that You are the Son of God, that You died for my sins and rose on the third day for the redemption of my sins and reconciliation with the Father. I accept Your gift of salvation offered to me based on Your love for me and not anything I can do for myself. From now on, help me live for You and with You in complete control. I ask this in the name of Jesus Christ. Amen.

Come join me as you begin to live the life you were created for. Now you too can become a fisher of men for our Heavenly Father El Shaddai and be that testimony of the mighty powerful God we serve.

★★★

Poem I wrote in my flesh:

¿Cómo No Amarte?

Si eres así hacia mi.
  Me proteges como lo Mas valioso de tu vida.
   Me mimas y me defiendes como un padre.
    Me alimentas de sabiduría y me tratas con ternura como una madre.

    Me comprendes y me escuchas como un amigo.
     Me celas y me deseas como un amante.
      Me amas como Dios ama a su iglesia, Dios
       Que dio su vida por ella como tú lo haces por mi.
       Te niegas a ti mismo para que yo pueda ser feliz.

How can I not love you?

If you are like this toward me.
  You protect me as the most valuable thing in your life.
   You pamper me and defend me like a father.
    You feed me wisdom and treat me tenderly like a mother.

    You understand me and listen to me as a friend.
     You are jealous, and you desire me like a lover.
      You love me as God loves His church, God
       Who gave His life for her as you do for me;.
       You deny yourself so I can be jubilant.

★★★

280

Poem Heart and Mind Transformation

Lo que yo aprendí, Y el porque me enamoré de Usted mi Papa Dios … … …

Pero Dios, Su plan es más deseable.
  No puedo comparar Le con nadie.
   Su paz es indescriptible.
   Su amor es infinito.

    Eres omnipotente; todo poderoso.
     Eres omnisciente; lo sabes todo.
      Y eres omnipresente; estas en todas partes.
       En este mundo no existe nada que se pueda comparar con Usted.
        Y nada que yo quiero si no es de Usted,
         Quien dios su vida por mi cuando yo no lo merecía.

What I learned, and why I fell in love with You, Abba God

But God, His plan is more desirable.
 I can't compare Him to anyone.
  His peace is indescribable.
  His Love is infinite.

   You are Omnipotent, all powerful,
    Omniscient; you know everything.
     And Omnipresent; you're everywhere.
      In this world, there is nothing that can compare with You.
       And nothing I want if it's not You,
        Who gave His life for me when I didn't deserve it.

Santo!

Joey's track pamphlet he created of his life story.

Have you ever heard of a dead man coming back to life? . . . Well, it happened to me.

Listen to my story!

At the age of 13, I was introduced to narcotics. I started out sniffing glue and next began using marijuana and alcohol.

I was looking for something to fill the emptiness of my heart. I was using drugs to find happiness . . . I didn't know about God.

Soon I started to take pills and then to shoot heroine into my veins. I thought I was only playing with drugs, but one day I made the startling discovery that the drugs were playing with me!

I had to steal night and day and would have done almost anything to feed my awful habit. . . . While I was using drugs, I thought there was no cure for me. That I would be a drug addict for the rest of my life. I was destroying myself with the God of heroine.

Finally, I was sent to prison. The Supreme Court of Puerto Rico was going to give me probation to go to the hospital in Lexington.

But—while I was in jail, a fine Christian who knew God, came to see me. He told me about the God of Love. He suggested I go to New York where they help addicts. . . . I agreed, and while I was there I found the Psychiatrist of psychiatrists—Jesus Christ!

He gave me a real joy and peace, and filled the emptiness of my heart. What drugs couldn't give me in five years, God gave me in one second!

I'm so thankful for what he had done in my life. God has given me a new purpose for living.

Look at yourself. You thought you were different from the others, and never get hooked. You never thought you would end up like a begger only living for a fix. You're hooked and you can't fool around anymore.

But Jesus can give hope, He said ". . . He (God) hath sent Me to heal the Broken hearted, to preach deliverance to the captives, and . . . to set at liberty them that are bruised." Luke 4:18.

You are dead in sin, but Jesus can give abundant life . . . It only costs a prayer to God. And, if you believe, this promise is for you.

"Verily, verily, I say unto you, He that heareth my word, and believeth on Him that sent me, hath everlasting life, and shall not come into condemnation, but is passed from death unto life." John 5:24.

WRITTEN BY: JOEY NEGRON

(312) 252-7888   *Prevention*, INC.
1336 NORTH HOYNE   CHICAGO   ILLINOIS 60622

ABOUT THE AUTHOR

A Heart for Jesus

Carmen Socorro Seguinot was born to Pablo Seguinot Ruiz and Felicita Cartagena Acevedo. Her paternal grandfather was Fernando Seguinot-Matias, and her paternal grandmother was Eularia Ruiz-Magandi. Her maternal grandfather was Rufino Cartagena-Jesus, and her maternal grandmother was Josefina Acevedo.

Her late husband was Jose Miguel Negron Rivera. She was married to him from 1974 to 1978. Her current husband is Pelegrino Sanchez Matos Jr., who she has been with since 1980 and married in 1983.

Carmen was born and raised in Chicago, Illinois, where she currently lives with her husband, Pelegrino. She has never ventured out of the city of Chicago. She's never felt the Lord calling her to do so, though she is sensitive to the cold weather.

She's had just about every job you can think of. She's worked in housekeeping; at four different clothing stores; as a factory laborer, a cashier at a pharmacy and a retail store called Jupiter's, and a teller at three different banks. She's worked at McDonald's and a currency exchange and been a youth counselor for the Title 20 Program. She's been a dental assistant and receptionist, a teacher's assistant at a monitory pre to first grade school, a DUI assessment counselor, and a medical assistant at a clinic. She also did some house cleaning during a short period of self-employment. She's been around, to say the least.

But who is Carmen really? Really, who is she? In *Open Book*, she has revealed who she is. Jesus Christ came after Carmen in 1999, and her life has not been the same since. She is a disciple of Jesus Christ, dying to herself and surrendering to Him daily. Currently, she attends New Life Covenant, where she serves as an elder and care team servant. Her greatest desire is to serve God by serving His creation. She yearns to see all mankind added to the Book of Life so they may live a life worthy of the Lord and please Him in every way—bearing fruit in every good work and growing in the knowledge of God while on earth, until they go home to Him (Colossians 1:10).

God uses a variety of different ways to help us become strong, vital servants of Jesus Christ. Instead of shrinking back in the face of the struggles and challenges of this world, let's look up to the Lord and seek His strength, plan, and purpose. As in Matthew 5:16, "In the same way, let your light shine before others, that they may see your good deeds and glorify your Father in heaven."

In Jesus's name, amen!

Carmen is a wife, the mother of four daughters, and grandmother to eleven grandchildren—who are the apple of her eye.

Printed in the United States
by Baker & Taylor Publisher Services